Psychoeducation
in Mental Health

Also Available from Oxford University Press

STRAIGHT TALK ABOUT PROFESSIONALS ETHICS
by Kim Strom-Gottfried

ENDINGS IN CLINICAL PRACTICE: EFFECTIVE CLOSURE IN
DIVERSE SETTINGS, 2/e
by Joseph Walsh, foreword by Thomas M. Meenaghan

SECONDARY TRAUMATIC STRESS AND THE CHILD WELFARE
PROFESSIONAL
by Josephine G. Pryce, Kimberly K. Shackelford, and David H. Pryce

WHAT IS PROFESSIONAL SOCIAL WORK?
by Malcolm Payne

EVIDENCE-BASED PRACTICES FOR SOCIAL WORKERS
by Thomas O'Hare

TEAMWORK IN MULTIPROFESSIONAL CARE
by Malcolm Payne, foreword by Thomas M. Meenaghan

AN EXPERIENTIAL APPROACH TO GROUP WORK
by Rich Furman, Diana Rowan, and Kimberly Bender

SHORT-TERM EXISTENTIAL INTERVENTION IN CLINICAL PRACTICE
by Jim Lantz and Joseph Walsh

MINDFULNESS AND SOCIAL WORK
edited by Steven Hick

SOCIAL WORK PRACTICE IN NURSING HOMES
by Julie Sahlins

SOCIAL WORK PRACTICE WITH FAMILIES
by Mary Patricia Van Hook

THERAPEUTIC GAMES AND GUIDED IMAGERY
by Monit Cheung

Psychoeducation in Mental Health

Joseph Walsh
School of Social Work
Virginia Commonwealth University

OXFORD
UNIVERSITY PRESS

Oxford University Press is a department of the University of Oxford.
It furthers the University's objective of excellence in research, scholarship,
and education by publishing worldwide. Oxford is a registered trade mark of
Oxford University Press in the UK and certain other countries.

Published in the United States of America by Oxford University Press
198 Madison Avenue, New York, NY 10016, United States of America.

© Oxford University Press 2016

Library of Congress Cataloging-in-Publication Data

Walsh, Joseph (Joseph F.)
    Psychoeducation in mental health \ Joseph Walsh.
      p. cm.
    Includes bibliographical references and index.
    ISBN 978-0-190616-25-0 (pbk. : alk. paper)
    1. Mental health counseling. 2. Patient education. 3. Psychotherapy patients—
Education. I. Title. [DNLM: 1. Family Therapy—methods. 2. Mental Disorders—
therapy. 3. Caregivers—education. 4. Patient Education as Topic. 5. Social
Support. WM 430.5.F2 W225p 2010]
    RC466.W35   2010
    616.89'14—dc22

                                                                    2009030621

ISBN 978-0-190616-25-0

3 5 7 9 8 6 4 2

Printed in the United States of America.

This book is dedicated to my grandmothers,
Theresa and Mary, and my aunts and uncles, Mary Francis,
Bill and Annamae, Joe and Mary Louise, Frank and Josephine,
Rosie and Don, Alyce and Ed, Helen Angela and Jim,
Millie and Aldie, Joe and Jinny, Marie and Dick, Rita and P.J.,
and Fred and Ruth.

Contents

Preface

Twenty-five years ago I read a book called *Families in Pain* by Phyllis Vine, which changed my professional life. The book chronicled the changes that had taken place during the 1970s in understanding the etiology of serious mental illnesses such as schizophrenia and bipolar disorder and the corresponding changing perspectives about the role of the family in the ill relative's life and recovery. Whereas families (especially parents and even more particularly mothers) had previously been considered major causes of the ill relative's disorder, it was now understood that those disorders were largely the result of disease processes in the central nervous system, the specifics of which were unknown but certainly had biological precipitants. Those family members who had once been stigmatized as pathogenic came to realize that the mental health professions had been hasty in highlighting their negative roles in their relative's disease process. It was like blaming the family for a person's diabetes. *Families in Pain* was filled with stories of family members fighting back, organizing into support groups largely outside the purview of the mental health professions, groups in which they provided each other with the education and support they were not getting from professionals. Family members could help themselves understand and learn how to better deal with a relative's mental illness. They could help each other become positive support systems and also combat the mental health profession's lingering theories of family pathology as central to the appearance of mental illness in a member.

All this was news to me. As a social worker educated in the mid-1970s, I had assumed that serious mental disorders were largely the result of psychological processes. I had already worked for eight years in a psychiatric hospital and community mental health center, where the roles of the social workers had included helping clients emancipate from their families of origin so that they could escape those toxic influences. Although this kind of thinking seems wrong-headed today, I want to emphasize that most of my colleagues and I were good, caring people who were merely working within the dominant theoretical perspectives of the time.

Vine's book was not the first to make these points, but it was one of the first, and it was the volume that changed my thinking, almost overnight. Coincidentally, the executive director at my mental health agency had received grant money for new programming, and she asked if I had any ideas. I immediately suggested that we offer a family education and support group that would attempt to form an alliance with the family members of our clients, offering education and support for them as survivors and potentially positive influences on the development of their ill relatives. This group, the first of its kind in central Ohio, was immediately successful. I ran the nine-week group program three times annually for seven consecutive years, until such groups had become so commonplace that they were available to families at most agencies in town. The family education and support group put my agency on the map in the region and was the major experience on which the rest of my practice career has been based. When I moved to Virginia some years later, I continued to offer the group (with variations in format) with the sponsorship of organizations, including the Mental Health Association of Virginia, the state chapter of the National Alliance for the Mentally Ill, and the Richmond Behavioral Health Authority's clubhouse program.

During the past thirty years, psychoeducational interventions have expanded in scope to address more than a dozen problems in living (as described in chapter 1). The interventions are suitable for helping persons, their families, and their significant others in coping with most mental, emotional, and behavioral disorders. The literature includes many articles, and a few books, about these topics. But there is no book that attempts to incorporate the theories and fundamental curative factors of all psychoeducational interventions or the ways in which education and support can be effectively conveyed to participants by professional leaders. Such is the purpose of this book.

Psychoeducation in Mental Health is written for all health and mental health professionals who provide, or are interested in providing, psychoeducational interventions to persons who experience or are affected by many disorders of mental, emotional, and behavioral functioning. The first five chapters (part 1) are focused on theories of psychoeducation, including what it is, its range of uses, how it works (through the lenses of several theories of human and family functioning), the components of effective education, and essential group leadership qualities. Part 2 is focused on nine topic-based applications of the modality, including what the research has to say about programs that are most effective. I emphasize that my intent is not to be comprehensive in addressing all types of psychoeducation that are being provided but to illustrate a range of practical interventions with which helping professionals may be involved. It is my hope that as a result of reading this book the human services professional will be better prepared to offer psychoeducation for a variety of populations.

Acknowledgments

Among the many people I wish to thank for their assistance in this project are students and colleagues who have provided me with information about various topics essential to an understanding of the theory and practice of psychoeducation. They include R. J. Arey, Linda Barker, Michael Buckley, Jessica Cann, Bill Farrington, Karen Gill, Leigh Ann Klipper, Elena Lamanna, Debbie McDermott, and Joan Pomeroy.

Author's Note: All client names used in this book are fictitious.

Part **1**

Theory and Research

Chapter 1

An Introduction to Psychoeducation

The term *psychoeducation* describes a range of individual, family, and group interventions that are focused on educating participants about a significant challenge in living, helping participants develop social and resource supports in managing the challenge, and developing coping skills to deal with the challenge (Griffiths, 2006). Although these three elements characterize all psychoeducational strategies, particular programs may have additional goals, including reducing participants' sense of stigma, changing participants' cognitions with regard to an issue, identifying and exploring feelings about the issue, and developing problem-solving skills related to the issue (see exhibit 1.1).

Exhibit 1.1:   *Definition of psychoeducation*

A range of programs that focus on the following:
  Educating participants about a challenge in living
  Helping participants develop *social and resource supports* in managing the challenge
  Developing *coping skills* to deal with the challenge
  Developing *emotional support*
  Reducing participants' sense of *stigma*
  Changing participants' *attitudes and beliefs* about a disorder
  Identifying and *exploring feelings* about the issue
  Developing *problem-solving skills*
  Developing *crisis-intervention* skills

Psychoeducation is a means of removing barriers to participants' understanding of complex, emotionally charged information and developing strategies for using the information in a constructive manner. The targets of change in psychoeducation may include the participants themselves, their significant others (usually family members), or the larger community (through promotion of advocacy efforts) (Roffman, 2004).

Psychoeducation serves the goals of both treatment and rehabilitation. It involves teaching people about a problem so that they can reduce the

---

Exhibit 1.2:   What psycho "education" does

Directly provides information through lectures, discussion, and other
     formal or informal means that are essential to the participant's
     biological, psychological, and social functioning
Provides participants with concrete resources and information
     regarding the nature and impact of a life challenge
Teaches participants how to gather information for themselves
Helps participants understand the effects of their behavior on others
Helps participants understand others' needs and motivations
Models techniques for self-advocacy

---

related stresses or prevent them from occurring again (see exhibit 1.2). It is
based on a model of lifestyle regularity and healthy habits, early detection of
warning signs, and treatment adherence. Psychoeducation is also based on
participant strengths, focusing on the present and future rather than
dwelling on past difficulties with the issue. It can serve as a forum for recognizing and normalizing participants' experiences and response patterns
as well as holding professionals accountable to high standards of service.
Other goals for psychoeducation programs may include increasing participant well-being, self-identity, social skills, and respite opportunities.

The Varieties of Psychoeducation

Psychoeducation has become extremely popular in human services practice
during the past thirty years in the United States and around the world. The
philosophy of psychoeducation has been applied to a variety of health,
mental health, and human-development challenges. A sample of such programs derived from a PsycINFO literature review revealed the following
applications:

     General parenting-skills development
     Families experiencing mental illness or substance abuse in a member
     Families of children with emotional and behavioral problems
     Families of persons facing various chronic and life-threatening phys-
         ical conditions
     Permanency planning for the adult offspring of aging parents
     The significant others of persons with HIV/AIDS
     Trauma recovery for youth in residential treatment
     Incarcerated male and female inmates
     University women who have experienced sexual assault
     Social workers who experience vicarious trauma
     Juvenile offenders incarcerated as adults

Women in substance-abuse treatment
Adolescent girls who experience negative social pressures
Persons experiencing bulimia
Children of divorce
Youth experiencing bullying behavior
Separation resilience groups for couples who spend much time apart
Families participating in family preservation services

Psychoeducational groups have been used successfully with racial and ethnic minority populations, including low-income Latino women with HIV/AIDS (Subramanian, Hernandez, & Martinez, 1995), Korean American families of persons with mental illness (Shin, 2004), black women adjusting to college, school children who desire to develop their racial identities (Candelario & Huber, 2002), black women in need of greater psychosocial competence (Jones & Hodges, 2001), American Indians who seek cultural identity development (Weaver & Brave Heart, 1999), and minority families of mentally ill clients (Jordan, Lewellen, & Vandiver, 1995). Although the versatility of the modality has been recognized, there are still challenges that remain in determining which kinds of content are most suitable for which kinds of members and how membership can be specified to meet common needs.

Psychoeducational programs are delivered in many service settings. It is not a one-size-fits-all approach to service delivery (see exhibit 1.3). Programs may be provided in one hour (Clemens, 2004), one day (Pollio, North, & Reid, 2006), and over a period of weeks, months, or years (Brennan, 1995), with open- or close-ended structures (Botsford & Rule, 2004). Some programs for youth are integrated into school curricula (Dore, Nelson-Zlupko, & Kaufmann, 1999). Human service professionals have leadership in most psychoeducation services, but consumers or family members of consumers lead some groups and others are co-led by professionals and consumers (Ruffolo, Kuhn, & Evans, 2006). For purposes of consistency in this book, providers of psychoeducation will usually be referred to as practitioners.

Exhibit 1.3: Varieties of psychoeducation

Program length: one hour, one day, one week, one month, several months, and up to several years
Program structure: open- or close-ended, with or without the ill relative, and with human service professionals, family members, or both as leaders
Program location: hospitals, agencies, homes, or "neutral" community locations

Psychoeducation can be a stand-alone intervention, but it is often used as one intervention among several for helping participants with a particular life challenge. The practitioner must always consider whether other important needs of the participants are being neglected, especially in group settings where material is generically presented. Further, psychoeducation programs should not try to do too much (education and psychotherapy) for participants, sacrificing breadth for depth.

The distinctiveness of psychoeducation can be seen in its didactic/educational approach, the partnership or nonhierarchical relationship between the leader and participants, and an open acknowledgment of participants' special expertise in the topic area (given their experience with the problem). As noted in the next chapter, it draws from several direct practice theories and is often utilized in mental health settings as one part of an intervention strategy that integrates counseling, medication, and case management.

What Psychoeducation Is Not

Psychoeducation is *not* synonymous with psychotherapy, but there is overlap between the two modalities in some cases. Although difficult to define, psychotherapy can be understood as a process of interaction between a professional practitioner and a client (individual, family, or group) for the purpose of ameliorating the client system's distress, disability, or malfunction in the areas of cognitive, affective, or behavioral functions. The therapist has a working theory of human development and change, along with some method of intervention logically related to the theory (Corsini & Wedding, 2000). Psychotherapy tends to be focused on the person, whereas psychoeducation has a much greater systems focus and tries to avoid pathologizing the participant. Still, psychoeducation is sometimes provided along with psychotherapy, and sometimes it is difficult to make a distinction, as will be seen in many of the examples included in part 2 of this book.

The Psychoeducation Change Philosophy

Although psychoeducation programs may differ in philosophy and technique, most facilitate movement toward the three goals of education, support, and improved coping. The first major function of these programs is to help participants reorganize their experience of a problem in living from a subjective ("I feel so alone with this problem") to an objective ("Other people deal with this as well—what a relief!") frame of reference, which facilitates a sense of cognitive mastery (Hayes & Gantt, 1992). The social work value of empowerment is always incorporated, as participants are helped to use new skills and information to better manage their challenges (Lee, 2001). Practitioners and participants are considered to be partners in treatment, with the premise that the more knowledgeable the participants are, the more positive the health-related outcomes will be for all.

Psychoeducational models do not see the family as the source of a problem but as a resource toward growth. Through family psychoeducation, the family's role is to create an atmosphere conducive to improved functioning of the individual with the problem at considerably less stress to family members.

Evolution of the Modality

The concept of psychoeducation has evolved over the past forty years. It was initially used to describe a process of educating practitioners about the nature of mental, emotional, and behavioral problems (Mykelbust, 1973) and also as a means of preparing clients to undergo analytic psychotherapy (teaching clients about the modality, communication, and how to handle aggressive impulses) (Authier, 1977). Contemporary uses of psychoeducation can be traced back to the 1970s, when knowledge about mental disorders began to focus on biological rather than family processes. The increasing emphasis on education for those with mental health problems was partially due to the consumer movement, with its advocacy for consumer rights and empowerment (Landsverk & Kane, 1998). Psychoeducation covers a fundamental right of the individual to be informed about his or her illness (Colom & Lam, 2005). Many health professionals have abandoned their expert and therapist images and become more collaborative with clients and families, eager to share information with them.

Contemporary psychoeducational models were first implemented in the late 1970s for individuals with schizophrenia and their families by such pioneers as Hatfield (1979) and Kanter (1980). The actual practice was underway before the current term was applied, with Anderson, Hogarty, and Reiss (1980) often being credited with its adoption.

The Effectiveness of Psychoeducation

Psychoeducation is said to be among the most effective of the evidence-based practices that have emerged in clinical trials and practice settings (Lukens & McFarlane, 2006). Many single-subject and quasi-experimental designs have been utilized to test the effectiveness of these interventions on client populations, and some experimental studies have also been conducted. Most studies show that psychoeducation is equal or superior to alternative interventions. One review found that there is an increasing body of evidence showing education to be an effective component in a comprehensive treatment approach to mental illness (Landsverk & Kane, 1998). This review revealed that psychosocial educational interventions can be beneficial for a wide variety of populations and problems in living. It also found that psychoeducation can empower participants and that the process allows them to collaborate more fully with their health care providers. In addition, this review emphasized the importance in psychoeducation of practitioner skills and attitudes and of peer-to-peer interactions. Psychoeducation is most effective when it includes educational content that is specifically targeted to its recipients. Much more will be said about the effectiveness of these services throughout the book.

Summary

Psychoeducation is an effective, adaptable intervention for helping individuals and their significant others develop knowledge of and coping skills for a variety of problems and challenges in living. Still, it is difficult to make generalizations about the effectiveness of psychoeducation, because there is such variety in the nature of programs and participant goals. Future research needs to be conducted to determine the structures, settings, and teaching tools that can optimize the effectiveness of psychosocial interventions. Each chapter in part 2 of this book reviews the effectiveness literature with regard to many types of programs and client populations. Before specific interventions are discussed, however, the general characteristics of psychoeducation are considered in the remainder of part 1.

Chapter 2

Psychoeducation and Human Behavior Theory

As described in the last chapter, psychoeducation can be effective with a variety of life challenges and in a variety of formats. This chapter identifies the common elements of psychoeducation programs that contribute to their overall effectiveness. Practitioners should keep these in mind as essential for any program in which they are participating.

Components of Effective Psychoeducation

The characteristics of psychoeducational programs that contribute to participant goal attainment can be summarized as follows:

Concrete information is provided about topics of concern.

Practical strategies are offered for behavioral change.

Self-esteem is enhanced with exposure to self-care resources.

Participants develop an increased resilience to stress as they acquire new coping and problem-management skills.

Participants develop new social networks.

Participants are introduced to a new (professional) language for understanding the problem issues.

Myths about certain problems in living are dismantled.

Clearer boundaries are created among participants, their significant others, and professionals.

Communication skills are enhanced, which facilitates problem resolution.

Barriers to personal and familial change are reduced through resource awareness and alternative ways of thinking.

Stigma and fear are decreased.

Hope for participants is generated. (Lukens & Prchal, 2002)

Group approaches to psychoeducation provide unique opportunities for participant socialization, exchange of experiences and information, and expanded social networks. Furthermore, participants' involvement in the planning of content for group programs has been identified as an effective means of increasing participant commitment to the process.

It is not often noted that psychoeducation includes benefits for participating human service professionals, but it does facilitate a constructive partnership between practitioners and consumers and promote ongoing self-education and professional growth and interaction among professionals of different disciplines.

The remainder of this chapter is devoted to a survey of the human behavior theories that are beneficial in providing effective psychoeducation.

The Theoretical Basis of Psychoeducation

Psychoeducation relies on six theories of human behavior and change (see exhibit 2.1), each of which is reviewed here in some detail.

Exhibit 2.1:   *Theoretical basis of psychoeducation*

Cognitive theory: nature and rationality of thinking processes (Berlin, 2002)

Learning theory: how people acquire, make sense of, and use new knowledge (Constas & Sternberg, 2006)

Psychodynamic theory: the nature of emotional life, self-awareness (Goldstein, 1995)

Developmental theory: stages of growth, illness, and adjustment (Hutchison, 2008)

Social support theory: relationships that provide assistance or feelings of attachment to others (Lang & Fingerman, 2004)

Empowerment theory: the process of increasing self-efficacy and influence (Lee, 2001)

Cognitive Theory

Cognitive theory is concerned with how people perceive and interpret information they receive from the environment (Berlin, 2002). More specifically, it is concerned with accurate perceptions, or drawing conclusions about perceptions based on available evidence rather than on biases or distortions of thinking (see exhibit 2.2). *Beliefs* are ideas that people hold to be true, but they may or may not be in accordance with the facts or evidence of a situation. Erroneous beliefs, which may result from misperceptions or from conclusions based on insufficient evidence, frequently contribute to problems in social functioning. For example, a mother who believes that schizophrenia is the result of poor parenting (an idea that has been invalidated) may experience guilt and continuously demean herself for producing an ill child. Conversely, a mother who believes that schizophrenia is largely a brain or thought disorder rooted in biology may feel better about herself and be more capable of living a full life, one that is not dominated by concerns about her son.

Exhibit 2.2:   Assumptions of cognitive theory

Thinking is the basic determinant of behavior. Thoughts and feelings are separate mental processes.

Most emotions and behaviors are a result of what people think, tell themselves, or believe about themselves.

People are active in constructing their realities, which emphasizes the subjectivity of perception and thinking.

Many problems result from cognitive deficits or misconceptions.

Rational thinking

Is based on external evidence,

Is life-preserving,

Keeps one directed toward personal goals, and

Decreases internal conflicts

From the perspective of cognitive theory, many problems in living result from incomplete information or misconceptions—conclusions that are based more on habits of thought than external evidence—that people have about themselves, other people, and their life situations. These misconceptions may develop for any of the following three reasons.

Cognitive deficits are when a person has not acquired the basic information necessary to understand a problem or formulate a solution. This situation is often evident in the lives of people who experience a complex problem or illness, and it can be largely remedied with education. For example, a child who is chronically in trouble for fighting with other children may not have learned social skills, and teaching that child how to be appropriately assertive may help to resolve the problem.

The other two sources of misperception are rooted in belief systems that have become too rigid to accommodate adjustment to new situations. For example, a person who has learned to interpret all psychological problems as learned may have trouble accepting the alternative explanation that manic behavior often results from a chemical imbalance.

Causal attributions refer to three kinds of assumptions that people hold about themselves in relation to the environment. First, a person might function from a premise that life situations are either more or less changeable ("I have bipolar disorder, and there is nothing I can do about it"). Second, a person may believe that if change is possible the source of power to make changes exists either within or outside the self ("My doctor is responsible for how well I function"). Finally, a person might assume that the implications of his or her experiences are limited to the specific situation or that they are global ("I get confused when I experience job stress; therefore, I can't handle any stress well"). Whatever the sources of these beliefs, they are arbitrary and can change, often with the assistance of a more objective outsider.

Cognitive distortions are misperceptions of reality, conclusions that are not sufficiently based on the external evidence. Because everyone develops habits of thinking, people often interpret new situations in biased ways. These patterns are generally functional because many situations people face in life are similar to previous ones and can be managed with patterned responses. These habits become a source of difficulty, however, when they interfere with a person's openness to consider new information. For example, a person who had several early life difficulties with ineffective health professionals may believe that none of them are trustworthy, even after coming into contact with one who gives no evident reason for that label. Exhibit 2.3 includes some widely held cognitive distortions.

Exhibit 2.3:   Common cognitive distortions

Arbitrary inference: drawing a conclusion about an event with no evidence, little evidence, or contradictory evidence

Selective abstraction: judging a situation on the basis of one or several details taken out of a broader context

Magnification or *minimization:* concluding that an event is either far more significant or far less significant than the evidence indicates

Overgeneralization: drawing a conclusion that all instances of some type will turn out a particular way because one or two such situations did

Personalization: attributing the cause of or accepting responsibility for an external event without external evidence of a causal connection

Dichotomous thinking: categorizing experiences at one of two extremes—complete success or utter failure

(Beck, 1967)

Interventions based on cognitive theory are extremely popular in psychoeducation, as shown in part 2. By utilizing cognitive theory in psychoeducation, a leader can help participants acquire new information on which to base future decisions, adjust their beliefs (often about competence) with regard to managing a challenge, or develop more flexible patterns of thinking (so that problem solving becomes more creative). When a participant's perceptions and beliefs about an issue do seem to be valid, the practitioner intervenes by providing education about the issue and implementing problem-solving or coping exercises. When the participant exhibits significant cognitive distortions, the practitioner and participant must together identify situations that trigger the misconceptions, determine how they can be adjusted, and then implement corrective tasks. This process is summarized in exhibit 2.4.

Exhibit 2.4: Change strategies in cognitive theory	
When a person experiences:	**The practitioner assists with:**
Rational thinking	Problem-solving skills development
Cognitive deficits	Education and coping-skills development
Cognitive distortions	Cognitive restructuring

Strategies for cognitive intervention in psychoeducation fit into three categories, as follow.

Problem-solving skills development Problem solving is a structured five-step method for helping participants who do not experience distortions but nevertheless struggle with problems that they clearly perceive (see exhibit 2.5). Participants in psychoeducational programs typically experience realistic problems related to the program topic that they are not sure how to address (such as, "I don't know how to reach out to other people when I'm depressed"). Through problem solving, participants learn how to produce a variety of potentially effective responses to their problems (Corcoran, 2006). The first step is *defining the problem* the participant wishes to overcome. As the poet Emerson wrote, "A problem well defined is a problem half solved" ("Famous Quotes by Author," n.d.). Solutions are easier to formulate when problems are clearly delineated.

Exhibit 2.5: Problem solving

A process that increases the number of effective alternatives for resolving a problem and the probability that the most effective response will be selected from the pool of alternatives

Steps:
1. Define the problem in concrete terms.
2. Compile a list of uncensored alternatives.
3. Evaluate each response alternative.
4. Implement the preferred alternative.
5. Evaluate and terminate, *or* return to an earlier step.

The next step in problem-solving skills development involves the participant and practitioner *brainstorming* to generate as many possible solutions for a presenting problem as they can imagine. At this point, evaluative comments are not allowed so that spontaneity and creativity is encouraged.

All possibilities are written down, even those that seem impossible or silly. Some supposedly ridiculous ideas may contain useful elements on closer examination.

The third stage of the process involves *evaluating alternatives.* Any patently irrelevant or impossible items are crossed out. Each viable alternative is then discussed as to its advantages and disadvantages. More information about the situation may need to be gathered as a result of the work in this stage. For instance, information might be gathered about other agencies and resources (including other people in the participant's life) that can assist in making some of the choices more viable.

The next stage, *choosing and implementing an alternative,* involves selecting a strategy for problem resolution that appears to maximize benefits over costs. Although the outcome of any alternative is always uncertain, the participant is praised for exercising good judgment in the process and is reminded that making any effort to address a problem is the most significant aspect of this step. The practitioner should remind the participant that there is no guarantee that the alternative will succeed and that other alternatives are available if needed.

During the following session, the practitioner helps the participant to *evaluate the implemented option.* If successful, the process is complete except for a discussion about how to generalize problem solving to other situations in the participant's life. The exploration of any failures must be examined closely for elements that went well in addition to those needing work. If a strategy has not been successful, it can be attempted again with adjustments, or the practitioner and participant can go back to the fourth step and select another option.

Cognitive restructuring   Cognitive-restructuring techniques are used when the participant's thinking patterns are distorted and contribute to problem persistence. Through a series of discussions and exercises, the practitioner helps the participant to experiment with alternative ways of approaching challenges that will better promote goal attainment. In order to change a participant's belief systems, three steps are necessary. The first is to help the person *identify the thoughts preceding and accompanying the distressing emotions and nonproductive action.* For example, the parent of a young, depressed woman may interpret the girl's withdrawal as disrespect and a lack of appreciation, and consequently the parent may argue with the daughter, who responds by retreating further. The parent believes that he is being disrespected rather than that the daughter is incapable of more social interaction at the time. The second step is to *assess the participant's willingness to consider alternative thoughts* in response to the problem situation, or in the example given, a variety of reasons for the daughter's withdrawal. The practitioner helps the person to consider and perhaps write down other possible interpretations of the event. The third step is to *challenge the participant's irrational beliefs* by designing natural experiments, or tasks, that he or she can carry out in daily life to test their validity. The parent may be given some ideas about how to approach the daughter differently, in the hopes of engaging her in a conversation. If the new strategy works, the man will be likely to give up his previous interpretation of the daughter's behavior, and their relationship may improve.

Cognitive coping   A third category of cognitive intervention is cognitive coping (Corcoran, 2006). The leader helps the participant learn and practice new or more effective ways of dealing with stress and negative moods. All of these interventions involve step-by-step procedures for the participant to follow in mastering new skills. Cognitive coping involves education and skills training with the goal of helping participants become more effective at managing their challenges. There are many such types of coping-skills development that will be described throughout this book, including assertion skills, parenting skills, relaxation skills, stress-prevention skills, and social skills. Participants will modify their cognitive distortions when they experience positive results from practicing new coping skills.

Behavior Theory

It has already been noted that in many psychoeducation programs participants are helped to learn a new skill and then *practice* the new skill in the natural environment. That is, participants are encouraged to behave differently in order to facilitate changed thoughts in themselves and behaviors in themselves or others. For this reason the educator should have familiarity with the behavior theory principles of operant conditioning. The leader helps the participant achieve new, desirable behaviors in themselves or others by manipulating the environment to promote rewards for those behaviors.

As an example, in the cycle of aggressive children, children and adults get caught up in a pattern that tends to increase the child's undesired behavior. The adult makes a request of the child (to do homework), the child reacts with hostility, the adult in turn acts with hostility and withdraws, and the child thus averts complying with the request. In other words, the defiant behavior is rewarded, or reinforced. Parenting-skills development is one model of psychoeducation that teaches parents the principles of reinforcement to break these frustrating patterns. Parents learn to reinforce desirable behaviors in their children and ignore or punish negative behavior. In the above example, the child may lose privileges for failing to do homework rather than win the argument with the parent. If the child does her homework, she may be permitted to spend more time with friends.

Learning Theory

The challenge of understanding how people learn, and what educational approaches facilitate their learning in ways that are most relevant to them, is at the heart of psychoeducation. Of the six theories reviewed in this chapter, learning theory may be the least known to human services practitioners outside the education profession. The utilization of learning theory in psychoeducation involves the practitioner understanding different levels at which learning objectives can be articulated, depending on the nature of the learners and the subject matter to be delivered. Education about breast cancer, for example, will be delivered differently depending on the age of the participants (adults vs. adolescents) and whether or not they actually have breast cancer (it could be a prevention program). Further, people have different ways of learning (through lecture, discussion, activity, etc.). These topics will be covered in depth in chapter 4, and only a few points are considered here.

Social learning theory is based on the behavioral principle of vicarious learning, or *modeling,* which asserts that people acquire many new behaviors by witnessing how the actions of others are reinforced (Bandura, 1997, 2001). Social learning theory emphasizes learning through observation, practice, and interaction between people and their environments. The focus in psychoeducation is on creating support for learning among participants and developing a social context in which that learning can take place. It rests on the belief that a supportive social context contributes to motivation, retention of information, and the ability to transfer knowledge across situations. This form of learning is emphasized in groups more so than in individual intervention.

Teaching communication skills is one important aspect of education for many psychoeducation participants, and it involves social learning. Positive communication builds relationships and closeness with others, which in turn helps improve mood and feelings about oneself (Hargie, 1997). These skills cover a wide range of behaviors that includes attention to participants' social, assertiveness, and negotiation skills. When a person can articulate his or her concerns, other people are more likely to constructively suggest how they might adjust their behaviors in response.

Role-playing is an effective teaching strategy that can be used with all of the above interventions (Hepworth, Rooney, Rooney, Strom-Gottfried, & Larsen, in press). In this strategy, the practitioner first models a skill, then the practitioner and participant rehearse it together. Role-playing offers several advantages for intervention. The practitioner demonstrates new skills for the participant, which usually is a more powerful way of conveying information than simple instruction. Also, when the participant takes on the perspective of another significant person in his or her life (family member, boss, or friend), he or she is better able to understand the other person's point of view.

Psychodynamic (Reflective) Theory

Psychodynamic theories, such as ego psychology and object relations, are more directly focused on participants' emotional lives—how their feelings can be affected by and play a role in the course of their problems—than cognitive theory is. These theories assert that development of insight through emotional reflection is essential for lasting personal change and growth. The reflective theories are quite complex and are reviewed here only to an extent that demonstrates their utility in psychoeducation.

Emotions are consciously experienced feeling states (Parkinson, Fischer, & Manstead, 2005), and they serve to motivate people to behave in certain ways. People who participate in psychoeducational programs often experience strong emotions about the problem issue. These emotions may be constructive in helping participants manage the challenge, but at times they may be destructive, prohibiting the person from thinking through the challenge in a more objective manner. The parent of an adolescent girl with an eating disorder may try so hard to suppress his frustration with her that he gradually withdraws support, leaving the daughter alone with the problem. Leaders of psychoeducational programs often emphasize the importance of members learning to recognize and manage their emotions related to the topic.

Human service professionals in general tend to place more emphasis on thoughts than emotions (Berlin, 2002). Cognitive theory suggests that if thoughts can be changed, emotions will subsequently change. Psychodynamic practitioners believe, however, that emotions are not created through such a linear process (Farmer, 2009). Developments in the neurosciences indicate that emotional information is actually processed faster than cognitive information and can often bypass conscious thinking (LeDoux, 1996). In fact, there are more neural connections going from emotional processing centers of the brain to cognitive centers of the brain than vice versa. Based on this perspective, a person's ability to regulate feelings (often called emotional competence) is equally important to cognitive processing abilities (often called mental competence) (Goleman, 1998).

Emotions can make people feel uncomfortable or comfortable and thus provide signals for them to respond in certain ways. When a person is trying to understand something or make a decision, he or she uses emotions to deduce whether what is concluded makes sense or is a good idea. For example, when people think about doing something that contradicts their values or could hurt them, their emotions tell them that it is a bad idea. Just by imagining what might happen, their emotions are triggered and hence help them make better decisions. If a person in a psychoeducation program feels angry at him- or herself or another person for some perceived failing, it is important for the person to understand the source of that anger before allowing it to guide his or her response.

Emotion is physiologically programmed into the human brain, but it also involves a cognitive labeling of these programmed feelings, which is at least partially a learned process. Many theorists distinguish between primary and secondary emotions (Parkinson et al., 2005). The primary emotions may have evolved as specific reactions with survival value (see exhibit 2.6). They

---

Exhibit 2.6:   *The nature of emotions*

Emotions are feeling states that are consciously experienced. They motivate people toward or away from some stimulus.

The primary emotions evolved as specific reactions with survival value for the human species. They include anger, fear, sadness, joy, and anticipation.

The secondary emotions are socially acquired. These include (but are not limited to) envy, jealousy, anxiety, guilt, shame, relief, hope, depression, pride, love, gratitude, and compassion.

---

mobilize people, focus their attention, and signal their state of mind to others. There is no consensus on what the primary emotions are, but they are usually limited to anger, fear, sadness, joy, and anticipation (Panksepp, 2005). The secondary emotions are more variable among people and are socially acquired. Their greater numbers also imply that people's cognitive processes are significant in labeling them (Plutchik, 2005). Because they are linked to beliefs, these emotions may be related to cognitive deficits or distortions. These emotions include (but are not limited to) envy, jealousy, anxiety, guilt, shame, relief, hope, depression, pride, love, gratitude, and compassion (Lazarus & Lazarus, 1994).

The concept of emotional intelligence refers to the ability to process information about emotions accurately and effectively, and consequently to regulate emotions in an optimal manner (Goleman, 1998). Researchers have determined that emotional stimulation is necessary for activating certain thought patterns. Recognizing and regulating emotions requires emotional self-awareness and empathy, but it also requires the intellectual ability to calculate the implications of different behavioral alternatives. Understanding how and why one feels as he or she does and other people feel as they do requires emotional acquaintance and intellectual reasoning.

Emotional intelligence requires emotional sensitivity, or the ability to evaluate emotions in a variety of contexts. A person who is angry but knows that certain expressions of anger will be counterproductive in a particular situation (for example, with a boss) and as a result constrains his or her expressions of anger is emotionally intelligent. On the other hand, a person with this same knowledge who behaves angrily in spite of this awareness is emotionally unintelligent. People are not necessarily equally emotionally intelligent about themselves and other people. This fact helps to explain why some people, practitioners included, seem to be better at giving advice to others than they are at helping themselves.

Emotional intelligence can be developed, and doing so may be a focus of psychoeducation program leaders. The psychodynamic (or reflective) theories enhance the practitioner's understanding of the origins of emotional experiences and his or her ability to describe how emotional states influence behavior. The practitioner can help the participant develop more constructive emotional responses by providing insight or corrective emotional experiences. The negative feelings that cause problems come not from primary emotional responses, which if experienced directly would tend to dissipate, but from distortions (known as defensive reactions in psychodynamic theory) of those responses.

It is when people experience primary emotions that they are functioning in an adaptive manner. In psychoeducation the practitioner attempts to activate the person's primary emotional reactions, making them more available to awareness within the safety of the relationship and making secondary emotional reactions amenable to change when necessary. The participant may then more clearly identify emotional reactions, cognitive appraisals, and action tendencies. Participants can be helped to acquire problem-solving and coping skills and to achieve insight (self-understanding) through reflection about their strengths, limitations, and potential resources. They can emerge from the intervention process with an improved capacity for self-direction.

A practitioner's psychodynamic interventions are best understood as abstract strategies rather than concrete directives. Practitioners need to tailor these general strategies to the specific needs of participants. The general strategies include *sustainment* (developing and maintaining a positive relationship), *exploration-description-ventilation* (encouraging the participant's emotional expressions for stress relief and to gain objectivity about problems), and *reflection* (about solutions to present difficulties) (see exhibits 2.7 through 2.9).

Exhibit 2.7: Sustainment

What the practitioner does:
  Listens actively and sympathetically
  Conveys an attitude of good will
  Expresses confidence or esteem
  Realistically reassures the person about potential for change
  Realistically encourages the person to persist

How this helps the participant:
  Promotes a confiding relationship
  Instills a sense of the leader's competence and caring
  Enhances morale and the determination to persist
  Inspires and maintains the expectation of help

Exhibit 2.8:   *Exploration-description-ventilation*

What the practitioner does:
  Elicits the person's feelings about an area of concern
  Helps the person express and explore those feelings
  Helps the person maintain a focus on relevant feelings

How this helps the participant:
  Feels less alone, less overwhelmed, and more in control
  Is freed from anxiety, guilt, and depression
  Sees problems as more manageable
  Is moved to action
  Develops greater hope, confidence, and self-acceptance
  Recognizes and understands his or her emotional reactions
  Acquires insight

Exhibit 2.9:   *Reflection*

What the practitioner does:
  Makes comments, asks questions, and offers tentative explanations
    that promote the person's reflective capacity
  Leads discussion of the pros and cons of the person's taking cer-
    tain actions
  Assumes a moderately directive and structured stance

How this helps the participant:
  Facilitates clearer evaluation of feelings, self-concept, attitudes,
    and values
  Produces a better understanding of others or some external situation
  Increases insight into the nature of behavior and its effects on others
  Improves judgment and the ability to consider a wider range of
    problem-solving options

Developmental Theory

Everyone experiences continuous biological, psychological, social, and perhaps spiritual development throughout his or her life span. Early developmental theorists, such as Jean Piaget (cognition), Erik Erikson (psychosocial aspects of life), Lawrence Kohlberg (morality), and Carole Gilligan (women's ways of knowing), made major contributions to the process of understanding the stages that people seem to share, as well as the demands on adaptation that accompany those transitions. People pass through life transitions in ways that are not universal but are largely prescribed by biology and culture. Themes related to human development are relevant to psychoeducation, because it is often an inability to successfully adapt to life transitions that contributes to, or exacerbates, the kinds of problems for which people seek assistance. Anorexia, for example, is often described in part as a problematic reaction to the onset of puberty.

Developmental theorists in the past few decades have been much more alert to the fact that stages of human development are not universally shared. Theorists such as those mentioned above usually worked within a single culture, perhaps with a single class of people, and perhaps with a single gender, and then speculated that their findings generalize to all people. It is likely that people of different cultures, races, and sexual orientations, for example, experience different developmental processes. Thus it is more respectful of human diversity and the special circumstances in which people find themselves to take a *broad* view of human development, to have few preconceived notions of specific ways that all people should be expected to behave at certain times of life.

Hutchison (2008) has developed a human-development framework that is adaptable to all models of psychoeducation. She considers human development to include not only age-related stages but also the interplay of social, cultural, and historical factors. She breaks down the life span into the eight categories listed in exhibit 2.10, asserting that people in these different age groups share general expectations for role behavior, but only in the context of certain influences. Notice that she breaks down adulthood into four parts, with two of these parts devoted to older adulthood. This breakdown acknowledges that people are living longer and are able to be productive throughout their lives.

Exhibit 2.10: A life course perspective

Infancy and toddlerhood
Early childhood
Middle childhood
Adolescence
Young adulthood
Middle adulthood
Late adulthood
Very late adulthood
(Hutchison, 2008)

A normal life transition may be related to problem development in three ways. First, it may be a major causal factor in the development of a problem. For empty-nest couples, the last child leaving home may precipitate depression in one spouse, who is not equipped to live without centering on the children. Second, a life transition may be closely associated with a major problem in living so that the person, and perhaps the family, confuses the transition as causal. For example, the age of onset of schizophrenia is generally between eighteen and twenty-two years, a period that in mainstream American society is often associated with the assumption of adult roles. A family's ability to cope with the onset of schizophrenia in one member might be complicated by the fact that they have been expecting the person to move on to college, apartment living, or full-time work. If the family perceives the transition to be the cause of the mental disorder, it will respond in ways that are not effective toward problem resolution, such as sheltering the person until the supposed crisis passes. Third, a person who experiences a serious problem in living may be less confident or capable of addressing an upcoming life transition, or the family may hold the person back from moving through certain transitions because of this fear. A young athlete who experiences a traumatic physical injury may lack the confidence to make his way socially in high school, and the family may become overly protective of him.

Clearly disorders, as well as other problems in living, do not exist in a social vacuum. In psychoeducation, leaders must be able to help participants understand processes of human development and how the context may assist or impede problem resolution. Exhibit 2.11 provides a means of summarizing some of the above points, as Hutchison (2008) articulates six common influences on the course of human development.

Exhibit 2.11: Major themes of the life course perspective

The historical context of one's life
The element of timing (roles and behaviors that are associated with one's biological, psychological, social, and spiritual ages)
Linkages with others (how the person interacts with family or social units, what supports he or she desires and achieves)
Personal power in making choices
Diversity in life course trajectories
Developmental risks and protections (how life experiences either help or inhibit one's ability to manage subsequent transitions and events)

This brief overview of developmental theory concludes with a summary of Hutchison's (2008) description of conditions under which a life transition may develop into a life crisis:

The transition occurs along with a separate crisis or is followed by another crisis. A person's movement into young adulthood may be accompanied by development of a major mental disorder. As a result the person is unable to carry out the roles inherent to his or her life stage, and his or her behaviors come to seem "adolescent."

The transition involves family conflict over the needs and wants of the individual and the greater good of the family unit. A young adult who wishes to leave home may be drawn back into the family unit because one parent is alcoholic and the young adult is needed to help parent the remaining siblings. This situation may present a crisis to the person, who feels angry about his or her desired life course being stunted. If the young adult does leave home, the family may face a crisis related to a lack of adequate parenting and the subsequent acting out of the remaining siblings.

The transition is "off-time" or doesn't occur at the typical stage in life. A child who loses a parent to cancer at age twelve is unprepared for life without substantial parenting.

The transition is followed by unforeseen negative consequences. A couple is married, only to have one spouse's parent turn against the couple due to disapproval of some choices they have made. The couple may suddenly be without anticipated social and financial support.

The transition requires exceptional social adjustments. A young adolescent may move from one geographic area to another, losing one set of established peers and having trouble developing a new peer group because of his or her outsider status in the new school.

Understanding the interplay between human development and health, mental health, behavior, coping, and adaptation is critical in psychoeducation. Problems always occur in a social context and must be addressed in large part by attending to areas of that context. In part 2 of this book, the integration of these themes into the educational content will be evident.

Social Support Theory

Social supports—the people individuals rely on to affirm and enrich their lives—can be invaluable when coping with the demands of daily life. *Social support* can be formally defined as the interpersonal interactions and relationships that provide people with assistance or feelings of attachment to persons they perceive as caring (Hobfoll, Freedy, Lane, & Geller, 1990). Social support resources can be categorized into three types, as follows:

> Material support: food, clothing, shelter, and other concrete items
>
> Emotional support: interpersonal support
>
> Instrumental support: services provided by casual contacts, such as physicians, auto repairmen, and landlords (Walsh & Connelly, 1996)

Some authors add social integration support to the mix, which refers to a person's sense of belonging. That is, simply belonging to a group and having a role and contribution to offer may be an important dimension of support (Lang & Fingerman, 2004).

Social support acts almost like medicine. The experience of stress creates a physiological state of emotional arousal, which reduces the efficiency of cognitive functions (Caplan, 1990). People become less effective at focusing their attention and cannot access the memories that normally bring meaning to their perceptions, judgment, and integration of feedback from others. Social supports compensate for these deficits in the following ten ways:

1. Promoting an ordered worldview
2. Promoting hope
3. Promoting timely withdrawal and initiative
4. Providing guidance
5. Providing a communication channel with the social world
6. Affirming one's personal identity
7. Providing material help
8. Containing distress through reassurance and affirmation
9. Ensuring adequate rest
10. Mobilizing other personal supports (Caplan, 1990)

Some of these support systems are formal (service organizations), and some are informal (such as friends and neighbors). Religion, which attends to the spiritual realm, also plays a distinctive support role (Caplan, 1990).

Many people perceive their support networks to be inadequate. McPherson, Smith-Lovin, and Brashears (2006) found that 43.6 percent of their 2004 sample reported that they have either no one or only one person with whom they discuss important matters in their lives, in contrast to an average of three such persons reported in a 1985 sample. People who experience marginalizing problems, such as chronic mental and physical disorders, tend to have smaller networks than people whose challenges are more universal.

Social support theory asserts that all people optimally benefit from supports that are particular to their personalities and life situations. That is, although social support is uniformly important, it is unique to each individual. In many psychoeducational programs, enhancing participants' social support networks is a primary goal. Many people who seek psychoeducation feel isolated and alienated from some of their peers who do not share their problem, perhaps do not understand it, and may be intimidated by the situation. Participants' quality of life can be greatly enriched if they can become part of a network of supportive others, both during the intervention and after it ends. The psychoeducator must assess each member's support needs relative to the presenting issue and subsequently encourage him or her to develop appropriate supports or use existing supports more constructively.

A *social network* includes all the people with whom a person regularly interacts (Moren-Cross & Lin, 2006). Network relationships often occur in clusters, such as the nuclear family, extended family, friends, neighbors, community relations, school, work, church, recreational groups, and professional associations. Network relationships are *not* synonymous with support, because they may be negative or positive, but the scope of the network does tend to indicate potential for obtaining support. Having supportive others in a variety of clusters indicates that a person is supported in many areas of his or her life. A *personal network* includes those from the social network who, in the individual's view, provide him or her with the most essential supports (Bidart & Lavenu, 2005).

There is no consensus about how psychoeducators can evaluate a person's level of social support. The simplest procedure is to ask for participants' subjective perceptions of support from family and friends. One useful model includes a focus on the following three social support indicators:

1. A listing of social network resources: the client lists all the people with whom he or she regularly interacts.
2. Accounts of supportive behavior: the client identifies specific episodes of receiving support from others in the recent past and gets a sense of whether these are sufficient in frequency.
3. Perceptions of support: the client subjectively assesses the adequacy of the support received from various sources. (Vaux, 1988)

With an awareness of the concepts of social support, social networks, and social network clusters, the psychoeducator can identify both subjective and objective support indicators with program participants and either build new networks or target underused clusters for the development of additional social support.

Empowerment Theory

Psychoeducation should always be delivered to enhance the capacity, or power, of individuals and their families to address their life concerns. In this context power includes a positive sense of self-worth and competence, the ability to influence the course of one's life, and the capacity to work with others to control aspects of public life (Lee, 2001).

Many people do not, or perceive that they do not, have power over themselves, their significant others, or the agencies and communities where they reside. This sense of powerlessness can be internalized and lead to a sense of helplessness and alienation from others in one's community. An empowerment orientation to psychoeducation represents the leader's efforts to positively influence participants' sense of worth, sense of membership in a community, and ability to create change in their surroundings (Rose, 1990; see also exhibit 2.12).

Exhibit 2.12: Empowerment

A psychological state characterized by feelings of self-esteem, efficacy, and control over one's life

A developmental process, existing along a continuum from individual growth to social change

Liberation from oppression, characterized by an ability to work more actively in the social arena to get one's needs met

Recipients of psychoeducation may be empowered at a personal level (changing their patterns of thinking, feeling, and behaving), an interpersonal level (managing their relationships more effectively), or perhaps a political level (changing their manner of interacting with larger systems) (Lee, 2001). Empowerment at the individual level is a process by which participants gain mastery and control over their lives and a critical understanding of their environment (Zimmerman, Israel, Schulz, & Checkoway, 1992). Psychological empowerment includes a person's beliefs about his or her competence, efforts to exert control, and understanding of the social environment (Zimmerman, 2000). The concept of perceived control is related to reducing psychological stress and increasing social action. Empowerment involves helping people learn decision-making skills, manage resources, and work productively with others. In groups, encouraging people to share information with others is an empowering experience, and the utilization of problem solving and role modeling increases participants' feelings of empowerment.

In psychoeducational practice, specific actions directed toward empowerment may be less important than the practitioner's general orientation toward helping participants become more involved in their communities (however defined) and feel more capable of exerting influence there. Toward this end, the practitioner must strive for collegiality so that participants feel assured that they have the final say in decisions that affect their lives.

Strengths-oriented intervention is a major aspect of empowerment. It implies that leaders should assess all participants in light of their capacities, talents, and competencies (Saleeby, 1996, 1997). The strengths perspective emphasizes human *resilience,* or the skills, abilities, knowledge, and insight that people accumulate over time as they struggle to surmount adversity and meet life challenges. It refers to the ability of people to persist in spite of their difficulties. The following are the major principles of strengths practice:

> All people have strengths.
> Problems can be a source of challenge and opportunity.
> Leaders can never know the upper levels of participants' growth potentials.
> There should be greater collaboration between practitioners and participants, to replace the traditional worker-participant hierarchy.
> Every environment includes many resources (many of them informal) that can be mobilized to help participants change.

Strengths-oriented practice mandates that practitioners give attention to both the risks and protective factors in a person's life.

Curative Factors in Psychoeducation

Before this chapter ends, it is important to note that the positive effects of psychoeducation may in fact be dependent on factors unrelated to its specific organization and content. The effectiveness of psychoeducation may ultimately depend on the leader's personal qualities and approach to the work. In one worldwide study of professional helpers, the following common characteristics of effective interventions were found:

> The participant enters into an emotionally charged, confiding relationship with the leader and perceives that the leader is competent and caring. This relationship enhances the participant's morale and promotes his or her determination to persist in the face of difficulties.
>
> The formal or otherwise "special" setting of the experience helps the participant feel safe and arouses the expectation of help.
>
> Content is based on what the participants perceive to be an understandable rationale and procedures that include an optimistic view of human nature. The leader's explanations are compatible with the participant's view of the world and thus help the participant make sense of his or her problems.
>
> The experience requires the active participation of all parties involved, all of whom believe the interventions to be a valid means of restoring health or improving functioning. Participants are given new opportunities for learning and success experiences to enhance their sense of mastery. (Frank & Frank, 1993)

Summary

Successful psychoeducational programs for individuals and groups may touch on up to six theoretical perspectives: cognitive theory, learning theory, psychodynamic theory, developmental theory, social support theory, and empowerment theory. Ideas about service delivery from each of these theories, respectively, encourage the leader to focus on participants' specific needs for education, new ways of thinking about their situations, ways to understand and act on their emotions constructively, participants' developmental histories, and ways of becoming effective at further work on their goals after the program ends. At the same time, some factors that help participants achieve their goals may be as rooted in the leader's personal presentation as they are in the specific program content.

The next chapter reviews several major theories of family systems and how they can be incorporated into psychoeducation-program development. These theories are essential to consider because psychoeducation is often provided to families as well as individuals.

Chapter 3

Psychoeducation and Family Theory

Many psychoeducational programs are conducted for families, either singly or in groups. In fact, the explosion in psychoeducation as an intervention for schizophrenia during the early 1980s featured family groups more than any other format. For this reason it is important for the practitioner to have an awareness of theories of family functioning, so that he or she can work toward enhancing family life in a proactive manner. It has already been emphasized in this book that psychoeducation is not a simple process of conveying information or facilitating support—the practitioner must have a sound theoretical knowledge of human behavior, including how people can make lasting changes in their lives. An awareness of family systems theory is essential for family work, both for the practitioner's effective presentation of educational material and for his or her ability to enhance members' efforts to provide support for one another (and for other families in multifamily groups).

Family theories bring the concept of interpersonal systems directly into the practitioner's focus. Working with families is qualitatively different than working with individuals. Assessing patterns of interaction and intervening with groups of people adds complexity to the process. Many practice theories specific to family work have been introduced into the literature since the 1950s, but two of them serve to adequately encompass the goals of psychoeducation—family emotional systems theory and structural family theory. These approaches are suitable for the purposes of psychoeducation because when families seek psychoeducation they are generally struggling with issues related to power and authority in a family or member's emotional ties or both. These two theories offer contrasting perspectives on family work and together provide the practitioner with a range of intervention options. In this chapter both theories are described in depth with a consideration of what they imply about the psychoeducation process.

A major difference between the family emotional systems and structural family theories is that the former was influenced by psychodynamic concepts and the latter is more cognitive-behavioral in its approach. Family emotional systems practitioners are concerned with the emotional attachments among members. As is true with the psychodynamic theories, many of their interventions are reflective in nature. Family structuralists are concerned with the architecture of the family. They assume that when a family constructs appropriate authority, rules, and boundaries for its members, their emotional lives will be satisfactory.

What follows is a detailed review of each theory, with an example of how each shapes the practitioner's activities.

Structural Family Theory

Structural family theory was developed by Salvador Minuchin in the 1970s and has continued to evolve through his ongoing work and that of others (Minuchin, 1974; Minuchin, Lee, & Simon, 1996). The focus of this theory is a family's structure, a concept that refers to the invisible and often unspoken rules that organize how members of a family interact. This theory developed in response to a perceived need for intervention methods that could be used with families having multiple problems, such as nontraditional inner-city families dealing with poverty and other issues contributing to family disruption. The theory was also influenced by the rise in prominence of the social learning, cognitive, and behavior theories and the growing demand for time-limited models of family intervention.

Structural family theory is particularly useful when working with families experiencing crisis and disorganization. Learning about effective and ineffective family structures can help persons who are experiencing disruption decide how best to reorganize their family units. Its interventions are suited to families plagued by acting-out members and problems such as drug addiction, some mental illnesses, crime, single-parenthood, and violence (see exhibits 3.1 and 3.2). The theory can, however, be used with any type of family.

Exhibit 3.1: Level 1 of family functioning: Meeting basic survival needs

Typical issues: food, shelter, safety, education, health, and an inability of the parental subsystem to provide adequate emotional nurturing
Examples: challenges related to meeting basic material needs, violence, physical abuse, academic problems, health needs, and crisis adjustment
Preferred intervention: structural

Exhibit 3.2: Level 2 of family functioning: Developing a clear family structure that maintains internal flexibility

Typical issues: appropriateness of executive (parental) authority, appropriateness of subsystems, and limit setting on member interactions
Examples: challenges related to parenting, balancing roles, communication, and changing roles due to life-cycle transitions
Preferred intervention: structural

Major Concepts

When a family experiences many types of problems or challenges regarding one or more members, its structure can be disrupted. The major concepts of structural family theory help practitioners determine where a family's structural problems are located and how to address them.

Roles are the functions provided within a family by each member. For example, in a traditional family unit, a father may have the role of bread-winner and the mother may have the role of caregiver. Roles change over time and in different contexts.

Rules are the behaviors, tasks, and responsibilities to which each family member is expected to adhere. They may be openly articulated or acquired as matters of circumstance or habit.

Each family includes *subsystems,* which are subsets of members who interact in certain contexts that are not equally open to the participation of other members. Subsystems may include parents, adult members, nuclear versus extended family members, siblings, and even subsets of siblings (depending, for example, on age or gender). Subsystems are normal and functional, but they can be problematic when serious conflicts develop between them (parents vs. children, for example) or if they exclude certain other members (such as a parent-child subsystem that excludes the other parent). Each family member usually belongs to more than one subsystem.

Alliances are conditions in which two family members or subsystems interact cooperatively. Alliances are positive when they contribute to the overall well-being of the persons involved and to the family as a unit. They are negative when they are rigid and exclusionary or otherwise contribute to family problems.

Internal boundaries are the invisible barriers that regulate the amounts of contact that members or subsystems have with each other. It is considered desirable that family members have some balance of access and privacy. Family boundaries may be rigid (members being physically or emotionally separated) or fluid (members being too close to one another and therefore being denied privacy or separateness). *External boundaries* refer to the separation of the family unit from external systems. It is appropriate for families to keep many of their interactions private from outsiders. The family may also interact as a unit within its community, for example, by attending church activities.

Executive authority and *power* are characteristics of the person or persons who are the primary rule and decision makers in the family. It is assumed that responsible adult members should have authority in a family. The persons who have power may shift, however, depending on the context. The power to decide whether to move the family to a new city may reside with the adult members, whereas the power to decide on a site for the annual vacation may rest with the children (within cost and time parameters set by adults).

Flexibility refers to the ability of the family to successfully adjust to predictable and unpredictable environmental demands. Family structure implies stability, but a healthy system must be adaptable to change. The family system must also be adaptable to life transitions, including the physical and emotional development of its members and the addition and subtraction of members through marriage, leaving home, birth, and death.

Communication is a concept that is universally important in human services intervention but receives extensive attention in structural family theory. It can be defined as all verbal and nonverbal practices of conveying messages to other persons or subsystems. Understanding family communication provides access to family rules. Functional family communications are characterized by verbal and nonverbal congruence and consistently observed rules.

How Problems Develop

Family structural characteristics that may contribute to problem development include power imbalances, disengaged members or subsystems, boundaries that are too rigid or too diffuse, the inability of members to mobilize support from one another when needed, members who rely too much on one another, member resistance to normal family processes (such as the growth and development of others), conflict avoidance, and the failure of the system to realign after a stressful event. When one member of a family experiences a problem that requires human services intervention, including issues of mental health, physical health, crisis, and developmental changes, the structure of a family may change. If the system becomes chaotic, structural interventions may be helpful for restoring family balance.

Goals of Structural Family Intervention

The goal of structural intervention is to adjust the existing family structure so that it becomes more functional for all participating members. This adjustment involves various strategies to strengthen, loosen, dissemble, or develop family alliances and subsystems. Change may also involve increasing the available supports for members outside the family system. The principle of structural family intervention that action precedes understanding suggests that the origin of a problem is largely irrelevant to the change process. One or more family members must take action, with the guidance of the practitioner, to change the nature of family interactions. Through restructuring processes that include practicing new ways of interacting and communicating, family members may experience significant relief from their presenting problems. Insight about the problem situation may occur after the fact, but this is not considered to be a necessary aspect of change.

Intervention Approaches

In structural family intervention, the practitioner acts as a stage director. This role is an active posture, as the practitioner becomes highly involved with family processes. He or she makes an effort to connect interpersonally with each family member in order to be perceived as credible and empathetic. To do so, the practitioner adjusts his or her natural interpersonal style to fit in with the family's style of interaction. The practitioner tries to convey an atmosphere of family competence when introducing any of the following specific interventions:

1. Teaching stress-management skills prior to initiating any anxiety-provoking interactions, to enhance the self-control of members.
2. Encouraging the family to track its problem behaviors between meetings so that members can more clearly perceive their structural patterns and get accustomed to working actively in the intervention.
3. Supporting the strengths of the system with compliments about aspects of family functioning that are going well, which includes affirming the dignity of the family with sympathetic responses and nonjudgmental comments.
4. Normalizing problems so that families do not feel badly about themselves.
5. Manipulating space in sessions. In this strategy, the practitioner asks family members to sit next to, closer to, farther from, or facing one another in ways that highlight structural characteristics, such as alliances, subsystems, and boundaries. The technique also demonstrates to families in a physical manner how their structures can be changed. For example, adults who lack power may be asked to sit closely together during sessions to provide support to each other.
6. Communication-skills development, since the root of many family problems lies in the inability of members to clearly communicate their needs, ideas, and feelings to one another. The practitioner may spend much time instructing families in methods of clear speaking and listening, using space (as described in number 5) to facilitate the process. As a part of this technique, the practitioner helps family members redirect the manner in which they process stress, such as withdrawing when communication becomes negatively charged.
7. Directing simulations (rather than relying entirely on discussions) of actual or possible family situations with role-plays as a means of illustrating and changing family interactions. Instructing members to practice interacting in new ways helps to adjust alliances and other structural characteristics to promote a more functional family system. For example, spouses may be asked to discuss how they want to respond to the negative behavior of a child in the presence of the children so as to enhance their executive authority. Detached chil-

dren in a family may be asked to interact as a means of strengthening that subsystem. In role reversals members are asked to play the roles of other family members to sensitize them to the feelings of others with whom they may be in conflict.

8. Assigning tasks, or homework, for members to complete between sessions insures the family is continuously working toward its goals. Tasks facilitate the implementation of new behaviors in the natural environment, and members can report on their ability to complete these tasks when they return to the practitioner's setting.

An Application of Structural Family Theory in Psychoeducation

Steve and Laura Booth attended a family program for the parents of adolescent and young adult children who had substance-abuse problems. Their twenty-one-year-old son, Paul, who lived with them at home, was a longtime alcohol abuser who had lost two jobs and his driver's license due to an inability to control his drinking. The Booth family also included a younger son (eighteen) and daughter (sixteen), both of whom used alcohol (according to the parents) but had never been in trouble for it outside the home.

A major goal of the program, which included four sets of parents and was conducted by a social worker, was to educate families about how substance abuse, whatever its origins, can be effectively reinforced or punished within the family system. That is, family responses to the substance abuser can have a major impact on whether the abuse persists. During the once-weekly three-session program, parents were helped to examine their family structure and consider whether any systems adjustments might reduce or eliminate the abuser's drinking and have positive effects on all members of the family.

During discussions, the social worker suggested that the Booth household lacked an effective executive authority. Steve could be a strict disciplinarian and had, in fact, told his oldest son on two occasions that he must leave the house if he didn't stop his drinking. But Laura, who seemed to be uncomfortable with conflict and guilty about the fact that she worked part-time, rarely followed through with her husband's stated limits. This difference in approach created tension between Steve and Laura, but their way of managing the situation was to avoid discussing topics (such as Steve's drinking) that might set them off. The three children, sensing their mom's ambivalence about punishment, often formed alliances when their dad was away in which they would together argue with her about one member's demand (they all benefited from supporting each other). They had even been able on occasion to talk their mom into purchasing alcohol for them to use at home. Laura's daughter said to her, "It's better than us drinking it somewhere else, don't you think?"

The social worker (and the other family group members) were able to point out to Steve and Laura that their children had been allowed to assume primary power in the family when it came to their own personal interests. Paul's problem behavior was the most striking, but given that adolescents cannot appropriately manage power in any family system, the other children were at risk for more serious problem behavior. The children had formed a close subsystem for the purpose of manipulating their mom, and in turn the parents, due to their tendency to be mutually avoidant when in conflict, had not established family roles (these might include grocery shopping, house-keeping, consistent attention to school, yard work, etc.) to insure that all of the children made unique contributions to total-family life; nor were they establishing (let alone enforcing) clear household rules for their children (or each other).

Although the above assessment might seem harsh, the practitioner handled it delicately, and the other families identified with the Booths' dilemma, seeing how their own households were structurally out of balance in some ways. This parents program was relatively brief, but the Booth couple was able to see the value of coming together and retaking control of the family system.

Family Emotional Systems Theory

Family emotional systems theory provides a rich and comprehensive framework for understanding how the emotional ties within families influence members throughout their lives in ways they often fail to recognize (Bowen, 1978; Kerr & Bowen, 1988; Titelman, 1998). Many adolescents and young adults, even when they have positive family relationships, believe that after years of relying on relatives they can become independent people, apart from family influence. This theory asserts, very much to the contrary, that the influence of the nuclear family is always with people. How adults manage other relationships, for better or worse, represents a continuation of patterns that they developed in early family life.

Family functioning is considered to be healthy when members can balance a sense of separateness from and togetherness with others and can appropriately control their emotional lives with a developed intellect. Family systems theory is particularly appropriate to guide practice when a family's (or individual's) difficulties are related to unstable relationships within their current family system, resulting in an inability of the members to achieve this balance. The kinds of problems presented by these families in clinical settings include relationships characterized by extreme emotional reactivity and the inability of members to break free from family ties to an extent that they can thrive outside the family unit (see exhibits 3.3 and 3.4). Clearly the emotional relationships among all members of a family unit may significantly change as a result of an illness or behavioral problem in one member.

Exhibit 3.3:   Level 3 of family functioning: Insuring adequate space and boundaries for all members

Typical issues: control and dominance, member isolation or distancing, and rigid relationships
Examples: challenges related to changing emotional relationships due to life-cycle transitions, grief, substance abuse, anger management, depression, sexual abuse, sexual identity, loss, and rejection
Preferred intervention: family emotional systems

Exhibit 3.4:   Level 4 of family functioning: Quality of life

Typical issues: intimacy and self-actualization
Examples: challenges related to blended families, emotional support needs (often due to life-cycle transitions), and improving quality of communications
Preferred intervention: family emotional systems

Major Concepts

The major concepts from family systems theory all have implications for the psychoeducational practitioner's interventions, if he or she determines that dealing with emotional relationships is a primary family need. Included in the descriptions of these concepts that follow are indicators of the causes of family system problems that can be addressed with psychoeducation.

In the *multigenerational perspective,* individual personalities and patterns of interaction among family members have their origins in previous generations. Further, the influence of extended family relationships might be as important to one's development as the nuclear family. In assessment, an understanding of family member characteristics and interaction patterns over three generations is ideal. This assessment can be done with a genogram, a diagram drawn by a program leader that includes two or three generations of a family with descriptions of how the members have related to one another. This process is useful in assessing family patterns of interaction and dealing with conflict over time, and it may also develop new insight among the family members that they can use in establishing new patterns.

Healthy individual functioning is characterized by *differentiation of self,* a concept with two meanings. First, it describes a person's capacity to distinguish between and balance his or her thinking and feeling selves. Thinking processes represent the ability to consciously recognize personal reactions or biases. Emotional reactions provide important information about the significance of situations. Differentiation also refers to one's ability to physically separate from his or her family of origin in a manner that preserves those emotional ties while not being constrained by them.

Triangles refer to family emotional systems theory's assertion that all intimate relationships are inherently unstable and require the availability of a third party to maintain their stability. That is, the price of intimacy is the experience of occasional conflict, and when in conflict people usually rely on a third person for mediation, ventilation, or problem-solving assistance. This reliance on a third party is a normal and usually healthy process. Serious problems related to one's differentiation may develop, however, when he or she is drawn into certain triangles within the family. When a weaker (younger or undifferentiated) person is drawn into a triangle in a way that does not facilitate the other two people's resolution of their conflict, that person may be deprived of the opportunity for individual development. He or she may, for example, assume the ongoing role of helping the other people avoid facing their problems with each other.

Anxiety is an unpleasant but normal affect that provides people with warning signs for perceived threats (Zvolensky, Lejuez, & Eifert, 2000). An anxiety-producing situation may be perceived as an opportunity for growth or a threat to well-being, and it is problematic only when it interferes with one's capacity for problem solving. All family systems include levels of anxiety, just as individuals do. Four relationship patterns that tend to foster family problems are marital conflict, problematic emotional functioning in one spouse, emotional impairment of a child, or emotional fusion in which two members distance themselves from each other to reduce the intensity of their relationship. A family system characterized by any of these patterns may develop an atmosphere of anxiety that is shared by all members.

Psychological defenses are processes by which people protect themselves from intolerable anxiety by keeping unacceptable impulses out of their awareness (Goldstein, 1995). *Projection* is a common defense in which one person attributes his or her unacceptable thoughts and feelings to someone else. The projector is not aware of having the feelings or thoughts but believes that the person on whom he or she is projected is experiencing them. Parents often use the defense of projection with their children as targets, because children are vulnerable family members. Within family systems, children may suffer if the parents frequently project negative feelings and ideas onto them. The children may believe that they possess these negative thoughts and feelings and behave as such. They become more emotionally reactive, and the quest for differentiation is compromised.

Fusion is the opposite of differentiation. It is a shared state involving two or more people, the result of a triangulation in which one member sacrifices his or her striving toward differentiation in the service of balancing the relationship of two other people. When one person is fused with another, his or her emotional reactivity to the other person becomes strong.

He or she does not think but only feels, and does so in response to the emotional state of the other person. Neither person is consciously aware of this state, because they both lack the capacity to adequately reason about, or reflect on, the situation. Fusion happens because for a significant length of time during childhood and adolescence prior to having an opportunity to differentiate, the fused person began to function within a triangle that served the needs of other family members.

People tend to lack insight into the fact that they are fused, but they experience high levels of emotional reactivity to the other person and may attempt to extricate themselves from the relationship. A common strategy is the *emotional cutoff*. This term refers to a person's attempts to emotionally distance him- or herself from certain members of the family, or from the entire family. Emotional cutoff is the result of a person's inability to directly resolve the anxiety related to fusion, and it prevents him or her from forming an identity or satisfying relationships with others. The pattern can continue after he or she leaves home. When physical distance alone is seen as a solution to ongoing family tensions, the person may be disappointed. A first-year college student may feel that he or she can at last take charge of his or her life when in fact fusion prevents the person from investing emotionally with other people.

Goals of Family Emotional Systems Intervention

The nature of change in family emotional systems theory involves an opening up of the system. Change requires detriangulation and the building of new alliances among members of the nuclear and extended family. The practitioner attends to the goals of lowering family system anxiety, increasing the reflective capacity of the members, and promoting differentiation by emotionally realigning relationships within the family system. Family emotional systems practitioners do not work with a set of explicit, concrete intervention techniques but rather with more general approaches, as will be described. The practitioner is challenged to adapt these approaches to a family's particular concerns.

Intervention Approaches

Genogram construction and review, as noted previously, is an excellent means of educating family members about their relationship patterns. It should be used only when working with individual families, however, as genograms include much sensitive information that a family may not want to share with a group.

Coaching is when the practitioner stands at the sidelines of the family system, asking questions that are intended to increase understanding and attachments among family members. This approach includes strategies known as person-situation and developmental reflection. With person-situation reflection, the practitioner makes comments, asks questions, and offers tentative explanations that promote family members' reflective capacity. The practitioner assumes a moderately directive stance and provides here-and-now interpretations of family behavior. This technique improves the family members' capacity to evaluate feelings and attitudes, understand one another and the nature of their behaviors, and consider a wider range of problem-solving options. With developmental reflection, the practitioner uses comments, questions, and tentative explanations to explore connections between the family's present and past patterns of behavior. The family may develop insight into patterns of behavior that stem from irrational feelings and fears and become able to consider new ways of thinking about the past and present.

Promoting the "I" position entails asking family members to take a personal stance when making comments, saying what they feel instead of what they observe. The practitioner should also use "I" statements. This approach helps to minimize confrontation, which increases anxiety and decrease one's ability to think clearly.

Therapeutic triangulation is taking the perspective of a family member who is at the point of a problematic triangle and asking questions of the other two members that bring attention to the negative aspects of the triangle. This approach is particularly effective when representing the perspectives of children, as well as other less powerful members. With couples, the practitioner becomes a member of a constructive triangle and poses questions aimed at toning down emotional reactivity and fostering more objective observation and thought.

Relationship experiments include any task strategies by which the practitioner opens up the family members to new, more functional alliances. These tasks may be performed within a meeting or between meetings, when members are at home. For example, some family members (such as children) might be encouraged to get to know extended family members (aunts, uncles, or grandparents). These experiments are similar to the enactments discussed in structural family theory, but they tend to be less detailed.

Displacement stories involve showing films or videos or telling stories to teach members about the functioning of other family systems, in ways that lower their defensiveness. The family is focused on an external group of people who are intended to represent what the family is experiencing, and they may apply any lessons learned to themselves.

An Application of Family Systems Theory in Psychoeducation

Barbara Lewis was a sixty-two-year-old widow with two grown children (Cyndi, thirty-seven, and Eddie, thirty-two) and a lifelong history of major depression. She had been taking antidepressant medications since her young adulthood and was hospitalized five times over the years for severe depressions in which she became delusional and could not get out of bed. These episodes each lasted about one month, and after a recuperative period of a few more months Barbara would again function at a normal level, with no evident symptoms until the next onset of depression several years later. Barbara had just been released from the hospital when she met Jane, her new social worker at the mental health center. When Jane met Barbara at the hospital, the client warned her to "get out of this submarine before it loses all contact with the navy and gets us all lost at sea." Since then, Barbara had bounced back nicely and was living at home alone, managing her personal affairs well and interacting with other women in her community.

Barbara's oldest child, Cyndi, had expressed concerns about her mother to the social worker because the client's husband, James, had died four years before and therefore would not be there to monitor Barbara's mental status, as he had always done. Cyndi's brother, Eddie, was emotionally cut off from their mother, having always been closer to his father and having only a superficial relationship with his mother. Cyndi felt responsible for taking care of her mother, even though at this time Barbara seemed fine and likely to adhere to her medication and counseling regimens.

Following an assessment, Jane decided to implement a psychoeducational intervention based on family emotional systems theory as part of her overall intervention plan. She wanted to educate Barbara and Cyndi about the patterns of interaction in the family and talk with them about trying to engage Eddie in the family system more substantively. The family was well-set materially, with a history of an appropriate authority, rules, subsystems, and boundaries. The family concerns were not related to structure but to emotional relationships. A system anxiety had developed since Mr. Lewis's death. Cyndi seemed to be somewhat undifferentiated from her mother, worrying about her excessively at the expense of her own family (she was married with two children). Eddie wouldn't reach out to his mother, always feeling that she hadn't been "good enough" for his father. Cyndi was thus located at the center of a family triangle. She was always trying to mediate between her mother and brother, trying to resolve their differences and make sure that everyone's needs were met. Cyndi and her brother got along well, but Barbara and Eddie communicated only through Cyndi. Jane concluded that Barbara's capacity for independent living was being constrained by Cyndi's well-meaning but controlling presence and that Cyndi's own family life was endangered by this pattern. Barbara and Cyndi both agreed to Jane's proposal for three sessions of psychoeducation, in which the health of the family would be addressed in light of Barbara's mental status.

The social worker identified a need to open up the family system with an increased presence of several relatives so that Barbara and Cyndi could be freer to pursue their own differentiated lives. To facilitate this process, Jane educated the women in the concepts of family emotional systems theory, praising both of them for contributing to the welfare of the family unit for so many years while pointing out the potential problems inherent in the symptomatic triangle. Cyndi was encouraged to invite two of her uncles into Barbara's life more prominently to assist in her support, and Barbara was encouraged to seek out a relationship with her son directly, instead of communicating through her daughter. Through relationship experiments, mutual reflection, Jane's own thoughts about what she would do if she were in Barbara's position (therapeutic triangulation), and the encouragement of both women to own their own feelings through the use of "I" statements, these goals were achieved. Barbara would continue to receive supportive counseling, medication management, and case-management services, but it seemed that she might now feel more comfortable with her family situation, which enhanced her long-term mental health prognosis.

Summary

Effectively providing psychoeducational programs for families requires that the leader have a working knowledge of one or more theories of family functioning on which to base the intervention activities. A family systems theoretical perspective enables the leader to have a lens through which he or she can evaluate how well the program material will be received and processed by the participants and how that material will be applied throughout a family. Structural family theory and family emotional systems theory, although only two of many family systems theories, are useful in most psychoeducational groups because together they address cognitive, behavioral, and reflective aspects of family life.

Chapter 4

Teaching Skills for Psychoeducation

To be effective psychoeducators, human service professionals must be effective teachers. Herein lies one of the paradoxes of psychoeducation: the teacher may have a depth of knowledge about a relevant topic but be unable to effectively convey that knowledge to others. It appears to be assumed in the psychoeducation literature that having knowledge qualifies one to dispense it, but this assumption is not necessarily true. Any college student will attest that some of his or her worst teachers were the professors, and some of his or her best teachers were the graduate students in training. For this reason it is important to review some essential components of effective teaching. Formal training in psychoeducation seems to be somewhat limited, as few programs offer course work in its foundations, principles, and theories. The purpose of this chapter is to introduce relevant topics related to effective teaching. There are entire textbooks devoted to each of these points, of course, so this review is brief.

Characteristics of Good Teachers

Some educators seem to have natural gifts in their craft, but they would probably all agree that becoming a good educator is a process that unfolds over a lifetime. Effective teaching is in part a function of one's personal qualities (the ability to make connections, inspire, be flexible to the needs of students, etc.) as well as mastery of some content area. That is, becoming a good teacher is partly a process of fusing one's natural interpersonal style with expertise in a topic area. This chapter considers some of the principles that psychoeducators can practice as they find their way to effectiveness. To begin, some characteristics of good teachers and, by extension, of psychoeducation providers are described here.

The practitioner must have broad and in-depth *knowledge about the subject* he or she is covering, for example, the nature of schizophrenia, its symptoms, its causes and course, the factors related to adjustment and recovery, the role of significant others in the course of the disorder, and what kinds of limits significant others should enforce to make sure they do not organize their entire lives around the disorder.

Organization skills, especially with groups, insure that the material to be addressed is interesting and well paced. Such skills include starting and stopping a presentation on time, preventing inappropriate interruptions, maintaining group momentum, and managing topic transitions.

Presentation (communication) skills refer to the practitioner's ability to deliver content and facilitate members' interactions clearly, with appropriate language, and in a variety of ways (lectures, PowerPoint presentations, discussions, etc.) to keep them engaged.

Practitioners must consistently demonstrate *positive attitudes about participants,* as people as well as learners, and have the ability to enthusiastically communicate belief in the participants' potential to grow.

Practitioners should be able to accurately *assess the motivational levels, paces of learning, and moods of learners.* These skills are unrelated to expertise in a subject area and instead reflect an appreciation of individual differences in how information is acquired and retained.

Related to the above point, the practitioner must have an *awareness of different learning styles* of participants (for example, people may be visual, verbal, or task-based learners) and be able to incorporate these styles into the learning process through variety in teaching activities.

The practitioner must have an *ability to think critically about the content area,* that is, to consider the limits to knowledge and the implications of knowledge for the lives of the participants. This is a deeper level of knowledge than simply having factual information.

The practitioner must possess the *ability to tolerate frequent repetition and a slow pace of learning.* The topics for which people seek psychoeducation are complex, and the practitioner's nature of interactions with "lay" learners will be quite different from those with professional colleagues.

The practitioner must *provide opportunities for learners to share their concerns and questions,* in other words, become participants in the learning process.

Evaluation skills are required for the practitioner to determine whether the psychoeducation process is having its desired effects. The practitioner must be able to evaluate the extent of learning that has taken place, the adequacy of the content, issues for program improvement, and the quality of his or her own performance.

An informal survey of graduate social work students at the author's university yielded these additional characteristics of good teachers: being approachable, nonjudgmental, entertaining, interactive, trustworthy, enthusiastic, and experienced with the material. Clearly many of these characteristics transcend simple knowledge about a topic. Some additional characteristics related to educating people in group settings will be presented in chapter 5.

Levels of Learning

Many years ago the educational philosopher Benjamin Bloom (1976) articulated six levels at which learning objectives can be formulated, depending on the nature of the subject matter, characteristics of the learner, and goals of the teaching. None of these levels is considered superior to the others; the point is that an educator must keep in mind the kind of learning he or she wants to instill in learners prior to developing a curriculum. The six levels can be described as follows.

Basic knowledge is being capable of reading and understanding words, facts, dates, classifications, principles, and theories. Many survey courses, which are intended to introduce learners to broad knowledge about a subject, are taught with these objectives. Teaching strategies associated with this learning level include presentations that are based on comprehensive outlines, the labeling and defining of important terms, and emphasizing fundamental principles about a topic area. In a group for parents of children with attention deficit hyperactivity disorder, for example, the psychoeducator will certainly be intent, at least in part, on many facts about the condition.

Comprehension involves the learner becoming able to interpret information and extrapolate from a certain body of knowledge. That is, the learner not only masters facts but also is expected to use that information to learn more on his or her own from that body of facts. Teaching strategies include summarizing for participants different types and sources of information about a topic, helping learners to absorb the information in their own words, and helping them to defend their ideas in different contexts. Education about HIV/AIDS may focus on the participants' ability to grasp the implications of the information on how they should conduct themselves in close interpersonal relationships.

Application is a process of helping the learner to become capable of remembering knowledge or principles in order to solve problems in the future. That is, learners can apply their knowledge to generate new solutions to challenges. Teaching strategies include proposing novel situations and possible solutions to learners and giving them complex demonstrations, perhaps through role-plays. Parents of children with diabetes will want to know how best to respond when their children experience a sugar deficiency, and the educator can engage all of them in discussions about how they would respond in a variety of situations.

Analysis refers to a teacher's ability to help learners become capable of identifying the common elements and differences of topic-related problem situations and the limitations of their knowledge. They need to be able to pick apart relevant versus irrelevant aspects of challenging situations as a means of more fully grasping how to make decisions. Teaching strategies involve breaking a problem down into parts and relating the elements to a variety of possible solutions. A safe-sex group will, among other things, help participants to differentiate the characteristics of appropriate and inappropriate interactions with potential romantic partners and to think about what interpersonal situations call for what kinds of actions.

Synthesis refers to the learner's ability to accomplish a personal task after devising a plan of action. Teaching strategies involve designing problem-prevention strategies and inventing new ways to accomplish tasks. Persons with bulimia may be helped to plan for avoiding further binge episodes and maintaining good dietary habits by summarizing the interacting risk and protective factors associated with their problem behaviors.

Evaluation is the learner's capacity to make effective critical judgments about a situation based on certain criteria. Teaching strategies include helping learners to specify their desired outcomes and weighing the pros and cons of different actions toward those ends, selecting best options with clear rationales, and critiquing both the processes and outcomes of the problem-solving behavior. For persons who are members of minority groups and working to increase their ethnic pride, such learning involves considering and evaluating a variety of lifestyle choices that will be consistent with the learner's short- and long-term personal goals.

Types of Student Learners

In addition to learning objectives, there are different types of learners, much as there are different personality types. The psychoeducator does not need to assess the preferred learning styles of his or her participants in advance but should integrate learning activities into programs that touch on each of them. Four general types of learners are described next (Kolb, 1984).

The *activist* learns best through experimentation of the type found in simulations, case studies, and homework assignments. This person learns best not by listening but by doing. Appropriate educational approaches for this person include problem-solving activities, small-group discussions, utilization of peer feedback, and homework. When learning about schizophrenia, for example, the activist may want to participate in simulated treatment-planning exercises to get a feel for what kinds of services might be most useful for the family member.

The *reflector* learns best through reflective observations and discussions about a topic. The use of learning journals and brainstorming activities are helpful to this process. The learner needs time to think about new material, to see how it fits with his or her view of the world. This person may try hard to get a feel for what it is like to experience an issue of concern. Lectures are helpful toward this end, and the educator should also provide general commentaries about the material that the learner can ponder.

The *theorist* learns best by abstract conceptualization, through lectures and supplemental readings that link the material to other ideas. This person may best learn about adolescent identity development, for example, by comparing the ideas formulated by such diverse theorists as Erikson (1968), who postulated common processes of psychosocial development, and Levinson (1978), who presented common stages of male development through the life span. Suitable educational approaches include theory readings and debates.

The *pragmatist* learns best with concrete experiences of the type found in laboratories, fieldwork, and personal observations. Peer feedback is helpful for this learner, and activities should be provided that help the learner apply new knowledge and skills. The educator serves as a catalyst for self-directed, autonomous learning by such learners. For learning about eating disorders, this type of learner may benefit from interacting with community treatment providers and learning about the various interventions they utilize. He or she may be particularly interested in the empirical evidence that supports these interventions.

Summary Considerations for Psycho "Educators"

Providers of psychoeducation need to attend to the following three factors in making informational presentations to members.

Educational methods must be consistent with the learning styles of participants. There are many types of intelligence and many ways that people can learn. Howard Gardner's (1999) theory of multiple intelligences constitutes a major step forward in understanding how people come to possess different types of cognitive skills and how the same person is able to effectively use cognitive skills in some areas of life but not in others. In this theory, intelligence is defined as a "biopsychosocial potential to process information that can be activated in a cultural setting to solve problems" (Gardner, 1999, p. 23). Gardner has delineated seven intelligences, which are summarized in exhibit 4.1. Two intelligences, *linguistic* (related to spoken and written language) and *logical-mathematical* (analytic), are consistent with traditional notions of intelligence. The five others, however, are not.

Exhibit 4.1: **Gardner's multiple intelligences**

Linguistic: the capacity to use language to express what is on your mind and to understand other people

Logical-mathematical: the capacity for mathematical calculation, logical thinking, problem solving, and deductive and inductive reasoning

Visual-spatial: the ability to represent the spatial world internally through visual discrimination, recognition, mental imagery, and image manipulation

Bodily kinesthetic: the capacity to use your body to solve a problem, make something, or put on some kind of production; the body can be trained to respond to the expressive powers of the mind

Musical: the capacity to think in music and to hear patterns, remember them, and perhaps manipulate them

Intrapersonal: the capacity to understand yourself, to know who you are, what you can do and want to do, how you react to things, which things to avoid and gravitate toward, and where to go if you need help; such people are aware of their range of emotions and can find outlets for them

Interpersonal: the ability to understand and communicate with others; note differences in moods, temperaments, motivations, and skills; form and maintain relationships; assume roles within groups; and adapt behavior to different environments

In consideration of the idea that different people have different intelligence strengths, the psychoeducator should design teaching strategies that may appeal to different intelligences. Instead of working from the traditional linguistic perspective that relies on spoken language, the leader can include variety in his or her curriculum, for example by using art, music, emotive, and interpersonal activities. In addition to encompassing the participants' intelligence strengths, variety will also make for a more broadly engaging program.

The nature of psychoeducation must be consistent with traditions in the participants' cultures. Components of diversity, including the leader-participant relationship and the selection of specific topics and activities, must be considered in selecting program formats and include attention to the following: socioeconomic class, gender, religion, ability and disability, ethnicity, and race (Jordan et al., 1995).

Dimensions of multicultural position have relevance to how content is integrated into the teacher and learner's experience, how they construct knowledge, the leader's attention to prejudice-reduction activities with participants, equity pedagogy (the amount of time used with auditory, visual, written, and practice educational methods), and how the individual or group culture can best experience empowerment.

Related to each mind's unique aspect of information processing, Jean Piaget's (1977) concept of the *schema* is important. Schema is defined as an internalized representation of the world, or ingrained patterns of thought, action, and problem solving. Schemas develop through social learning (watching and absorbing the experiences of others) or direct learning (one's own experiences). Both processes may involve assimilation (responding to experiences based on existing schemata) or accommodation (changing schema when new situations cannot be incorporated within an existing one). Any experience (or new information) that one cannot assimilate creates anxiety, but if schemas are adjusted to accommodate the new experience, a desired state of internal equilibrium will be restored. The psychoeducator's appreciation for differences in information processing, based on the participant's existing cognitive sets, can facilitate learning.

The stage of the participant's level of knowledge and needs must be considered with regard to his or her readiness to accept certain types of information. Psychoeducation is often provided for people who are confronting a grave situation in their or their family members' lives. They may know a lot or very little about the situation, and care must be taken to introduce content at a level at which the learner can comprehend it and not be overwhelmed by its implications. People are often initially in denial about certain problems (such as mental illness, alcoholism, and physical disease), and their defenses need to be respected as they gradually develop the ability to accept and cope with the issue.

The challenge for the leader to be sensitive to the learner's stage of knowledge can be clearly seen in group work. For example, in a multiple-family group, the leader must be careful about including family participants whose disabled relative has dealt with a frustrating chronic condition alongside other families who are newer to the condition. Although this may be an opportunity for the constructive sharing of experiences and perspectives, the "younger" family may become overwhelmed with grief if they are not ready to consider the possible duration of their family challenges. As another example, some leaders of grief groups do not include participants who have been bereaved for less than six months, on the grounds that they are not ready to fully process the implications of their life change.

The points described above suggest that designing effective instructional materials for psychoeducation takes careful planning, with attention to the needs, personal characteristics, existing knowledge bases, and demographic backgrounds of the participants. Implications of these issues for the educator are discussed next.

Components of Effective Instruction

When educational material is to be disseminated, the leader needs to further attend to the principles of effective instruction, as described in the following:

Orient participants to the subject matter at the first meeting, and orient them to each related subject that is subsequently introduced. For example, participants should be thoroughly introduced to the nature of bereavement at the first session of such a group. Later the stages of grief should be separately reviewed in depth as they become a focus of discussion.

State all learning objectives clearly, and invite the participants to articulate their own objectives.

Break down information about complex topics into units that can be addressed sequentially. This is particularly helpful for learners who feel overwhelmed or have difficulty keeping focused on their concerns. One example is to slowly describe the identifiable steps of the progression of AIDS and the steps involved in its treatment.

Review any prerequisite knowledge that participants must have in order to comprehend new material. Prior to a psychoeducational presentation on disruptive behavior disorders, for example, the practitioner may survey a participant about his or her prior knowledge of some causes of disruptive behavior and then offer reading material to supplement this level of knowledge.

Present the new material in ways that the audience can appreciate, be it through DVD presentations, shared activities, or lecture, for example.

Ask questions of the participants regularly as new material is being presented to test whether it is being received as intended.

Provide practice of new content through discussion, role-playing, hypothetical problem-solving exercises, and perhaps through implementation outside the session. As an example, participants can be encouraged to practice new communication or relaxation strategies between meetings.

Assess participant learning regularly, through the use of formal or informal measures.

Provide regular feedback to participants on their progress in grasping new information, and be prepared to review or present the information again in another way.

Understand that discussion of material is always indicated when dealing with controversial topics, particularly difficult topics, and when the educational experience includes emotional processing. Practitioners should not assume that participants will share their feelings about sensitive topics without being encouraged to do so.

The structure of a psychoeducation program should depend on the characteristics of the desired participants. Some structures have been recommended for persons with mental illnesses. For persons with depression, education should facilitate the acquisition of problem-solving skills and the reframing of negative memories (Klausner et al., 1998). For persons with schizophrenia, who have problems with attention, concentration, and memory, it is important for the leader to focus on cognitive-skills enhancement (Hogarty et al., 2004). Both types of participants benefit from instructional methods that include constant repetition of content to reinforce learning.

One group of researchers has found that intellectually higher functioning participants learn significantly more when the information is presented in an unstructured format (Emer, McLarney, Goodwin, & Keller, 2002). They argue that structured formats interfere with higher functioning participants' own varied learning approaches. The same researchers found that lower intellectually functioning participants show no preference for either structured or unstructured formats, but they do require additional support (and more time) with their information-processing needs. In addition, Greenberg, Fine, Cohen, and Larson (1988) argue that lower functioning participants are more likely to find group formats overstimulating. When in doubt, it seems, the psychoeducator should develop unstructured teaching formats, which will meet the needs of a greater proportion of participants.

Summary

For psychoeducation to be effective, the provider needs to pay as much attention to how he or she organizes and presents the intervention as to the content of that intervention. In an effort to alert service providers to the importance of program organization, some characteristics of good teachers, levels of learning, types of learners, types of intelligence, and other guidelines have been reviewed in this chapter. The points presented here will be elaborated in more detail in part 2, as the book looks at how they are addressed in specific programs.

Chapter 5

Group Development and Leadership

Psychoeducation programs are often provided in group formats. This practice is compatible with the goals of the modality because all intervention groups set out to provide members with education and new skills, behaviors, and ways of understanding themselves and their surroundings (Toseland & Rivas, 2006). All groups also attend to the interpersonal needs of members through mutual support and perhaps social learning (see exhibits 5.1 and 5.2). Although group interventions may feature a variety of theoretical perspectives, almost all groups can be provided in formats based on the cognitive, behavioral, and psychodynamic theories described in chapter 2. The purpose of this chapter is to provide an overview of psychoeducational group development, leadership, and assessment. (Because this is a chapter on groups, the practitioner will be referred to as the leader.)

Exhibit 5.1:   Therapeutic factors in groups

Instillation of hope from the support of other members
Greater self-understanding
Positive role modeling (imitating the strengths of others)
Learning from interactions (both verbal and nonverbal feedback)
Universalizing of experiences ("you are not alone" with the problem
    or challenge)
Group serves as a reflection of society (reality testing)
Acceptance by others
Support for healthy self-disclosure (as an antidote to isolation)
Opportunities to help others (altruism)

Exhibit 5.2:   Beneficial factors in family groups

Presence of positive peer models
Opportunities to express and validate concerns and questions
Positive collaborative relationships infuse members with hope, optimism, and mutual respect

Member commitment is enhanced when they participate in the planning of group content

A focus on practicality (concrete problem solving and specific and attainable goals)

The group process facilitates the integration of information into each participant's unique experience

Peer instructor's role modeling and credibility

Interventions enhance the sense of dignity and self-esteem due to increased tools for self-care

Interventions increase resilience to stress, coping skills, and problem manageability

Mastery (success) experiences increase levels of empowerment

As mentioned in chapter 1, psychoeducation groups may be led by professionals or by persons who share the life challenge of the group members. For example, Rummel, Hansen, Helbig, Pitschel-Walz, and Kissling (2005) trained individuals with schizophrenia or schizoaffective disorder to deliver psychoeducation to their peers, and outcomes were comparable to professionally led groups. The researchers attributed the effectiveness of this delivery of psychoeducation to the leaders' creditability with their peers and their function as role models.

Forming Psychoeducational Groups

Regardless of their level of formality, intervention groups need to be planned with clear purposes and procedures. What follows are steps to take in forming psychoeducation groups (Zastrow, 2006). I will use the example of my own family education and support group to illustrate each step.

Articulate the purpose of the group. This step requires a concise statement that clarifies for all persons involved what the group will attempt to accomplish. My family education and support group was developed with the purpose of helping families to accomplish the following:

Become educated about current theories of the mental disorders that affect their relatives, including causes, course, interventions, and prognosis

Become educated about the purposes and actions of the medications used to treat their relatives

Act as an ongoing mutual support system in day-to-day interactions with relatives, with an emphasis on reducing and controlling behaviors disruptive to the family

Become informed about local agencies that provide relevant services to clients and families

Become well educated enough about the mental health service system that they can advocate for quality services on behalf of their
relatives
Reduce their feelings of guilt and social isolation
Become able to pursue activities that do not center on the client
member

The sponsoring agency may have additional goals for the group. My
agency director saw the above group as a means of better integrating our
agency with the network of other agencies in the city by offering a unique
program.

Identify a guiding theoretical framework. This step refers to the general approach (such as cognitive or behavioral) that the leaders will take in
delivering the service to group members. The importance of selecting a theoretical approach is to bring consistency to group activities. Cognitive theory, with its emphasis on learning, is pertinent to educational groups, and
behavior theory is relevant to groups that are intent on changing member
behaviors, such as skill-building groups. Psychodynamic theory emphasizes
the role of emotions, some of which may lie below the surface, in shaping
one's responses to a life challenge. The family education and support group
utilized all three perspectives, the second one to help the members reinforce their impaired relatives' behaviors differently.

*Identify the level of learning (see chapter 4) that the program will tar-
get.* Most leaders will want to organize presentations and interactions to
enhance participants' basic knowledge, comprehension, and application
skills (as the family education and support group did). More ambitious (or
academic) programs will also help participants to develop analytic, synthesis, and evaluation capabilities.

Articulate the roles of the leaders. Leaders should decide what roles
they anticipate playing during the meetings. These roles will depend on the
purposes and membership of the group. It is possible that group leaders
will be highly directive and active, more facilitative, or perhaps more
focused on monitoring the activities of the members. Leader roles may
change over time depending on the group membership and through trial
and error to discover what works best. Leaders should be flexible in how
they approach their roles. In the family education and support group, I
hoped to be an active leader but yielded leadership roles to the participants
after the group had been together for several weeks and they became more
relaxed and active.

Select techniques and activities for the group. This step is related to the
theoretical framework but refers more concretely to how the leader will use
time in the group. That is, what will the leader and members do? These decisions should be based on a thorough literature review to determine what
types of activities have been found helpful for particular populations. In the

family education and support group, the coleaders divided up each ninety-minute session into providing lecture material, discussing handouts, and informal discussion of member concerns. By the time recruitment begins, leaders should have most of these materials selected, even though they may make changes during the member screening process.

Locate space for the group. Space is often at a premium in agencies, so the leader should not forget the step of reserving adequate space for the group. I once had a nightmarish experience with this issue, as I mistakenly assumed that a certain room on a certain evening would be available for my group. I was forced to make some last-minute inquiries and wound up conducting the group in the meeting room of a nearby church. (This location turned out to be good, as the church was a neutral site and members felt less stigma by meeting there.)

Consider the financial aspects of conducting the group. What will be the costs to the sponsoring agency of adding the group to its range of services, in terms of staff time and supplies? Along the same lines, what will be the financial benefits to the agency? My director was willing to take a financial loss on a new group (not charging participants any money), because he saw a long-term financial benefit in terms of positive agency exposure. This scenario, however, is not always possible, so the leader needs to consult with the administration about funding or any charges to members.

Consider the composition of the group. Some groups are homogeneous, meaning that members are much alike in their presenting challenges and perhaps demographic characteristics, whereas other groups are heterogeneous, with wide variability in member characteristics. Examples of this difference can be seen in groups that address mental illness in general versus those that address depression specifically, groups that include persons who are experiencing a challenge versus those that include their families, and groups that are open to parents versus those that are open to partners or siblings. Heterogeneous groups are challenging in that the members have less in common and therefore do not connect as easily. In the family education and support group, membership was primarily homogeneous, including middle-aged parents with children who had a mental illness. This homogeneous nature presented problems at times for younger parents or siblings who joined the group, because they tended to feel out of place in the general context.

Decide if the group will have open or closed status. Open groups are willing to accept new members after they have begun. These groups incorporate the benefits of accommodating more participants, providing immediate support to members, putting less pressure on members for personal disclosure, and tolerating a changing membership well. On the negative side, open groups are less stable and members are slower to trust each other. Closed groups accept no new members after beginning. They tend to encourage more intensive interactions, are more stable and cohesive over time, and ensure greater predictability of member behavior. On the negative side, they require long-range commitments from members and are more adversely affected by member dropouts. The family education and support group was closed, as it was considered essential to promote a level of trust and cohesion that would be possible only with a stable membership.

Determine group size. Some groups are as small as four or five members, whereas others can be quite large, with twenty-five to thirty members or more. The leader will often have an ideal group size in mind, but this number may need to be compromised depending on the success of recruitment and other unpredictable factors. Clearly how the group operates will depend very much on its size. With more members, interactions tend to be less personal. Group leaders need to be aware that the group size should not be such that its purposes are defeated or that the leaders cannot present group material effectively in ways they desire. The family education and support group appeared to function best with ten to sixteen members, which encouraged participation but also helped members feel that they would never be put on the spot about sharing.

Determine frequency and duration of meetings. Most groups function with a regular schedule. As a general rule, no meeting should last for more than ninety minutes, as members will begin to tire and their attention spans will wane. For children and young adolescents, who are physically restless, meetings of thirty to forty-five minutes may be sufficient. The family education and support group featured nine weekly meetings of ninety minutes each.

Choose recruiting strategies. This step refers to methods that will be used to advertise the group, how extensive they will be, who will be involved, and whether a budget is required for this service. In my position as an agency social worker, I assumed sole responsibility for recruiting members for the family education and support group. I wrote and distributed flyers to the mental health agencies in the metropolitan area, gave presentations about the program to staff at those agencies, and called prospective members to discuss the group after they were referred. I devoted two months to these activities before starting the first group. Later groups did not take so long, as a referral network fell into place.

Screen candidates in advance. Advance screening allows the group leaders to provide all interested candidates with an orientation, in person or perhaps by phone, about the group. Candidates can learn about the program, get to know the leader, and ask and answer questions related to their suitability for such a group program. They may describe their previous group experiences, their presenting concerns, their specific goals, relevant background information relative to group content, and any potential obstacles to their participation in the group. In the family education and support group, candidates were screened during a phone call that followed their referral.

The leader can use information ascertained during the screening process to identify what kinds of learners will compose the group. Recalling the four types of learners from chapter 4, the leader can attempt to identify activists (who learn best through simulations, case studies, and homework assignments), reflectors (who learn through reflective observations and discussions), theorists (who learn by abstract conceptualization), and pragmatists (who learn best through the concrete experiences of fieldwork and personal observations). With this information the leader can make final decisions about the types of learning activities to include.

Develop rules. Rules are sometimes set in advance by the leaders and can be communicated as part of the screening process. It is also considered advantageous to group process to help members take responsibility for the group by setting some rules with their participation. Rules generally include such issues as attendance expectations, behavioral guidelines, policies about visitors and new members, policies about individual member contact with the leader between meetings, and details such as eating, use of language, and cleaning up. The only rule that I stressed prior to beginning my group is that participants commit to attending three times before deciding whether the experience was worth their ongoing time investment.

Rules should be either planned in advance or established at the first meeting. There should be leader-member cooperation in rule setting, and members should be given much responsibility for setting them. In that way their investment in the process of a constructive group is maximized.

Psychoeducation Group Stages

Once a psychoeducation group is developed and operational, the leader should be aware of the more or less predictable stages of group evolution, as his or her activities may depend on processes in a particular stage. Although there is no single standard outline of group stages, the four-stage model presented in exhibit 5.3 is useful.

Exhibit 5.3: *Psychoeducation group stages*

1. Pre-affiliation
2. Power and control
3. Shared working
4. Separation

(adapted from Anderson, 1997)

The *pre-affiliation* stage is characterized by a mixture of approach and avoidance behavior among the members. They do not know one another well, and may not know the leader, so members will likely feel normal anxiety and ambivalence about participating in the new group. They will not be ready to share much of their experience with one another.

In the *power and control* stage, members work out issues of status and role with the leader and one another. Put another way, they integrate their personalities into the group system. Those people who are relatively dominant will tend to present as such, and those people who are more passive will fall into those roles. Some members may test their influence with other members and the leader and test the leader's limits with regard to rules and discussion topics.

The *shared working* stage is characterized by the members working well together on the group's purposes. After they have been together for a while, they may fall into a predictable, relatively comfortable pattern of interaction. It is possible that the leader is not quite as active in this stage, at least with regard to managing group process. The members achieve a sense of group identity and self-direction.

The *separation* stage is characterized by member awareness of the upcoming end of the group, or perhaps their own individual ending with the group. Members begin to break away physically or emotionally in ways that may be quite distinct from one another. They will share less about their day-to-day challenges and instead focus more on the future. The leader becomes more active in order to insure that all essential group material is covered and that the members have time to reflect on their experiences with the group.

It is important to emphasize again that not all groups progress through these stages. These stages, in fact, represent an ideal type. In some educational groups, for example an adolescent conflict resolution group, the leader may be highly active for the duration, and member interaction may be limited. Further, some client populations may not be expected to move fully into the working stage. Children with behavioral problems, persons with mental retardation, and persons with serious mental illnesses may have limited interpersonal skills or cognitive abilities that inhibit their moving much beyond the second stage. Still, in every group the leader should consider the goals, timeline, and characteristics of its members and with this information think ahead to the type of group process that is unfolding.

Each of these four group stages is characterized by a different set of processes, or patterns of interactions among members. Because the leader's activities are influenced by the stage of the group, it is useful to consider how they change over the life of the group (Hepworth et al., in press).

Group Leadership Activities

This consideration of group stages should not obscure the fact that the leader's ongoing ability to inspire confidence is key to a group's success. One study of psychoeducation groups concluded that the group needs to experience not only that the leader can help them understand their illness but also that he or she has the ability to guide them through vulnerable emotional states (Hayes & Gantt, 1992). Still, leadership activities during the four stages of group evolution generally unfold as follows.

In the pre-affiliation stage the leader

> Presents the group goals and general structure to the members,
> Clarifies expectations for member interaction,
> Assures all members of their opportunities for participation,
> Encourages members to discuss any anxieties or ambivalence they feel,
> Encourages the development of trust, and
> Models desired member behavior.

I was often exhausted after my opening meetings from all of my talking and caregiving, as the members were looking to me for content and direction. The mutual support process was usually not evident until the second or third meeting.

Group leaders can enhance members' levels of motivation to participate in the group by ensuring a supportive environment, helping to set meaningful objectives for the group, encouraging participation and effort from all persons, and developing appropriate levels of challenge for participants. A summary of group leader activities during the first meeting is outlined in exhibit 5.4.

Exhibit 5.4:   Group leader activities for the first meeting

Brief opening statement (encourage comments, questions, and feedback and accentuate member similarities)
Clarify the leader's roles
Clarify participant roles (perhaps later in session)
Round robin (for introductions)
Facilitate motivation (help members develop explicit goals)
Address ambivalence and resistance
Clarify mutual expectations (confidentiality) and norms (by word and example)

In the power and control stage, the leader

> Encourages regular attendance and membership stability (in close-ended groups),
> Encourages balanced member participation,
> Draws out less involved members,
> Provides feedback about the quality of member communication,
> Encourages member-to-member rather than member-to-leader exchanges,

> Creates and models norms for group behavior,
>
> Promotes decision making by consensus, and
>
> Discourages the formation of subgroups (which tend to marginalize some members and detract from the whole-group process).

I always noticed that a few members tended to be overpowering in their level of emotional expression, and I worked hard to draw out the more reserved, and perhaps intimidated, members.

The group leader must deal with some inattention or disruptive behavior during this stage of the group. He or she can do so by monitoring the entire group process, ignoring minor misbehavior (as it will probably not persist), intervening in sustained minor misbehavior, and being directive enough to make appropriate directive corrections. Clearly it is the responsibility of the group leader to minimize disruptions to the overall process.

In the shared working stage, the leader

> Becomes less verbally active (as members take more responsibility for the agenda),
>
> Supports the development of positive internal leadership,
>
> Highlights common group themes,
>
> Balances time allotments among members,
>
> Keeps members focused on goals and tasks, and
>
> Helps members appreciate both their individuality and value to the group.

It was always a joy for me to see how members became a mutual support system for one another after two or three weeks, helping one another understand more about mental illness and providing one another with useful suggestions about coping.

It is difficult for the leader to balance support and education activities. When considering what educational material should be presented to the participants, the leader should insure that the material is not readily accessible from other sources, represents an integration of material from different sources, presents alternate points of view about a topic, and arouses interest among the participants (Good & Brophy, 1997). It is also recommended that members be introduced to all topics prior to their presentation, so that members have an opportunity to review them in advance.

In the separation stage, the leader

> Becomes more directive in bringing the group to a constructive conclusion,
>
> Encourages members to look toward the future,
>
> Helps members review their learning or rehearse new skills,
>
> Identifies areas for each member's continued work,
>
> Shares his or her reactions to the group's ending, and
>
> Asks members to evaluate the group (see exhibit 5.5).

Exhibit 5.5: *Group leader activities for the separation stage*

Label the onset of the ending stage
Become more active and directive
Encourage a future orientation in conversations
Consider the group less as a unit and more as individuals with distinct agendas
Address separation issues if appropriate
Resolve unfinished business prior to the final session
Structure the final session (including member reflection activities)
Celebrate the group's significance

I utilized a structured means of encouraging each member to share their impressions of the group experience with one another, as well as asking for formal and informal evaluations.

Assessing a Psychoeducation Group in Process

Group assessment includes the leader's observations about the functioning of a group over time. It involves elements of content and process. *Content* refers to the verbal statements of participants, and *process* refers less concretely to the ways members interact with each other (Toseland & Rivas, 2006). Further, member roles in a group, although varied, may be classified as task-focused (keeping the group moving toward its explicit goals) or process-maintenance (being more concerned with how members are interacting and getting along). The group assessment may be done formally or informally, perhaps with a coleader or supervisor, through file charting (my primary strategy), summary notes made after the group, or occasional meetings between the leaders. The following topics are useful in the assessment.

Descriptions of group members   Descriptions include notes about each member with regard to his or her attitudes about the group and each person's strengths and limitations as they pertain to the group's functioning. The following list does not describe types of learners but how members are inclined to interact in the group setting.

Independent learners are self-initiated and self-directed. They may be deficient, however, in collaborative skills, which may be problematic to other members.

Participants get the most out of sharing experiences. They tend to be deferential to others, however, and may spread themselves thin or put others' needs ahead of their own.

Collaborative learners are skilled in working in teams. They may also depend too much on others, however, and not work well alone.

Competitive learners are motivated by their sense of competition with other participants in setting and achieving goals for learning. On the negative side, they may turn off less competitive people, and their style is not conducive to collaboration.

Avoidant learners prefer to keep to themselves. They can focus well on independent tasks, but they also tend to be highly sensitive to any negative feedback.

Dependent learners have a strong need to maintain contact with others to help them manage their anxiety and obtain clear directions. They are not autonomous and self-directive, and they do not manage uncertainty well.

Group structure   Assessment requires that the leader reflect on the following questions: Does the group work together as a unit? Are there subgroups of members who tend to talk with one another and exclude the rest? How active must the leader be in helping the group function as a unit rather than as a collection of disconnected individuals?

Communication and interaction   This topic includes the exchange of verbal and nonverbal messages, the extent to which members seem to like or dislike one another, the relative attention or inattention of members to one another, the assertiveness versus passivity of members, and the intensity or lethargy of their interactions. These characteristics are determined by group size (some people may become lost in a large group), the status relationships among members, their emotional bonding, any subgroups that may develop, and the expectations and reinforcements that members receive from the group experience.

Decision making   To what extent do group members share responsibility for decision making as relevant issues come up? What are the group norms for making decisions? Is it primarily the leader's role? Do a few people tend to monopolize the process?

Group cohesion   This term refers to the relative sense of unity among the members. It is determined by their needs for affiliation, their perceived incentives to coalesce, and their expectations about the consequences of the group. In other words, what's in it for them?

Group norms   Norms pertain to standards of acceptable and unacceptable behavior, both formal and informal, that preserve order. These norms result from, and also reflect, member attitudes toward task orientation, the shared sense of responsibility for goal attainment, their attitudes toward the leader(s), their attitudes about receiving feedback, the subject matter of the group, accepted ranges of emotional expression, and personal characteristics (their values, beliefs, and traditions).

Evolving leadership style   This topic refers to how active the leader(s) are, the topics about which they tend to be more or less focused, their sensitivity to each member, how they differentially interact with each member, and how they divide up roles and tasks.

Summary status statement   Based on the above considerations, the leader should develop a concluding statement about how well the group is moving toward goal achievement. This statement should include the leader's impression of the group's overall strengths, weaknesses, and ongoing potential. Following this process, the leader will be better prepared to make any leadership or strategic adjustments for upcoming sessions.

Summary

Providing psychoeducation in group settings holds particular challenges for the educator. Devising appropriate group content and facilitating an effective group process requires that the leader understand issues related to group development and the learning styles of participants. In this chapter, a number of major themes, including the stages of group process, appropriate leadership styles for use in each of those stages, and strategies for ongoing group assessment, have been provided. Of course, psychoeducation groups must also be developed in ways that are suitable for the particular subject matter and the types of participants who will be involved. That is, group format will depend on whether persons with certain life challenges, their significant others, or both will be included and on their readiness to absorb and work with the educational content. With this foundation, part 2 addresses specific applications of psychoeducation.

Part 2

Applications

C h a p t e r 6

Schizophrenia

Schizophrenia was the first mental illness to become the subject of psychoeducational interventions on a widespread basis. It was first because the disorder is chronic, highly disabling, and caused by a yet-unknown nervous system pathology. It was once believed to be caused by pathological family systems. Early family theorists used such terms as *emotional divorce* (Bowen, 1960), *communication deviance* (Lynne, Cromwell, & Matthysse, 1978), the *double-bind* (Bateson, Jackson, Haley, & Weakland, 1956), and family *schisms* and *skewes* (Lidz, 1975) to describe problematic parent-child interactions that supposedly caused a child to withdraw into psychosis. When the biological theories of schizophrenia became prominent in the 1970s, family advocacy groups organized to provide mutual education and support programs. They often had antagonistic feelings toward mental health providers, whom they viewed as stigmatizing (Vine, 1982). This chapter reviews the mental disorder of schizophrenia and a range of psychoeducational programs that have been shown to be helpful to the client's and his or her family's adjustment to the disorder.

The Nature of Schizophrenia

Schizophrenia is characterized by a person's abnormal patterns of thought and perception, as inferred from his or her language and behavior. The fact that it is primarily a disorder of *thought* distinguishes it from severe disorders of *mood*, such as bipolar disorder and depression. Schizophrenia includes two types of symptoms (American Psychiatric Association [APA], 2000). *Positive* symptoms represent exaggerations of normal behavior. These symptoms include hallucinations, delusions, disorganized thought processes, and tendencies toward agitation. *Negative* symptoms represent the diminution of what would be considered normal behavior. These symptoms include flat or blunted affect (the absence of expression), social withdrawal, noncommunication, anhedonia (blandness) or passivity, and ambivalence in decision making.

A person with schizophrenia experiences pronounced sensory changes (Benioff, 1995). Visual changes include heightened sensitivity to light and color, illusionary changes in faces and objects, and distortions in size. Auditory changes include hallucinations (described in the next paragraph), heightened sensitivity to noise, an inability to screen out background noise, the muting of sounds, and distortions of the sounds of voices. Physical changes include heightened sensitivity to touch, an inability to interpret internal sensations, and tactile and olfactory hallucinations. Cognitive changes include loose associations, the inability to filter out irrelevant information, distractibility, overstimulation of thoughts (flooding), feelings of enhanced mental efficiency, increased or decreased speed of thinking, fragmentation (the inability to create a whole from the parts), delusions, and idiosyncratic explanatory systems.

Among the major symptoms of schizophrenia, *hallucinations* are sense perceptions of external objects that are not present. Hallucinations may be auditory, visual, gustatory (the perception of taste), tactile (feeling an object), somatic (an unreal experience within the body), and olfactory (a false sense of smell). *Delusions* are false beliefs that a person maintains even though the beliefs are overwhelmingly contradicted by social reality. They include persecutory (people or forces are attempting to bring one harm), erotomanic (another person is in love with the individual), somatic (pertaining to body functioning), and grandiose (an exaggerated sense of power, knowledge, or identity) beliefs, as well as thought broadcasting (one's thoughts are overheard by others), thought insertion or withdrawal (others are putting thoughts into or taking thoughts out of one's head), delusions of being controlled (thoughts, feelings, or actions are imposed by an external force), and delusions of reference (neutral events have special significance for the person).

Schizophrenia has an approximate 1 percent worldwide prevalence, and there is remarkable consistency in prevalence among most nations of the world (Murray & Jones, 2003).

There are five subtypes of schizophrenia:

1. Paranoid schizophrenia features a preoccupation with delusions or auditory hallucinations but a preservation of cognitive functioning.
2. Disorganized schizophrenia is characterized by disorganized speech and behavior and flat or inappropriate (exaggerated) affect.
3. Catatonic schizophrenia features disturbances of immobility or excessive mobility, mutism (not speaking), odd gestures, echolalia (repeating the words of others), or echopraxia (repeating the movements of others).
4. Undifferentiated schizophrenia describes persons who exhibit a range of symptoms but do not meet the criteria for the above three subtypes.
5. Residual schizophrenia describes persons who display only negative symptoms after an active episode. This form of the disorder may be transient or persist for many years. (APA, 2000)

Many individuals who develop schizophrenia display *premorbid*, or early warning, signs. These signs include a slow, gradual development of symptoms, social withdrawal, a loss of interest in life activities, deterioration

in self-care, and a variety of odd behaviors. These behaviors are often difficult for families and other loved ones to understand. The signs can exist for
many years, but when present they do not guarantee the eventual onset of
schizophrenia.

The Course of Schizophrenia

The onset age for schizophrenia is between fifteen and forty years. Men
tend to have their first episodes between the ages of eighteen and twenty-
six, whereas for females they occur between the ages of twenty-six and forty
(Seeman, 2003). There is an equal prevalence for males and females, however, and an equal geographical distribution throughout the world. Approximately 10 percent of persons with schizophrenia experience its initial
onset during late childhood and adolescence (Mengelers, van Os, & Myin-
Germeys, 2007). The disorder is rare before the age of eleven or twelve. In
children, delusions and auditory hallucinations are less prominent,
whereas visual hallucinations and disorganized speech are more common.
The duration of schizophrenia is the same regardless of age of onset,
although there is a correlation between age of onset and chances for adapting positively to its symptoms (McClellan, McCurry, Snell, & DuBose, 1999).

Complete remission in schizophrenia is uncommon, and its course is
variable. A person with the disorder experiences a chronic course, either
with symptoms being more or less florid but never really disappearing or in
which periods of psychosis are interspersed with periods of remission. An
accurate prediction of any individual's course is impossible. Although the
causes of schizophrenia are uncertain, there are clues for differentiating better and worse prognoses.

Persons with schizophrenia have a high rate of comorbidity with substance-
related disorders, up to 60 percent in some studies (Potvin, Sepehry, & Stip,
2006).

The Effects of Schizophrenia on Families

When a person has schizophrenia, a chronic state of emotional burden
develops that is shared by all nuclear family members (Lenoir, Dingemans,
Schene, Hart, & Linszen, 2002). Common reactions include stress, anxiety,
grief, depression, and resentment of the impaired member. Spouses tend to
blame each other for the family turmoil, and siblings tend to blame parents.
There is little time available for family leisure activities, and one adult, usually the mother, becomes the primary caretaker of the impaired member.
Siblings have some reactions unique from parents, including emotional con-
striction in personality development, isolation from peers, and jealousy
about the attention given to the impaired member (National Alliance for the
Mentally Ill, 1989).

As a result of these reactions, the concept of family (or caregiver) expressed emotion (EE) has been prominent in the schizophrenia literature for the past thirty years (Kymalainen & Weisman de Mamani, 2008). It has been operationalized to include ratings of family member hostility toward the ill relative, emotional overinvolvement with the relative, the degree of warmth with which the relative refers to the client, and the frequency of critical and positive comments made about the client. People with schizophrenia from families that express high levels of criticism, hostility, or overinvolvement have more frequent relapses than people with similar problems from families that tend to be less expressive of their emotions. As a research measure, EE provides one means for determining the kinds of family environments that put the person with schizophrenia at risk of or keep them protected from symptom relapses. Many family advocacy groups have objected to EE measures, arguing that they blame the family for a member's illness (Mohr, Lafuze, & Mohr, 2000). Professionals do not use the concept to blame family members for the course of a relative's illness but to affirm that families need support in coping with the disorder.

Because the majority of persons with schizophrenia reside with or near their families, it is important for professionals to understand what is effective in working with those persons to facilitate the adjustment of all members. In Butzlaff and Hooley's (1998) meta-analysis of twenty-seven studies, EE was consistently shown to correlate with symptom relapse. The authors also found that the relationship between EE and symptom relapse was strongest for clients with more unremitting symptoms. Family interventions in schizophrenia usually focus in part on producing a more positive atmosphere for all members, which in turn contributes to the ill relative's adjustment.

Regarding protective factors, persons with schizophrenia tend to function best with a moderate amount of face-to-face interaction with significant others (Chambless, Bryan, Aiken, Steketee, & Hooley, 1999). Likewise, they manage moderate amounts of social stimulation well. They respond favorably to attitudes of acceptance, reasonable expectations, opportunities to develop social and vocational skills, and a relatively small number but broad range of social supports. These supports may include family members, friends, neighbors, work peers, school peers, informal community relations, and perhaps church members. Factors that influence the family's coping well or poorly include the severity of the disorder (people actually seem to cope better when the disorder is more severe), the preservation of time for other activities, the ability to be proactive in seeking assistance, and the availability of outside support (Lenoir, Dingemans, Schene, Hart, & Linszen, 2002).

General Components of Psychoeducation with Schizophrenia

Family psychoeducation increases participants' sense of self-efficacy regarding the ill relative (Pekkala & Merinder, 2002). In some models of family intervention, services are provided in the home in an effort to secure the participation of all members. All programs have many elements in common, including those listed in exhibit 6.1.

Exhibit 6.1:   *Common elements in family psychoeducation for schizophrenia*

Empathic engagement with all members
Clear expectations for participation by all family members
Education about the nature of schizophrenia and how to cope with it
Family assistance with utilizing available treatments and community
   resources
Mutual support provision within the group
Social network enhancement outside the group
The teaching of stress-management techniques
The teaching of communication and problem-solving skills
Encouragement for family members to pursue their own well-being
(Dixon et al., 2001; Kopelowicz, Liberman, & Zarate, 2002; SAMHSA, 2009)

Exhibit 6.2 provides one example of a psychoeducational program (designed by the author) that attempts to incorporate the elements described in exhibit 6.1. Exhibit 6.2 also notes the theoretical focus of each meeting.

Exhibit 6.2:   *Family education and support group schedule of meetings*

Session 1: orientation and introductions
Session 2: group discussion on the range of services available in the
   county for persons with mental illness and the feelings of family
   members about the quality of the service agencies they have dealt
   with (education, mutual support, human development)
Session 3: leader presentation on current theories about the causes,
   course, and treatment of the severe mental illnesses (education)
Session 4: follow-up group discussion on week 3 presentation (mutual
   support, reflection, problem solving, structural family theory)
Session 5: leader presentation on the uses and limitations of medications in the treatment of mental illness (education)
Session 6: follow-up group discussion of week 5 presentation (mutual
   support, reflection, problem solving, structural family theory)
Session 7: group discussion about the various intervention modalities
   commonly used in mental health agencies and how families can
   best involve themselves in that process (education, mutual support, reflection, problem solving)

Session 8: a representative from the Mental Health Association speaks
about family advocacy for quality services from mental health professionals on behalf of their client relatives (education, mutual
support, structural family theory, problem solving)
Session 9: wind-up discussion on matters of interest to members;
evaluation forms distributed, completed, and discussed; and
group members can decide whether they wish to continue meeting beyond the nine-week course

One research study has shown that families place greater emphasis on
dealing with negative symptoms and family relationships than professional
leaders do. Leaders instead tend to give at least equal emphasis to diagnosis and medication issues (Pollio, North, & Foster, 1998). Some program
developers emphasize that, when working with clients or families, the
potentially supportive roles of religion and spirituality should be addressed
or at least welcomed (Phillips, Lakin, & Pargament, 2002). Further, the issue
of leaders being able to appreciate the cultural contexts of families' lives has
recently been highlighted as an important component of psychoeducation.
Such cultural sensitivity enables the leader to explore member needs and
biases and establish a sense of mutuality in goals (Shin, 2004).

Attention should always be paid to the types of family members who
compose a given psychoeducational program. When the client is an adult,
families tend to be interested in family relationship issues and the client's
denial, noncompliance with intervention, and positive symptoms. When the
client is an adolescent, families tend to be more concerned about mood and
problem behaviors (Pollio, North, Reid, Eyrich, & McClendon, 2006).
Spouses of persons with schizophrenia tend to enjoy spouses-only groups,
but they tend to drop out of more heterogeneous groups (Mannion, Mueser,
& Solomon, 1994). The same is true of siblings for siblings-only groups
(Lukens, Thorning, & Lohrer, 2004). Older adult caregivers in groups want
help in permanency planning for their child (Lukens & McFarlane, 2006).

Psychoeducation Program Outcome Studies

Psychoeducation research regarding schizophrenia is quite extensive, more
so than that for any other problem in living. A number of meta-analyses have
been performed in the literature with regard to schizophrenia. This process
involves summarizing all studies of a certain type (usually experimental)
into one overarching review that attempts to combine all findings into consistent themes. In one meta-analysis of randomized controlled trials it was
found that family education resulted in greater medication compliance and
significantly decreased relapse or readmission rates for the ill relative at
nine- to eighteen-month follow-up, compared with standard care (Pekkala &
Merinder, 2002). For every one hundred clients whose families participate

in such groups, it was estimated that twelve will avoid or postpone relapses for one year. Another review of the literature on EE showed that family intervention designed to reduce expressed levels of criticism, hostility, or over-involvement decreases relapse and increases compliance with medication, although families are still left with a significant burden (Pharoah, Mari, Rathbone, & Wong, 2006). The intervention also has a positive effect on participants' sense of well-being.

Another review noted that single-family interventions reduced the ill relative's readmission rates in the first year and that after two years family interventions lowered relapse and readmission rates as well as increased medication compliance (Pilling et al., 2002). A fourth review (Butzlaff & Hooley, 1998) showed that group interventions designed to reduce levels of intrafamily tension decreased relapse and increased compliance with medication, although families still experienced a significant burden. Family EE was consistently shown to correlate with symptom relapse, especially for clients with a more chronic disorder. Low EE family environments were associated with fewer symptom relapses and rehospitalizations than high EE environments were.

A fifth review of forty randomized controlled studies indicated that four outcomes are significant: (1) education improved members' knowledge of mental illness, (2) behavioral instruction helped members ensure that their ill relative takes medications as prescribed, (3) relapse-prevention skills development reduced the ill relative's relapses and rehospitalizations, and (4) new coping-skills development reduced the distress associated with caregiving (Mueser et al., 2002).

The Center for Mental Health Services is a federal agency within the U.S. Substance Abuse and Mental Health Services Administration (SAMHSA) that leads national efforts to improve prevention and mental health treatment services for Americans. SAMHSA has introduced six resource kits to encourage the use of evidence-based practices, and one of these kits is for family psychoeducation. Its literature review indicates that the practice is effective, resulting in decreased relapse and hospitalization rates within the first year, providing psychosocial support for recovery, facilitating workforce reentry, and providing social-skills development for participants (SAMHSA, 2009). Families feel less stress, and employment rate gains are two to four times that of baseline when combined with supported employment programs.

In their literature review of programs that include the person with schizophrenia, Ascher-Svanum and Whitesel (1999) found that individuals who had taken part in an educational intervention experienced improved compliance with the medication regimen, lower relapse rates, longer participation in aftercare programs, improved social functioning and quality of life, decreased negative symptoms, improved insight into their illness, improved skills acquisition, improved attitudes toward medication intake, and a better understanding of mental illness.

Given these literature reviews, the general characteristics of family groups that appear to produce positive outcomes include a longer program (ten sessions or more), participation of families with relatives who have a similar disorder, inclusion of the ill relative in some or all meetings, and a focus on education and support rather than therapy (Pekkala & Merinder, 2002).

Examples of Family Psychoeducation Programs

What follows are examples of programs that have been widely used and shown to be effective with various types of participants. This section begins with a survey of the first formal psychoeducational programs and then considers more recent programs. All of these programs emphasize the importance of member education about the nature and course of schizophrenia. Although it is rarely stated explicitly, all such programs work to empower the members, both the people with a mental illness and their family members, by helping them to develop the skills and confidence necessary to assume greater control over their lives. Further, with the consistent program focus on improved behavior-management skills for the impaired member, participants are encouraged to restructure their family systems so that greater authority lies with the caregiving members.

Early Programs

In the early 1970s a parents group known as Thresholds was developed at a psychosocial rehabilitation agency in Chicago. Mental health professionals provided education and behavioral-management strategies to family members (including the client relative in one meeting) in a weekly open-ended twelve-session program (Dincin, Selleck, & Streicker, 1978). Positive outcomes included parents' reports of more positive attitudes toward the ill relative, their improved ability to manage family stress, and a greater appreciation of their own needs. Information about the importance of social support was critical in working toward the third outcome.

In another early program, single families attended six weekly meetings provided by mental health agency professionals immediately following the client's hospital discharge. Leaders integrated skills-development themes with educational opportunities to improve family stress management (Goldstein & Doane, 1984). Noteworthy outcomes included rehospitalization rates during a six-month follow-up period.

A purely supportive psychoeducational program was developed in Europe at this same time to enhance families' ability to cope with the stress of caring for an ill relative without overtly attempting to change their behaviors (Byalin, Jed, & Lehman, 1985). That is, the focus was on only education and support development. A mental health professional met with a family in the home only as often as the family requested. The professional attempted to affirm that the family was not responsible for the ill relative's mental disorder and offered whatever support might be helpful to the family.

Another program included families and professionals in a ten-week group series, meeting once weekly with guest speakers every two weeks (McClean, Greer, Scott, & Beck, 1982). The purposes of the program were to provide families with information about mental illness, enable them to take more time for themselves, and help them acquire behavior-management skills for use in their households. One finding in this program was that an informal coffee hour at the end of each meeting helped with member sharing. This finding supports the assumption that families who come together can offer much assistance to each other without professional facilitation. It appears that participant opportunities to reflect on their own needs was significant, although it was not explicitly stated as such.

In a social intervention program, professionals led a nine-month biweekly relatives group focused on member sharing of client behavior-management strategies (Leff, Kuipers, & Berkowitz, 1983). What was unique about this program is that, through a screening process, families who tolerated client behaviors poorly were matched with families characterized by greater attitudes of acceptance. Within the groups, the more accepting members were described as having a positive effect on the attitudes of the more critical members.

Anderson, Reiss, and Hogarty (1986) developed a one-day survival-skills workshop for families whose ill relative was in a psychiatric hospital (see exhibit 6.3). Representatives of various mental health disciplines provided information to families about the relative's illness during a single eight-hour session. Although this (and other) intensive program was beneficial, it could

---

Exhibit 6.3: Anderson's survival-skills workshop topics

Information about the causes, course, and outcome of schizophrenia (one hour; education)

The treatment of schizophrenia, including medications, other treatments, and illness management (seventy-five minutes; education)

The family and schizophrenia, including needs of the patient and family, family reactions, common problems faced by clients and families, family guidelines, and problem solving (two hours; mutual support, reflection, problem solving, structural family theory, human development)

Questions regarding specific problems (thirty minutes; mutual support, reflection, problem solving, structural family theory, human development)

Informal discussion during breaks and lunch

not provide participants with opportunities to reflect on their own needs or on the developmental challenges faced by their family members. Families were helped to formulate reasonable expectations for change, develop limit-setting and home-management strategies, and organize ongoing support networks for themselves. The workshops consisted of four units: (1) the development of a working alliance between participants and professionals, (2) the survival-skills workshop, (3) discussion groups about ways to utilize the didactic material, and (4) planning for the ongoing use of workshop information. It was intended that the educational material would be incorporated into participants' individual work with other treatment providers. The daylong session was followed by single-family sessions every two to three weeks for six months to one year, in which information from the workshop was applied. During the individual work, participants could spend more time reflecting on their personal challenges brought on by the onset of mental illness in a family member.

Another set of family intervention approaches is known as behavioral family therapy (Falloon, Boyd, & McGill, 1984). These interventions are based on a rationale that families can become attuned to the warning signs and ongoing risks of relapse with schizophrenia and can become effective, self-directed problem solvers. These skills were provided through educational workshops, communication-skills development with multiple families, problem-solving skills development (a rational process rooted in cognitive theory), and home-based interventions. The interventions were designed to educate families about mental illness, improve family communication, instruct families in problem-solving skills, and promote the application of problem-solving strategies to specific family concerns.

One example of this approach involves two single-family educational sessions provided by several mental health professionals in the client's home, with all family members present. The first session is educational, focused on the nature of the client's disorder, and the second session considers issues of medication adherence and home behavior management. Follow-up studies confirm that family members retain information presented in this format over an extended period of time. Another intervention model involves four months of weekly sessions of continuing education for family groups. Content is focused on teaching behavior-modification techniques that families can use to shape the ill relative's behavior. Outcome measures for these programs include rehospitalization rates, client adherence to intervention plans, and measures of family cohesion.

During the late 1980s, the Family Psychoeducation in Schizophrenia Project was tested in New York State. Its goals were to educate and support participants and empower them to exercise more control over their lives. Clients and their families were randomly assigned to one of two psychoeducational treatments at the time of hospital admission. One was a multi-family group with two therapists, and the other included individual family intervention with one therapist. The work continued for two years, with twenty-four-hour-per-day on-call coverage and the client relative joining the intervention at discharge. It was found that the multifamily group members experienced lower relapse rates and, regardless of treatment, clients had fewer psychiatric rehospitalizations. Of the 170 families included in both studies, 16 percent of the clients in the multifamily group relapsed versus 27 percent in the other group (national relapse rates run between 50% and 65% for persons with schizophrenia in general). Although hospitalizations were reduced for all participants, ill relatives in the multifamily group had significantly fewer in the last six months of treatment.

All of these programs (and others) represented useful efforts to provide families with the kinds of education and support they wanted, and all of them were found to be effective in various ways.

More Recent Programs

Multifamily group intervention William McFarlane (2002) and his associates have developed and evaluated a multifamily group intervention (MFI) that includes family members and their impaired relatives. MFI is a two-year program for adults with schizophrenia that integrates educational and behavioral interventions and is intended to compliment individual work with clients. The intervention targets each client's and family's cognitive deficits, continuity of care concerns, stress levels, stigma, quality of life, and expressed emotion (see exhibit 6.4). Each family's development of stronger and more consistent social support is another major goal. MFI

Exhibit 6.4: Multifamily groups

Goals:
Prevent relapse and recover functional losses (short-term)
Maximize potential (long-term)

Key elements:
Alliances with professionals
Information about schizophrenia
Guidelines for managing the disorder
Practice in problem solving related to the disorder

Intervention stages:
Joining
Educational workshop
Relapse prevention via problem-solving groups
Vocational and social rehabilitation

provides education about illness symptoms and management and encourages the development of social support, with the overall goals of decreasing psychiatric symptoms, relapse, and hospitalization and increasing the ill relative's social and vocational functioning. The program includes four phases:

1. A minimum of three sessions devoted to worker/family engagement, conducted with single families
2. A daylong, or two- to three-session, multifamily workshop, based on the survival-skills workshops of Anderson et al. (1986)
3. Regular meetings every two weeks for one year, focused on social and vocational functioning
4. After one year of biweekly meetings, monthly meetings, with a continuing focus on social and vocational functioning

The multiple-family interventions are delivered by two mental health professionals to groups of five to eight families over a two-year period, with twenty-nine sessions during year one and twelve sessions during year two. After the joining and psychoeducational workshop phases, which are completed in one month, the final and extended two phases are delivered using a structured problem-solving group format. Through the thirty-six problem-solving sessions, consumers and families are helped to set individual family and client goals and are then taught to use a systematic problem-solving strategy for overcoming illness and non-illness-related difficulties. Although group processes (the interactions of leaders and members with one another) are hypothesized to contribute to the overall efficacy of MFI, the cognitive-behavioral strategies delivered through the problem-solving formats are the main focus of the intervention.

Leader activities are organized into the following four components.

Self-triangulation is a process by which the leader places him- or herself at the point of a triangle to mediate the interactions of the client and family members. (This strategy is based on family emotional systems theory.) The leader then puts problems into a context of family management challenges, directs and mediates problem-solving activities, blocks interruptions between the ill relative and other family members, and controls potentially harmful displays of affect by all group members.

Group interpretation is enacted by the leader's setting and processing discussion themes, praising inter-family assistance, and managing conversation among members so they stay focused on productive topics.

Cross-family linkages include leader actions toward helping members of different families participate in one another's problem-solving reflections.

Inter-family management refers to activities in which the leader helps each family to cooperatively develop appropriate roles, responsibilities, and behavioral consequences for each member. (This strategy is consistent with structural family theory.)

MFI outcome studies have shown that the programs are successful in expanding the client and family's social network (a variable that is associated with lower client relapse rates and fewer hospitalizations). Clients and families become more open, cooperative, and appropriately involved across family boundaries. Harmful intra-family interactions also diminish. The programs have been found best suited for young, community-based, relapse-prone clients who live in close proximity to their nuclear families.

The family survival workshop   Pollio, North, and Reid (2006) have built on the work of Anderson et al. (1986) by developing a one-day workshop of their own, known as the Family Survival Workshop (see exhibit 6.5). This program features information about schizophrenia (its etiology, course, outcome, and treatments, including medication) and family issues (needs of the client and family, family reactions to the illness, common problems faced by clients and families, setting family rules, and the problem-solving method). The leaders make a point of allowing ample time to answer questions from participants regarding specific problems.

Exhibit 6.5:   One-day Family Survival Workshop structure

Leaders consult with families in advance to determine workshop content.
Families are surveyed in the morning about their areas of interest.
A plenary presentation is given on the nature of mental illness, the brain, and the treatment of mental disorders.
At a midday luncheon, family issues are discussed in groups at tables of eight to twelve people, with placards drawing participants to particular topics.
The afternoon consists of two sets of hour-long breakout sessions, which include education and discussions on area resources, success stories, "ask the doc," religious resources, and legal rights.

This workshop provides family members with much information, but it does so quickly, and thus participant follow-up with their treatment providers is necessary to build on and clarify this knowledge. The program also allows little time for individual reflection on particular concerns.

The authors report in their program evaluation that there are gains from pre- to posttest in participants' feelings of control, ability to manage crises, knowledge of resources, and knowledge of the illness, along with reduced feelings of guilt.

National Alliance for the Mentally Ill programs   The National Alliance for the Mentally Ill (NAMI) is a nonprofit, self-help support and advocacy organization for people with mental illness and their families (NAMI, 2009). It includes statewide organizations as well as 1,100 local affiliates. Staffed by professionals and consumers, it sponsors psychoeducational programs for persons with mental illness, among many other services. Because NAMI is a family and consumer organization, its programs are focused on empowerment, education, improved family structure through behavior management, and social support development. The programs do not feature the kinds of therapeutic elements favored by some professionals with respect to encouraging personal reflection, examining cognitive assumptions, and attending to developmental processes in individuals and families.

NAMI provides a variety of groups for several consumer populations. For family members it sponsors the Family-to-Family Education Program and MESA (Mutual Education, Support, and Advocacy). For consumers, it sponsors the Peer-to-Peer and NAMI Care support groups. For mental health service providers and the public, it provides "In Our Own Voice": Living with Mental Illness. Several of these programs will be reviewed here. NAMI provides skills-training programs for support group facilitators, reflecting its belief that consumers can not only become effective leaders in psychoeducation but may also be more effective than professionals, given their firsthand experience with the array of challenges related to mental illness.

Family-to-Family   A twelve-week program for NAMI members, Family-to-Family has weekly meetings of two to three hours (NAMI, 2009). Two family members serve as instructors, and classes are held in community settings rather than mental health agencies. Its primary focus is on family member outcomes through better understanding of the illness and reduced stress. Client well-being is a secondary goal, achieved through improved communication and the development of a calmer family atmosphere. The program is not diagnosis-specific; there is an emphasis on common issues, needs, and concerns of family members whose ill relatives have a variety of mental illnesses (see exhibit 6.6). Each class utilizes a combination of lecture, class participation, and interactive exercises and includes up to twenty-five members.

Exhibit 6.6:   Family-to-Family program content

Session 1: stages of emotional reactions to the trauma of mental illness, goals for family members, understanding symptoms

Session 2: features and diagnostic criteria of psychotic illnesses, getting through critical periods, keeping a crisis file

Session 3: features and diagnostic criteria of mood disorders, bipolar disorder, borderline personality disorder, and anxiety; dual diagnosis; "telling our stories"

Session 4: basics about the brain (functions of key brain areas, brain abnormalities and imbalances in mental illness, genetic research)
Session 5: problem-solving skills development
Session 6: medication review (how they work, the psychopharmacology of mood anxiety and schizophrenia, adverse effects, adherence to medication, warning signs of relapse)
Session 7: the experience of coping with a brain disorder (problems in maintaining self-esteem and positive identity, the struggle to overcome demoralization, protecting one's integrity)
Session 8: communication-skills workshop (how illness interferes with capacity to communicate, how to process sensitive topics, talking to the "person behind the symptoms")
Session 9: self-care (learning about family burden; sharing in relative groups; handling anger, entrapment, guilt, and grief; how to balance our lives)
Session 10: the vision and potential of recovery (principles of rehabilitation, model programs of community support, a first-person account of recovery)
Session 11: advocacy (challenging the power of stigma, learning to change the system, meeting people who are advocating for change)
Session 12: review, sharing, and evaluation; certification ceremony; party

Outcome studies indicate that Family-to-Family results in significantly improved caregiver satisfaction, decreased problem-management information needs, and decreased social-functioning information needs. Program participation is also associated with lower rates of psychiatric hospitalization. It is only marginally associated, however, with lower use of crisis services and is not associated with the amount of outpatient service time utilized by the ill relative. The positive changes appear to be maintained over at least six months.

Peer-to-Peer consumer training The Peer-to-Peer course is provided by mental health consumers for other mental health consumers and is delivered in two-hour meetings held weekly for nine weeks. It is taught by teams of trained peer instructors. All participants interested in establishing and maintaining wellness are welcome to the courses. This program is similar to the Family-to-Family course in that each class contains a combination of lecture and interactive exercise material (see exhibit 6.7). No formal data are available on the effectiveness of this program; it is included here as an example of a consumer-run psychoeducation group.

Exhibit 6.7: *Peer-to-Peer course content*

Session 1: stigma, discrimination, begin relapse-prevention planning
Session 2: schizophrenia, bipolar disorder, depression, thoughts, feelings, sleep, continue relapse-prevention planning
Session 3: panic disorder, obsessive-compulsive disorder, senses, behavior, relapse-prevention planning
Session 4: storytelling
Session 5: language, emotions, relapse-prevention planning
Session 6: addictions, spirituality, medication, complete relapse-prevention plans
Session 7: coping strategies, decision making
Session 8: relationships, begin advance directive
Session 9: empowerment, advocacy, "complete" advance directive, evaluation

Summary

Psychoeducation programs have been provided for more than thirty years for persons with schizophrenia and their significant others. The program philosophies developed in part from family members feeling stigmatized and blamed for having an ill relative, which is one reason why the content is, and has always been, practical in focus. Professionals, laypersons, and consumers alike can effectively provide these programs. There is much research evidence that these programs are beneficial to all participants in a variety of ways, although it remains true that participating persons with schizophrenia and their families still experience much burden and emotional pain afterward. What remains to be determined is the differences in content and methods of presentation that may be useful for specific client populations, including parents, siblings, and friends.

Figures 6.1 and 6.2 are samples of surveys that can be provided to family support group participants prior to joining the program, at the first meeting (pretest), and at the end of the group experience (posttest). Both surveys have been developed by the author and demonstrated high content validity with a panel of experts.

Figure 6.1: Phone survey for new group members (a recruiting instrument)

Opening remarks: In order to be most helpful to you, I am interested in learning how much you understand about your family member's mental disorder and what kinds of help you are seeking. I would appreciate your taking a few minutes to answer some questions. All of your responses will be confidential. The answers that you and other new group members provide will enable me to prepare subject matter most relevant to your needs.

Name: _____ Relationship to client: _____

1. How long has your family member been in treatment at this and other mental health agencies?

    _____ years   _____ months

2. How long has your family member been living with or close by you?

    _____ years   _____ months

3. Clients of mental health agencies are given a diagnosis, which is a professional term used to describe their problem. Are you aware of the diagnosis that your family member has been given?

    _____ yes   _____ no

    If so, what is it? _____

4. Have you ever been invited by your family member's case manager, physician, or other providers to participate in joint meetings?

    _____ yes   _____ no

    If so, please explain the nature of your participation. _____
    _____

5. Is your family member taking any medications as part of the treatment program?

    _____ yes   _____ no

    If so, what kind? _____

    Can you describe what the medication is supposed to do? _____
    _____

6. Is your family member involved with any other social service agencies to get help with his or her problems?

    _____ yes   _____ no

    If so, which ones? _____
    _____

7. Have you heard of any other social service agencies that you would like to learn more about?

    _____ yes   _____ no

    If so, which ones? _____
    _____

8. What are some of the main challenges you experience in living with or near your client relative?

    a. _____
    b. _____
    c. _____
    d. _____
    e. _____

9. In what ways do you hope that the family education and support group can be of help to you?

a. _____
b. _____
c. _____
d. _____
e. _____

10. If you have any other questions or comments about the group, the agency, or me, please list them here.

_____
_____
_____

Figure 6.2: Pre- and post-group evaluation form

The Family Education and Support Group Member Assessment

Name: _____   Date: _____

In this first series of statements, please assess the independent living skills of your family member with mental illness. Please remember that these can be possessed in degrees and do not necessarily indicate that your family member is living on his or her own at the present time. As you consider each item, use the past month as a time frame in deciding on your response. Circle the response that most closely matches your assessment of each statement as demonstrated by the example.

Example: My family member   Very   Rarely (Occasionally) Frequently
           is afriendly person.   Rarely

This respondent feels that the family member is sometimes friendly but not as friendly as he or she might be. Now, please proceed to complete the scale below and elaborate on each of your responses in the space beneath each item.

My family member with mental illness:

1. Uses money to pay his/her   Very   Rarely Occasionally Frequently
    personal expenses in a   Rarely
    reasonable way.

Explain: _____
_____
_____

2. Takes care of housekeeping tasks without being reminded.   Very Rarely   Rarely   Occasionally   Frequently

Explain: _____

_____

_____

3. Maintains an adequately balanced diet.   Very Rarely   Rarely   Occasionally   Frequently

Explain: _____

_____

_____

4. Arranges for transportation promptly when needed.   Very Rarely   Rarely   Occasionally   Frequently

Explain: _____

_____

_____

5. Spends time with friends outside the home.   Very Rarely   Rarely   Occasionally   Frequently

Explain: _____

_____

_____

6. Engages in recreational activity outside the home.   Very Rarely   Rarely   Occasionally   Frequently

Explain: _____

_____

_____

7. Makes an effort to secure income from a source outside the family.   Very Rarely   Rarely   Occasionally   Frequently

Explain: _____

_____

_____

8. Keeps his/her clothing clean.   Very Rarely   Rarely   Occasionally   Frequently

Explain: _____

_____

_____

9. Maintains reasonable expectations   Very   Rarely   Occasionally   Frequently
   of the family for companionship.   Rarely

Explain: _____
_____
_____

10. Takes the initiative to achieve   Very   Rarely   Occasionally   Frequently
    or maintain a job.   Rarely

Explain: _____
_____
_____

11. Takes medication as prescribed.   Very   Rarely   Occasionally   Frequently
                                         Rarely

Explain: _____
_____
_____

12. Has a physician whom he/she   Very   Rarely   Occasionally   Frequently
    visits when physically ill.   Rarely

Explain: _____
_____
_____

13. Purchases his/her own clothing   Very   Rarely   Occasionally   Frequently
    and household supplies.   Rarely

Explain: _____
_____
_____

14. Meets at least monthly with a   Very   Rarely   Occasionally   Frequently
    mental health counselor or   Rarely
    case manager.

Explain: _____
_____
_____

Next, rather than thinking about your family member, please consider your own situation. Listed below is a series of statements reflecting various types of personal relationships and activities. These statements refer to different ways in which persons may cope with the stresses associated with mental illness in the family. There are no right or wrong answers to these items, since all people cope with stress differently. Next to the statements below, please circle the response which best describes your level of participation. Again, you may elaborate on your responses in the space below each item.

Example: I exercise to work off
            tension.   (Very Rarely)   Rarely   Occasionally   Frequently

This respondent hardly ever gets exercise, if at all. Please go on now to complete the
scale items below.

1. I engage in personal hobbies   Very   Rarely   Occasionally   Frequently
    outside the home.   Rarely

Explain: _____
_____
_____

2. I participate in at least one   Very   Rarely   Occasionally   Frequently
    community social group.   Rarely

Explain: _____
_____
_____

3. I have contact with my family   Very   Rarely   Occasionally   Frequently
    member's mental health service   Rarely
    provider.

Explain: _____
_____
_____

4. I spend time with my friends   Very   Rarely   Occasionally   Frequently
    for purposes unrelated to my   Rarely
    family problems.

Explain: _____
_____
_____

5. I can devote uninterrupted time   Very   Rarely   Occasionally   Frequently
    to my job *or* my own routine   Rarely
    daily activities (if unemployed
    outside the home).

Explain: _____
_____
_____

6. I visit a mental health professional   Very   Rarely   Occasionally   Frequently
    for help with my own problems.   Rarely

Explain: _____
_____
_____

I confide in the following people about my family problems:

7. Neighbors   Very   Rarely   Occasionally   Frequently
                                       Rarely

Explain: _____
_____
_____

8. Extended family members (aunts,   Very   Rarely   Occasionally   Frequently
    cousins, grandparents, etc.)   Rarely

Explain: _____
_____
_____

9. My physician   Very   Rarely   Occasionally   Frequently
                                       Rarely

Explain: _____
_____
_____

10. My pastor   Very   Rarely   Occasionally   Frequently
                                       Rarely

Explain: _____
_____
_____

My family member with mental illness is a:

_____ son   _____ brother
_____ daughter   _____ sister
_____ mother   _____ spouse
_____ father   _____ other (please specify: _____)

He/she lives in:

_____ my house or apartment
_____ a group home for persons with mental illnesses
_____ an agency-managed or supervised apartment
_____ his/her own house or apartment
_____ other (please specify: _____)

He/she is now _____ years old and has received services at this and other mental health agencies or psychiatric hospitals for approximately _____ years.

Other comments? _____

_____

_____

_____

THANK YOU VERY MUCH FOR YOUR COOPERATION

Bipolar Disorder

Bipolar disorder is a disorder of mood in which, over time, a person experiences one or more *manic episodes* that are usually accompanied by one or more *major depressive episodes* (APA, 2000). Bipolar disorder is primarily a disorder of brain functioning and is both recurrent and chronic. Medication is always a major, and sometimes the only, intervention for this disorder because of its demonstrated effectiveness. Still, the medicalization of bipolar disorder has tended to obscure the fact that it has an uncertain etiology and psychosocial risk influences. Research has continued to support hypotheses that there are psychological and social, as well as biological, components to the onset and course of the disorder. The person at times seems normal but at other times behaves in bizarre, even psychotic, ways. Persons afflicted with the disorder benefit from understanding and learning to cope with it. Psychoeducation has become a primary intervention for persons with bipolar disorder and their significant others. What follows is an overview of the disorder and material that can be useful in educating persons with bipolar disorder and their significant others.

Description of Bipolar Disorder

Bipolar disorder features both manic and depressive episodes (APA, 2000). A manic episode is a distinct period in which the person's predominant mood is elevated, expansive, or irritable to a degree that there is serious impairment in occupational and social functioning. Manic episodes may be characterized by any of the following symptoms (at least three must be present): unrealistically inflated self-esteem, a decreased need for sleep, pressured speech, racing thoughts, distractibility, an increase in unrealistic goal-directed activity, and involvement in activities that have a potential for painful consequences. Manic episodes are rapid in onset and may persist for a few days or up to several months.

A major depressive episode is a period of at least two weeks during which the person experiences a depressed mood or loss of interest in nearly all common life activities. Symptoms may include (five or more must be present) depressed mood, diminished interest or pleasure in most activities, significant and unintentional weight loss or gain, insomnia or hypersomnia, feelings of physical agitation or retardation, loss of energy, feelings of worthlessness or excessive guilt, a diminished ability to think or concentrate, and persistent thoughts of death or suicide.

Another feature of bipolar disorder is the hypomanic episode (APA, 2000). This term refers to the person's gradual escalation over a period of several days or weeks from a stable mood to a manic state. It is a mild form of mania that may be pleasurable for the person. He or she experiences higher self-esteem, a decreased need for sleep, a higher energy level, an increase in overall productivity, and more intensive involvement in pleasurable activities. Its related behaviors are often socially acceptable, and consequently hypomanic behaviors may receive positive reinforcement from others. At these times, however, the person's decreased insight may lead him or her to believe that the disorder has permanently remitted and there is no need to continue with medication or other interventions. The potential for a full manic episode thus becomes greater. Poor insight, or the lack of awareness of having a mental illness, is a prominent characteristic in the active phases of bipolar disorder (Conus et al., 2006).

The overall prevalence of bipolar disorder is estimated at 1 to 2 percent, but there are two types of the disorder (APA, 2000). Bipolar I disorder is characterized by one or more manic episodes, usually accompanied by a major depressive episode. Bipolar II disorder is characterized by one or more major depressive episodes accompanied by at least one hypomanic episode. In other words, bipolar I disorder features a mix of mood episodes whereas in bipolar II disorder depressive episodes predominate. Bipolar I disorder is highly recurrent, with 90 percent of persons who have a manic episode developing future episodes (Evans, 2000). The number of episodes tends to average about four in ten years (APA, 2000). The typical age of onset of a manic episode is the midtwenties, but bipolar disorder may begin at any time from childhood through midlife (Post, Leverich, King, & Weiss, 2001). In one study, 59 percent of respondents reported experiencing their first *symptoms* of bipolar disorder during childhood or adolescence (Lish, Dime-Meenan, Whybrow, Price, & Hirschfeld, 1994).

In childhood and adolescence, bipolar disorder almost always appears differently than in adulthood. The childhood disorder presents as a nonepisodic, chronic, rapid-cycling mixed state featuring agitation, excitability, aggression, and irritability rather than "classic" mania (Carlson, 2002). The validity of childhood bipolar disorder, however, is hotly debated, as it has only been studied extensively during the past twenty years (Smith, 2007).

Risk and Protective Factors for Bipolar Disorder

Studies indicate a higher than average aggregation of bipolar disorder in families. Children with a bipolar parent are at an increased risk for mental disorders in general, and their chances of developing bipolar disorder are between 2 and 10 percent (Youngstrom, Findling, Youngstrom, & Calabrese, 2005). Twin studies further support the heritability of the disorder. A study of identical and fraternal twins in which one member of the pair had bipolar disorder showed a concordance rate of 85 percent (McGuffin et al., 2003). Researchers once speculated that the potential for bipolar disorder emanated from a single gene, but studies are now focusing on polygenic models of transmission (Ryan, Lockstone, & Huffaker, 2006). The core of bipolar disorder remains elusive. There are various proposed sites of dysfunction in the brain for bipolar disorder. Four areas under study include the roles of neurotransmitters, the endocrine system, physical biorhythms, and physical complications during the mother's pregnancy and childbirth (Scott, McNeill, & Cavanaugh, 2006; Swann, 2006).

Stressful life events play an activating role in early episodes of bipolar disorder, with subsequent episodes sometimes arising in the absence of clear external precipitants (Ingram & Smith, 2008). Persons with bipolar disorder who have a history of early life adversity (such as physical or sexual abuse) show an earlier age of onset, faster and more frequent cycling, increased suicidality, and other problem conditions, including alcohol and substance abuse (Post et al., 2001). Adolescents with bipolar disorder are more vulnerable to mood episodes when they experience stress in family, romantic, or peer relationships. The frequency of these episodes is predictive of less improvement in mood fluctuations (Kim, Miklowitz, & Biuckians, 2007). Persons who experience high levels of life stress in general after the onset of bipolar disorder are four times more likely to have a relapse than clients with low levels of stress. Events that can cause these episodes include disruptions in social rhythms (daily routines or sleep-wake cycles, such as air travel and changes in work schedules) (Frank, 2007). Stressful events in social and family support systems appear to affect the course of bipolar disorder in combination with genetic and biological vulnerabilities (Miklowitz, 2007).

Family Conflict and Other Problems Associated with Bipolar Disorder

It should not be surprising that persons with bipolar disorder tend to experience serious social and occupational problems. These problems include social withdrawal, low self-esteem, the loss or absence of intimate relationships, increased dependence on others, family conflicts, job loss, and disruptions in social routines (Sierra, Livianos, Arques, Rojo, & Castelló, 2007). An adolescent who develops bipolar disorder often experiences an arrest in psychological development, acquiring self-efficacy and dependency problems that endure into adulthood (Floersch, 2003). The person's mood swings and erratic behavior may be a source of ongoing turmoil in family, peer, and professional relationships (Johnson, Winett, Meyer, Greenhouse,

& Miller, 1999). Manic individuals test the limits of their relationships until others are exhausted, frustrated, and drained of empathy. Because the mean age of onset is in young adulthood and there is a higher risk of recurrence as the client ages, many spouses, family, friends, and peers do not experience the client in a manic state until their relationship has already developed. Significant others become confused by perceived changes in the client's personality.

There is much evidence that expressed emotion (defined in chapter 6 as excessive amounts of face-to-face contact and hostile and critical comments between persons and their relatives) is associated with poorer outcomes in bipolar disorder (Miklowitz, Wisniewski, Miyahara, Sachs, & Otto, 2005). Although the bipolar person's ratings of family member criticisms do not themselves predict mood symptoms, those persons who are more distressed by relatives' criticisms have more severe manic and depressive symptoms and proportionately fewer well days. Persons who report that their relatives become more upset by their own criticisms have less severe depressive symptoms at follow-up, probably because the emotional release is helpful to them. Again, this data does not suggest that family members merit blame but underscores the disruptive impact of bipolar disorder and shows that changing family interactions through psychoeducation can be beneficial to all persons involved. Higher levels of social support are associated with more rapid recovery from an episode of bipolar disorder (Johnson et al., 1999).

Married persons with bipolar disorder are at a high risk for divorce (Lam, Donaldson, Brown, & Malliaris, 2005). They become dependent on the spouse for support in times of crisis, but spouses tend to see the mania at least in part as a willful act. The well spouse's self-esteem can diminish while being blamed for the family's problems, acting as a buffer between the client and community, and making many concessions to the person in an effort to maintain family stability. If the marriage continues, other problems may include the well spouse's guilt feelings, growing need to control the relationship, and at times even a learned dependence on the client's pathology for the relationship to persist. Further, the person may drain the family's financial resources with spending sprees, debt accumulation, and treatment costs.

These same interpersonal patterns contribute to the bipolar person's occupational problems. One study indicated a stable working capacity in only 45 percent of individuals, and 28 percent experienced a steady decline in job status and performance (Hirschfeld, Lewis, & Vornik, 2003). Missed work, poor work quality, and conflicts with coworkers all contribute to the downward trend for persons who cannot maintain mood stability. Even though bipolar persons experience lengthy periods of normal mood functioning, occupational functioning can be irreparably damaged by behaviors occurring during mood swings. If the disorder becomes manifest at a young age, the person may not achieve adequate education and skills to establish a productive work career.

The individual's denial or lack of insight into the disorder poses another problem. When manic, the person may be reluctant to accept the need for medication and other interventions (Swartz & Frank, 2001). Episodes of mania and depression tend to be brief in comparison to the duration of normal mood activity, and the person may decide after a period of stability that there is no longer a need for precautionary interventions. This decision is a major concern because it is recommended that most bipolar persons take medication during periods of stability as well as the active phases of the disorder (Sachs, Printz, Kahn, Carpenter, & Docherty, 2000). This problem is accentuated by the diminished ability of the person to distinguish normal from abnormal mood states.

The bipolar person may experience additional emotional problems related to fears of the recurrence of mania and to dealing with the loss of relationships and his or her former sense of self. The lifetime risk of suicide for persons with bipolar disorder is 19 percent, the highest of any mental disorder (Sands & Harrow, 2000). It is also well established that persons in both manic and depressive cycles often abuse drugs and alcohol in an effort to treat the symptoms. There is a 60 percent lifetime risk of substance abuse among persons with bipolar disorder (Goodnick, 1998).

Psychoeducational Interventions

Psychoeducation has an important role in educating persons with bipolar disorder about the illness and its repercussions so that it can be controlled (Rothbaum & Austin, 2000). The chronic nature of bipolar disorder is difficult for people to come to terms with, and psychoeducation can help them deal with the effects of past episodes on their lives, comprehend the impact of the disorder on their self-image, and make plans to minimize future problems. Many people who develop bipolar disorder have already made major life decisions (career, marriage, lifestyle) and thus are often faced with the difficult task of making adjustments to their future plans. The more that a person and those in his or her environment understand about the disorder, the better able they will be to manage it. The general goals of psychoeducation for bipolar disorder are to

> Increase participants' knowledge about the disorder,
>
> Increase awareness of intervention options,
>
> Recruit family and partner support as appropriate (to generate social support and assess family structure),
>
> Decrease the risks of manic or depressive relapses (identify stresses that may trigger mood episodes),
>
> Enhance long-term medication compliance (through reflection on one's attitudes about medication), and

Enhance social and occupational functioning through coping-skills development (cognitive and behavioral interventions). (Miklowitz & Goldstein, 1997; Rouget & Aubrey, 2007)

Professional literature reviews consistently show that psychoeducation has a positive effect on the course of bipolar disorder. Along with cognitive-behavioral intervention it is the most effective means of preventing recurrences of manic and depressive episodes (Colom & Vieta, 2004). Other researchers come to the same conclusion, adding that interpersonal, family structure, and social rhythm (described in this chapter) therapies should be included in these programs (Geller & Goldberg, 2007; Zaretsky, Rizvi, & Parikh, 2007). Psychoeducation helps individuals become active, informed participants in the management of the disorder and promotes a collaborative relationship between persons and their caregivers (Vieta, 2005a). Researchers in one study found that persons most likely to participate in a psychoeducation program were young adults with relatively high education levels, a shorter duration of the disorder, a better initial knowledge of medication, and a lesser external locus of control orientation (Even, Richard, & Thuille, 2007).

Social rhythm interventions are popular psychoeducational behavioral strategies for treating persons with bipolar disorder and major depression. These interventions emphasize the importance of the person's adherence to a structured daily schedule that includes planned activity and rest periods. Such normal social rhythms serve to balance the person's tendencies to engage in erratic, unpredictable behaviors when in an active phase of bipolar disorder; they also run counter to the depressed person's tendencies to isolate. Some professionals encourage the person's use of formal time logs for developing and carrying out social rhythms. These logs resemble daily appointment schedules in many ways but are more personalized in breaking down the person's day into planned formal and informal (including leisure) activities. An example of a social rhythm scale is found in figure 7.1.

In summary, psychoeducation empowers participants by providing both a practical and theoretical (cognitive-behavioral) approach for understanding and dealing with the symptoms and consequences of bipolar disorder (Vieta, 2005b). It identifies bipolar disorder as a biological abnormality that requires regular medication and teaches persons to cope with symptoms and maintain regularity in social and occupational functioning. Participants consistently demonstrate improvements in treatment adherence and in other clinical outcomes, including reduced mood episodes and hospitalizations and increased time between episodes. Because bipolar disorder shares many of the same clinical characteristics as schizophrenia, including a relapse-remission course, significant psychosocial impairment, the need for ongoing medication compliance, and the negative impact of family stress on clinical outcomes, some psychoeducational approaches developed for schizophrenia have been adapted for use with persons with bipolar disorder.

Figure 7.1: The social rhythm metric

ACTIVITY	Check if did not do	Clock time	AM	PM	Check if alone	Spouse/partner	Children	Other family	Other persons
Out of bed									
First contact with another person (in person or by phone)									
Have morning beverage									
Have breakfast									
Go outside for the first time									
Start work, school, housework, volunteer activities, child or family care									
Have lunch									
Take an afternoon nap									
Have dinner									
Physical exercise									
Have an evening snack									
Watch evening TV news program									
Watch another program									
Activity A (describe)									
Activity B (describe)									
Return home (last time)									
Go to bed									

Source: Monk, Flaherty, Frank, & Hoskinson, 1990

Program Examples

In this section several psychoeducational programs will be described briefly, followed by two extended program descriptions.

For Individuals

Group psychoeducation in one program in Canada had a positive effect on the participants' quality of life, defined as a subjective state of well-being. This outcome variable was assessed in an eight-week time-limited psychoeducation program (Michalak, Yatham, Wan, & Lam, 2005). The program addressed the following five goals, which were incorporated into all eight sessions, with emphases depending on the expressed wishes of the participants during the first meeting.

1. To help participants identify the signs and symptoms of bipolar disorder and to enhance their knowledge about the course of the disorder, including relapse risk factors (requires attention to education and participant learning styles)
2. To raise awareness of the impact of bipolar disorder on psychological, cognitive, physical, emotional, and social functioning (education and human-development themes)
3. To improve participants' knowledge about pharmacologic treatments for bipolar disorder and their common side effects
4. To provide guidelines for insuring medication effectiveness and safety (an opportunity for member reflection on their own situations and personality styles)
5. To provide cognitive strategies for coping with bipolar disorder (involving problem-solving and family structure themes)

The researchers found that participants in this program demonstrated a significant improvement in quality of life in terms of reported physical functioning and general life satisfaction.

Colom et al. (2003) conducted a randomized trial of the efficacy of group psychoeducation in the prevention of episode recurrences for 120 bipolar clients whose disorders were in remission (the controls attended nonstructured group meetings). Through twenty-one sessions, each of which included the formal presentation of material and group discussion, the featured topics were medication adherence, coping with environmental stress triggers, and issues related to social and occupational functioning.

Through two years of follow-up, the researchers found that the experimental program significantly reduced the number of client relapses and increased the time span between recurrences of depressive, manic, or mixed episodes. Clients in the experimental group also experienced fewer and shorter hospitalizations. The authors concluded that the differences between the two groups were due to the experimental group's emphasis on early recognition of symptoms of relapse and modifications of participants' daily routines.

Additional support for individual intervention in another culture comes from a Spanish control-group study by Colom and Lam (2005). In this study, participants took part in an educational program covering twelve sessions that taught recurrence identification and improved lifestyle regularity in a group setting. The researchers found that the program was successful in improving illness awareness and treatment adherence at the six-, eighteen-, and twenty-four-month follow-up points.

For Families

A variety of family intervention models have shown to be effective in influencing the course of bipolar disorder. One inpatient family intervention program consisted of six one-hour sessions focused on

> Understanding and accepting the illness,
> Identifying possible precipitating stresses,
> Understanding and making adjustments to family interactions that promote stress,
> Planning for stress management through problem-solving discussions, and
> Accepting the need for ongoing intervention after discharge. (Clarkin et al., 1990)

To study the effectiveness of this program, researchers randomly assigned twenty-one clients to experimental and control conditions. At six and eighteen months after discharge clients in the psychoeducational program demonstrated better outcomes, but surprisingly the treatment effect was limited to females. The researchers speculated that women may be more socialized to work with their families whereas men might be prone to move toward independence too quickly. This finding has not been reported or addressed in other studies, but it underscores the importance of attention to gender issues in program development.

One example of a highly structured psychoeducational family intervention is found in a multiple-family group for persons with bipolar disorder (Brennan, 1995). This intervention is a fourteen-week program including six to nine clients and fifteen to thirty family members who meet weekly for two hours. Two to three mental health professionals lead the program. The program is primarily didactic and attends to the two goals of educating members about bipolar disorder and its treatment and enabling members to achieve a measure of control over the symptoms. The program addresses the following topics in sequence.

Introductions   In the first session members are helped to feel at ease, discuss the purposes of the group, elicit their individual and collective hopes, and develop a set of questions to be answered over the fourteen weeks in small groups.

What is bipolar disorder?   Following reintroductions, a presentation is made on the symptoms, causes, and course of bipolar disorder, using DSM criteria as illustrations. The viewing of a video about bipolar disorder is followed by a group discussion.

Medications and other interventions A presentation (by a physician or other knowledgeable professional) is given on the positive and adverse effects of the major medications used in the treatment of bipolar disorder. The viewing of a video about medications is followed by a group discussion.

Clients and families are seen separately, part 1 Clients and family members divide into separate groups and discuss their reactions to the burden of bipolar disorder, which enables participants to reflect on their particular situations and on the human-development stage of the ill relative. Leaders help family members to consider structural changes that might benefit their coping. Each group task includes the construction of a message (what they would like the others to understand about themselves).

Recognizing and preventing relapse A presentation is given on the identification of the early warning signs of relapse of persons with bipolar disorder. Through problem-solving activities each family learns what to do when those signs are present.

Understanding the mental health system Group members discuss the local mental health treatment system and any perceived service gaps with regard to inpatient, outpatient, crisis intervention, and private sector services. Participants share their positive and negative experiences with the service system and formulate a set of family-related problem scenarios to present and process the following week.

Role-play demonstrations by guest professionals Using the participants' suggestions from the previous session of situations they would like to see portrayed, visiting mental health professionals role-play those situations without a script and then open up the group for a discussion of ways to resolve the problems or challenges presented. (The use of visiting professionals is optional.) Such situations may include persuading a client to take medication, urging an ill relative to resume a greater level of social functioning, and managing parent fears of relapse when warning signs are present. During this meeting participants have time to reflect on their particular situations, engage in mutual problem solving, and provide one another with emotional support.

Client and families are seen separately, part 2 This optional session is organized the same as part 1. Near the end of the session the families, in small groups, formulate a series of questions about a range of issues related to bipolar disorder to ask a visiting professional (psychiatrist, psychologist, or social worker) scheduled to appear the next week. Leaders encourage the family members to consider the stage of human development of the ill relative and how the challenges related to bipolar disorder are significant to those stages.

Presentation by a guest professional The professional discusses topics and answers questions raised during the previous week.

Understanding suicide A discussion is generated among all participants about coping with the emotional effects of attempted suicide, threatened suicide, or the fear of suicide. Because this is such a sensitive topic, any members who are not comfortable with it are excused from this session (although few participants opt out).

Presentation of a documentary on bipolar disorder Discussion follows the presentation of the documentary. This session also includes preparations for the following two weeks, in which members choose among two dozen or so prepared topics of special interest to them on managing the symptoms of bipolar disorder.

Review of intervention guidelines for clients and families Over two sessions, the leader shares guidelines about managing high-priority items chosen during the previous session, followed by member sharing of their experiences in successfully managing the symptoms of bipolar disorder.

Program evaluation and summary Participants review key ideas developed in the program and provide feedback to the leader on how to design the next group. The meeting ends with a review of the questions developed in the first session, to see if they have been answered.

The program evaluations indicate universal approval of the program, even though many participants admitted initial skepticism. Participants report that the content about bipolar disorder was important to their learning how to manage the course of the illness. They further valued the knowledge that they were not alone with the problem and were relieved to be able to talk about their challenges with supportive others. No long-term data on the impact of the program has been made available.

Family-focused treatment (FFT) is a well-researched psychoeducational intervention that attempts to improve family functioning by training members in the three topic areas of education, communications skills, and problem-solving skills (Rea et al., 2003). Two practitioners trained in the approach meet weekly with participants for the first three months, every other week for the second three months, and monthly for the final three sessions. The twenty-one individual sessions are an hour in length, and the leaders address all three program components during each meeting (see exhibit 7.1).

Education	Communication	Problem solving
Symptoms	Active listening	Cognitive-behavioral
Course	Structured feedback	processes
Causes	(positive and negative)	Relapse drills
Interventions	Making positive behavior	
Risk factors	requests (via role-playing)	
Protective factors		

Exhibit 7.1: Components of family-focused treatment

The educational component includes information about symptoms, course, causes, and treatment, presented within a vulnerability-stress framework, with attention paid to risk and protective factors. Communication-skills training includes active listening, giving structured positive and negative feedback, and making positive requests about one another's behaviors. These activities include role-playing and between-session practice. Problem-solving training includes the structured cognitive-behavioral process (see chapter 2, "Cognitive Theory") with special attention given to family problem solving around a "relapse drill." A variation of this FFT structure includes addressing each of the three major components separately for two to nine sessions, depending on the assessed needs of the families (Miklowitz & Goldstein, 1997).

The FFT intervention has been evaluated with regard to several outcome measures. In one control-group study (with controls receiving individual family intervention and medication management), the program led to a reduced risk of relapse and hospitalization (Rea et al., 2003). Interestingly, this impact was strongest after, not during, the year of active intervention. It was speculated that this result is due to the fact that experimental group families had learned and retained skills that they could utilize after the program ended, more so than participants in the control group. Additionally, the more severely ill clients were better protected from relapse in the FFT group than in the control group. The higher functioning clients tended to have low rates of rehospitalization regardless of the group they were in.

In another FFT evaluation study, 101 clients were randomly assigned to a one-year program of FFT or to medication and crisis-management services (Miklowitz et al., 2000). Results indicated that clients receiving FFT achieved longer periods without relapse than clients in the comparison groups. The greatest effects were found for depressive symptoms. Further, after nine months of FFT, clients and family members were found to be using more positive communication skills, which predicted later symptom amelioration, as in the earlier study. Clients from the FFT program were found to have more positive nonverbal interaction patterns during a one-year posttreatment problem-solving assessment than those who were involved in the control intervention.

Another FFT group was developed especially for families with adolescent ill members to see if outcomes were comparable to adult groups (Miklowitz et al., 2004). Program modifications include addressing the developmental issues common to adolescents (see exhibit 7.2) and the unique clinical presentations of bipolar adolescents (a non-episodic, chronic, rapid-cycling mixed state featuring agitation, excitability, aggression, and irritability). This example is the first in this book of a program that specifically attends to the psychosocial stages of the clients' lives and considers how these developmental challenges affect the presentation and course of a mental disorder. Because the presentation of adolescent bipolar disorder is different from that of adults, it is difficult for families to distinguish symptoms from normal behavior relative to one's stage of life. Families are helped to understand the interactions of psychosocial development and biological illness and taught not to assume that all challenging behavior is indicative of a mental disorder.

Exhibit 7.2:   *Major developmental characteristics of adolescence*

Biological: onset of puberty and sexual maturity, growth spurts
Cognitive: engages in more complex and abstract reasoning, can follow complex instructions, separates reality from possibilities, predicts consequences of actions, develops moral principles (Depending on the cognitive skill level, interventions may focus on changing thinking patterns, through discussion and perhaps in groups, or behaviors, rewarding more positive behaviors.)
Psychological and social: conforms to the peer group, dresses for peer approval, criticizes parents and formulates own opinions and views, establishes independence from parents, seeks a sense of identity and self-worth, fears failure

---

The program was successful, as participants reported improvements in depressive symptoms, manic symptoms, and behavior problems over a one-year period. Another group of researchers determined that parents of children with bipolar disorder are more knowledgeable about mood symptoms than parents of children with depression. The study also determined that children with bipolar disorder had greater histories of hospitalization, outpatient treatment, medication trials, and placement in special-education classes than children with depression (Fristad, Goldberg-Arnold, & Gavazzi, 2002). Both types of families expressed knowledge gains, skills, support, and positive attitudes during an FFT intervention.

Miklowitz (2006) emphasizes that FFT can have a preventive effect on the ill relative's suicide potential. Persons with bipolar disorder are at a high risk for suicidal ideation and attempts, which in turn is associated with poor family communication and high inter-family conflict, especially with adolescents. Actively raising the issue of suicidal ideation (as was also done in the Brennan [1995] group described earlier) enables it to be addressed in all three components of family-focused therapy.

Other researchers have shown that multifamily groups lead to a decrease in expressed emotion among families. In one such study the caregivers of forty-five persons with stabilized bipolar disorder were randomly assigned to two groups; the experimental group received twelve ninety-minute psychoeducational sessions about understanding the disorder and developing coping skills (Reinares et al., 2004). Participants significantly improved their knowledge about bipolar disorder and reduced both the subjective burden and the caregiver's beliefs about the link between the subjective burden and the ill relative.

Summary

The modality of psychoeducation has become widely used to help persons with bipolar disorder and their families understand and cope with the disorder. The programs are based largely on those initially developed with regard to schizophrenia, due to the similarities of the two disorders, including chronicity, psychosocial problems experienced by the ill person, and the need for ongoing monitoring and medication use. Although these programs have not been evaluated as thoroughly as those used with schizophrenia, they appear to produce positive outcomes along a variety of measures and to help persons to maintain productive lives in spite of the disorder.

Chapter 8

Depression

Depression is a commonly experienced short- or long-term mood condition that ranges from mild to incapacitating. It is considered normal when it is relatively short-term and based on reactions to difficult external conditions, but it is a disorder when judged to be caused, at least in part, by biological factors. The focus of this chapter is on those depressions that tend to be long-term and significantly disruptive to one's social functioning. Like bipolar disorder, depression is classified as a mood disorder (APA, 2000), but it has unique characteristics that account for differences in how it is addressed by professionals. There is clearly a role for psychoeducation in the treatment of depression, as it can be a chronic condition with an irregular course that creates ongoing challenges for those persons who experience it, as well as for their families and friends. Many such programs for adolescents and adults have been developed and will be described in this chapter. The discussion will focus on the two diagnostic categories of major depression and dysthymic disorder.

A *major depressive episode* is a period of at least two weeks during which a person experiences a severely depressed mood or loss of interest in nearly all life activities. Symptoms are evident in the following five domains:

Affect: sadness, anxiety, anger, irritability, emotional numbness

Behavior: agitation, crying, flatness of expression, slowness of physical movement and speech

Attitudes toward the self: guilt, shame, low self-esteem, helplessness, pessimism, hopelessness, thoughts of death or suicide

Cognition: decreased ability to think and concentrate

Physiology: inability to experience pleasure, changes in appetite and sleep patterns, loss of energy, fatigue, decreased sex drive, somatic complaints

Dysthymic disorder represents a general personality style featuring symptoms that are similar to, but less intense than, those of major depression. Many people with major depression experience this disorder when in remission from the major episode, but it occurs more often by itself. The diagnosis requires two years of a continuously depressed mood. It generally has an early age of onset (adolescence through early adulthood) and produces impairments in school, work, and social life.

The Experience of Depression

Although many mood disorders are considered to be biological in origin, it is important for psychoeducators to grasp the human experience of depression. In a landmark qualitative study of persons with recurrent depression, Karp (1995) identified themes in the course of the disorder that can be of practical use to the psychoeducator. First, he characterizes long-term depression as a disease of isolation with the following four stages.

An initial period of "inchoate troubling feelings" The person lacks a vocabulary to label his or her experiences. He or she knows that something is not right but has no clear sense of what is happening or that it may represent a persistent problem state. The person may perceive these ill feelings as related to a transient developmental stage.

The person concludes, "Something is really wrong with me" For the first time, the person perceives his or her negative mood state as significant but still is not sure how to label it, whether as an emotional problem or some other type of life challenge.

A crisis brings the person into a world of "therapeutic experts" The crisis may not be a sudden traumatic event but rather any situation in which the person clearly recognizes that he or she needs professional help. Perhaps a significant other convinces the person to seek such help.

The person comes to grips with an "illness identity" The person accepts that he or she has long-term depression and must evaluate how to cope with it, through lifestyle choices as well as professional intervention. The person recognizes that he or she must learn to live with the depression and make sense of it in some way (possibly through spiritual reflection). The person may not ultimately see him- or herself as having a disorder but accepts that he or she is a depressed person, which is not the same thing.

Next Karp (1995) identifies the following commonly experienced stages of a person's coping and adapting to chronic depression.

Diversion of attention away from the problem Rather than confront the problem directly (because it is not perceived as a circumscribed problem), the person occupies him- or herself with other activities so as not to be so focused on the troubling mood. Such diversions may include work, hobbies, substance abuse, and many other activities, some of which are productive and some of which are potentially harmful.

Attempts to fix the problem, alone or with the help of significant others The person realizes that he or she is depressed but tries to overcome the problem without professional help. For persons with so-called minor depressions, such self-help strategies may be effective.

A search for the right professional   Karp (1995) found that people with chronic depression have high expectations for empathy from professionals and that, over the course of many years, they start and stop working with many such persons before finding one who has an appropriate orientation toward helping. For persons with long-term depression, this professional is one who does not have a purely medical perspective on the disorder.

The person incorporates the depression into his overall personality Rather than expect a cure for the depression, the person eventually accepts that it will remain a chronic condition, a part of one's personality and lifestyle. It becomes a part of who the person is, no longer something that exists outside the core self.

Interestingly, as noted previously, persons with depression are often ambivalent about working with professional practitioners of all types, wondering how well they can empathize with the mood problem. Karp (1995) learned that what people with depression most wanted from a professional was to be listened to and understood. They did not want the professional to rush into any type of intervention protocols. These findings seem to support the potential value of psychoeducation, which is a less stigmatizing and more collaborative method of intervention with persons who are depressed.

Depression in Adulthood

The prevalence of major depression in Western nations is approximately 2 to 3 percent for men (with a lifetime risk of 7% to 12%) and 4 to 9 percent for women (with a lifetime risk of 20% to 25%) (Kraaij, Arensman, & Spinhoven, 2002). The point prevalence of dysthymia is 3 percent, with a lifetime prevalence of 6 percent (APA, 2000). Episodes of untreated major depression typically persist for at least four months, but 50 to 85 percent of people experience one or more additional episodes (Karasu, Gelenberg, Merriam, & Wang, 2002). A worldwide study found that depression was continuously sustained for a twelve-month period for one-third of persons with the disorder (Barkow et al., 2003). Residual symptoms and social or occupational impairment continue between episodes for 20 to 35 percent of persons (Karasu et al., 2002).

Major depression tends to run in families, which supports, in part, a process of genetic transmission. Based on an analysis of twin studies, the heritability for major depression is in the range of 31 to 42 percent (Sullivan, Neale, & Kendler, 2000). The genetic potential for depression may be transmitted as an affective temperament that makes one susceptible to a mood disorder depending on other factors. Late-onset depression (after age sixty) is less associated with family transmission than early-onset depression (before age twenty) is and includes the risk influences of bereavement and medical disabilities (Cole & Dendukuri, 2003). Biological theories of depression have been formulated from the hypothesized actions of antidepressant medications. Many depressions are thought to be associated with deficiencies of certain neurotransmitters in the limbic area of the brain. There are limitations to these biological theories, however, as there is no test to establish biological depression and it is not possible to precisely measure levels of neurotransmitters in the brain (Brown & Harris, 2008).

The risk of recurrence of depression is related to the number of prior episodes that a person has experienced (Karasu et al., 2002). Recovery from depression is associated with less severe initial depression, receiving adequate intervention for managing the disorder, an absence of general personality problems, and being married (Barnett et al., 2002). For older adults, factors that impede optimal treatment response include an accumulation of negative life events and unresolved grief (Cuijpers, van Straten, Smit, & Andersson, 2009). Problems related to dependence on others, the role changes associated with old age, and social isolation may also pose barriers.

Depression in Childhood and Adolescence

Adolescence is a time of physical, psychological, social, and spiritual change. With some cultural variations, teenagers begin to separate from their parents and exert newfound independence, and this process sometimes leads to family conflicts. Physically, their bodies begin to mature and hormonal changes can cause mood swings. For some adolescents, the move into puberty can intensify a depressed mood that ultimately may affect sleep patterns, energy levels, concentration, and school performance (Rudolph, 2008).

Depression in children and adolescents is manifested differently than it is in adults (Waslick, Kandel, & Kakouros, 2002). *Irritable mood* is a criterion for youth but not adults, although adults often experience irritability as part of their depression. The *weight loss* criterion is not used with children and adolescents, because they are developing physically and are subject to weight fluctuations. Youth can only meet the appetite and weight disturbance criteria by not sustaining normal standards of growth and weight. For dysthymia, only one year's duration is required for adolescents as compared to the two-year criterion for adults. Depression in adolescents is further marked by separation anxiety, somatic complaints, and behavior problems (Fergusson & Woodward, 2002). Children and adolescents rarely experience hypersomnia (excess sleep) and are less likely to show psychotic symptoms than adults (Waslick et al., 2002).

Lifetime prevalence rates for adolescent depression range from 15 to 20 percent, and at least 9 percent of adolescents report moderate to severe symptoms (Rushton, Forcier, & Schectman, 2002). Prevalence rates for major depression in adolescence are estimated at between 4 and 8 percent. For dysthymia, prevalence rates range from 2 to 5 percent (Fonagy, Target, Cottrell, Phillips, & Kurtz, 2002). Rates of depression for females are double those for males (Lewinsohn & Essau, 2002).

Episodes of major depression for children and adolescents last for a median duration of six months (Cottrell, Fonagy, Kurtz, Phillips, & Target, 2002). Almost all (90%) episodes remit within a two-year period, but relapse is common. About half of youths will experience another episode within two years, and a majority (70%) will have relapsed at five years (Cottrell et al., 2002). Dysthymia takes longer to remit. The recovery rate is 7 percent two years after onset, and its median duration is 3.9 years (Kovacs, Obrosky, Gatsonis, & Richards, 1997). Youths with dysthymia tend to have an episode of major depression two to three years later. Adolescent depression tends to continue into adulthood (Fergusson & Woodward, 2002), with additional episodes estimated for approximately 60 to 70 percent of teens (Rao et al., 1995).

Several risk and protective influences have been identified for depression in adolescents. Research reviews have found that families with a depressed adolescent often feature weak attachment bonds, ineffective parenting, enmeshed family relationships, and greater family stress (Jewell & Stark, 2003). Parental depression is a particular risk factor. By the time a child with a depressed parent reaches age twenty, there is a 40 percent chance that he or she will have had an episode of major depression (Beardslee, Versage, & Gladstone, 1998). Genetic factors may be involved, although evidence for heredity is stronger in adults (Goodman & Gotlib, 1999). Other biological factors may include the abnormal neuroendocrine functioning that has been found in women who are depressed during pregnancy. The fetus may be exposed to increased cortisol levels and experience a reduced blood flow, leading to slower growth and less movement.

Psychosocial explanations have also been articulated for depression in youths (Duggal, Carlson, Sroufe, & Egeland, 2001). Parents may model depressive affect, thinking patterns, and behaviors for their children. Depressed parents also tend to see their children's behavior in a negative light, using low rates of reward and high rates of punishment in response to the child's behavior. Marital problems are associated with an increased risk for depression in children (Beardslee et al., 1998), and a number of studies have indicated a relationship between adolescent depression and childhood abuse (Brown, Cohen, Johnson, & Smailes, 1999).

The Families of Depressed Persons

The family members and loved ones of people with depression are also at risk for significant stress as they try to help their loved ones cope with and recover from depression. Their efforts change in relation to the duration of the illness, as follows.

1. There is initial bewilderment about the nature of the problem and its persistence.
2. The family member engages in active learning about the disorder and its associated problems.
3. The family member embarks on sustained intervention efforts to save the person from ongoing depression.
4. Eventually there is a moderation of caregiving efforts in order to take better care of the self. In other words, there is an eventual tempering of the loved one's involvement with the depressed person, as he or she realizes that the disorder is long-term and resistant to radical change. (Karp, 1995)

Karp's (1995) study participants provided further useful information about how significant others determine the extent of their supportive behaviors:

How much supportive reciprocity can be expected as the depressed person demands sympathy from the other. The loved one will be more likely to provide ongoing support if he or she also receives support from the depressed person in some ways.

The balance between relationship status and the width of sympathy. For example, spouses expect more from their partners and close friends than they do from their children or coworkers. If they do not receive reciprocal support from a partner, they will be less willing to provide ongoing support.

The need to strike a balance between taking care of oneself and taking care of the other person.

The relationship between the time span of the problem and the amount of sympathy offered. Interestingly, this is a curvilinear relationship: significant others are more sympathetic at the onset of the depression and if it becomes chronic, but they are less sympathetic during an intermediate period when the course of the depression is uncertain.

Some additional themes of interest that Karp (1995) identifies relative to significant others is that a loved one's misery can actually energize the caregiver, and the existence of ongoing turmoil may deepen some relationships. Men are better at sociability than at intimacy in how they provide support to a loved one, but for both genders the significant other ultimately develops a greater sense of social isolation while interacting with the loved one.

Psychoeducation and Depression

A biopsychosocial model of depression is helpful in psychoeducation (Schotte, Van den Bossche, De Doncker, Claes, & Cosyns, 2006). The core of the model is the concept of risk and protective mechanisms that may occur at the biological, psychological, and societal levels. Life events with stress-inducing value interact with a person's internal and environmental vulnerability, triggering distress that affects the person's resilience and leads to symptoms of depression. The onset and course of depression is symbolized as a negative downward loop in which interactions among symptoms, vulnerability, and stressors drive the client toward a depressive condition. The experience of depression influences future vulnerability to stressors and increases the risk of further relapse.

Persons with depression who attend psychoeducational programs experience a lower rate of relapse than persons who do not attend such groups (Franchini et al., 2006). Specifically, interventions based on cognitive-behavioral theory have been clearly documented as effective treatments for major depression in a meta-analysis of fifty-six studies (Lewinsohn, Clarke, & Hoberman, 1989). Such interventions offer participants new behavior skills and new ways of thinking about themselves. Treatments derived from the cognitive perspective are aimed at depressive thought processes, whereas those derived from behavioral positions are aimed at increasing pleasant activities and time-management skills and improving social, relaxation, and problem-solving skills.

All cognitive-behavioral interventions for depression should include the following components:

> A well-planned rationale that encourages the participant to believe that he or she can change
>
> A focus on skills development so the person can become more effective in managing his or her daily life
>
> An emphasis on the independent use of skills outside the meetings
>
> An encouragement of the participant's "owning" that improvements in mood are due to his or her own increased skills (Lewinsohn et al., 1989)

Interestingly, practitioners with a variety of personal characteristics can have equal success in facilitating positive outcomes for depressed persons. In a study of eight practitioners who conducted the same structured psychoeducational program for depression, significant leader differences were noted in the amount of group participation encouraged, group cohesiveness, session length, warmth, enthusiasm, clarity, on-task activity, specificity of feedback, and expectations of participant response. Still, all group outcomes were positive and similar (Antonuccio, Lewisohn, & Steinmetz, 1982). This finding supports the point made in chapter 4 that being a good educator is in part a matter of finding a teaching style that fits well with one's basic personality.

Programs for Adults

Coping with Depression

Coping with Depression (CWD) is a structured course that teaches participants techniques to cope with problems related to their depression.

It addresses the four areas of discomfort and anxiety in social situations, the importance of pleasant activities, managing irrational or negative thoughts, and developing new social skills (Swan, Sorrell, MacVicar, Durham, & Matthews, 2004). The course also works to promote improved self-monitoring of mood and personal goal attainment. CWD is provided in group settings that allow participants to practice and role-play new interpersonal behaviors and other skills. The program consists of twelve two-hour sessions conducted over eight weeks. Sessions are held twice weekly for the first four weeks and then weekly for the remaining four weeks. Groups typically consist of six to ten adults and a single group leader. One- and six-month follow-up sessions, called class reunions, are held to support treatment gains. There is an instructor's manual for this course, and it also makes use of a text called *Control Your Depression* (Lewinsohn, Forster, & Youngsen, 1992) from which reading assignments are given. The program structure is given in exhibit 8.1.

Exhibit 8.1:   The Coping with Depression program schedule

Sessions 1 and 2: presentation of course rules, rationale, and the social learning view of depression (people learn behaviors by modeling the behavior of significant others, and those behaviors can either reinforce depression or reinforce different emotional responses); teaching of several self-change skills, along with the principles of monitoring behaviors by developing a baseline, realistic goals, a plan, and a contract for change

Sessions 3 and 4: relaxation skills, featuring progressive muscle relaxation

Sessions 5 and 6: increasing pleasant activities through a review of a list of potentially pleasant activities provided by the leader

Sessions 7 and 8: identifying and changing irrational thoughts

Sessions 9 and 10: social-skills development, featuring assertion, planning more social activities, and strategies for making more friends

Sessions 11 and 12: an integration of skills learned, maintenance of gains, and prevention of relapse; each participant develops a personal emergency plan, detailing the steps they will take to counteract feelings of depression in the future

---

The Coping with Depression course has been shown to be an effective intervention for depression in several experimental trials, and the rate of relapse is comparable to that of other therapy interventions. The course has utility as either a preventive or a remedial intervention.

CWD has been adapted for use with several other client populations. The empirically validated Adolescent Coping with Depression course emphasizes skill building to promote control over one's mood and enhancement of coping skills through group activities and role-playing (Lewinsohn, Clarke, Rohde, Hops, & Seeley, 1996). There are sixteen two-hour sessions conducted over an eight-week period with up to ten adolescents, along with parallel weekly two-hour sessions for the parents. Using a workbook with short readings, quizzes, structured learning tasks, and homework assignments, the sessions are designed to increase social skills and pleasant activities; decrease anxiety through relaxation training; reduce depression-supporting cognitions through cognitive restructuring; resolve conflict through learning communication, negotiation, and conflict-resolution skills; and assist in planning for the future. Booster sessions are available for relapse prevention. This course can be modified for individual treatment tailored to the needs of individual adolescents. Still, the authors point out advantages of the group format. Two clinical trials have supported the efficacy of this intervention.

Bibliotherapy

A minimal-contact cognitive bibliotherapy experience has been found to be superior to a wait-list control group in helping depressed adults with their recovery (Jamison & Scogin, 1995). The researchers asked all voluntary community participants to read David Burns's (1999) *Feeling Good: The New Mood Therapy*, which is written at a sixth-grade level. The book instructs readers in activities, graded task assignments, role-playing, cognitive rehearsal, and assertion techniques. It is based on the tenets of cognitive theory in that it

> Provides readers with a rationale for the utility of cognitive therapy;
> Explains the relationship between thoughts and feelings;
> Instructs the reader in the identification, examination, and testing of automatic thoughts;
> Teaches reattribution skills (more rational understanding of the external causes of one's moods);
> Teaches how to generate alternative interpretations of situations that produce depressive symptoms and solutions to related problems; and
> Teaches the identification and modification of assumptions readers hold about their self-worth and ability to influence the environment.

Participants were asked to read the book within four weeks. During that time period a research assistant called them once weekly for conversations that did not exceed ten minutes. The researcher answered questions the participants had about the study and administered a depression inventory. Most participants' questions pertained to clarification of intervention procedures rather than advice about dealing with depression. The group was assessed before treatment, immediately after treatment, and three months later. More than 90 percent of participants continued in the study; on average they read 83 percent of the book, with a range of 23 to 100 percent. Results of the study indicate that there was a significant amelioration of symptoms, with gains persisting after three months.

Women with Depression

Some program developers believe that same-sex interventions may be particularly effective in that women and men experience unique challenges in dealing with depression. One group of researchers evaluated a brief group intervention for women of limited financial means with depressive symptoms (Lara et al., 2003). They utilized a comparison-group design with pre, post, and four-month follow-up assessments for ninety-three women in a group intervention condition who received six two-hour sessions of psychoeducation and for forty-two women in an individual condition who received twenty minutes of support in addition to the educational material. Both conditions were effective in motivating participants to engage in self-help activities (making time for themselves every week, using written journals as a means of sorting out problems, talking to someone about their problems, and carrying out the reflection and cognitive-behavioral exercises) and to seek further professional help when necessary. The intervention condition was positively evaluated. Participants regarded it as producing improvements in their mood, understanding and ability to cope with problems, constructive thinking, self-knowledge, and self-acceptance.

Programs for Families

Emotionally Attuned Parenting

Emotionally attuned parenting is a cognitively based intervention for helping children with severe depression and anxiety (Flory, 2004). It is based on evidence that

> Emotional isolation results in poor mental health;
> Punitive and unsupportive parenting is related to negative internalizing and externalizing behaviors in children and increased child distress;
> Psychiatric disorders are associated with poor verbal and affective communication, tension, distance, and lack of warmth in parent-child relationships; and
> Children's psychological well-being is affected by parental cognitions about the child.

The author argues that parental cognitions facilitate or hinder parents' empathy toward their child by producing a pattern in which (1) parental interpretation of the child's behavior affects parental affect and behavior, which (2) determines whether or not the child's emotional needs are met, which (3) causes either an increase or decrease in the child's depression and anxiety. The four most common negative cognitions that lead to non-empathic parental care are that the child is hostile, unreasonable, not genuine in demonstrating emotions, and not appropriately dependent on his or her parents. The loosely structured intervention consists of five to thirteen sessions for parents, including

> Education about the child's disorders and the negative cycle of parent-child interactions,
>
> Exploration of past parent-child interactions and the resulting interpretations,
>
> Challenging and restructuring negative parental cognitions and resulting responses, and
>
> Problem solving about strategies for soothing and calming the child.

One clinical trial found that the intervention produced a significant reduction in the number of child-reported anxiety and depressive symptoms and parenting stress (Flory, 2004). Child behavior problems, however, were marginally reduced.

The Multifamily Psychoeducation Group

Psychoeducation is considered an essential element of medication treatment for children with mood disorders. Such interventions should consist of education, support, and skill building and should help families become informed consumers of mental health services, including medication management. The Multifamily Psychoeducation Group (MFPG) is an eight-session, manual-driven treatment for children with mood disorders that is designed as an adjunct to medications and psychotherapy (Cummings & Fristad, 2007). Its goals are to educate parents and children about medications and their management, increase communication with the prescribing physician, and manage adverse effects of medication. The MFPG targets eight- to eleven-year-old children and is conducted in a series of ninety-minute sessions. It trains families in communication, social problem solving, and emotion-regulation strategies to address management of the child's mood symptoms. Each session covers a specific topic. Children and parents are seen together for the first fifteen minutes of the group and again for the last few minutes. Otherwise, parent and child group sessions occur separately. At six-month follow-up, participants show increased parental knowledge about the child's mood symptoms, more positive family interactions, improvement in the child's perception of parental support, and a better service utilization rate.

Programs for Children and Adolescents

Problem Solving for Life

Problem Solving for Life is a teacher-implemented, classroom-based intervention to prevent depression among adolescents (Spence, Sheffield, & Donovan, 2003). The program was tested with 1,500 eighth-grade students from sixteen high schools in Australia. The schools were randomly divided so that eight schools received the intervention and eight received no intervention. Twenty-eight teachers implemented the curriculum (including worksheets, overheads, and a teaching workbook) that included eight forty-five-minute lessons taught over an eight-week period. The curriculum was based on cognitive-restructuring activities and encouraged problem-solving skills and optimistic thinking styles. Students who exceeded a certain threshold on a depression inventory at intake were categorized as high risk for depression. All others were placed in a low-risk category. Measures on general pathology, social functioning, problem solving, attribution style, negative life events, and family conflict were conducted at intake, immediately following treatment (sixteen weeks), and twelve months after completing the intervention. The high-risk and low-risk students were evaluated separately. Immediately following the intervention, the high-risk students showed significantly greater reductions in depressive symptoms compared with the control group, and the low risk group showed a small decrease in symptoms. At the twelve-month mark, however, there was no difference of depressive symptoms between the treatment group and the control group.

Self-Control Therapy and Behavioral Problem-Solving Therapy

The purpose of this school-based study was to evaluate the efficacy of two cognitive-behavioral interventions, self-control therapy and behavioral problem-solving therapy, to treat depression in children (Stark, Reynolds, & Kaslow, 1987). Through use of didactic presentation, in-session exercises, and homework assignments, the self-control treatment was designed to teach children more adaptive skills for self-monitoring, self-evaluating performance, accurately attributing the causes of positive and negative outcomes, and imposing self-consequences for behavior. Topics covered in the twelve sessions include

Learning to monitor pleasant activities and positive self-statements,
Learning to monitor delayed rather than immediate consequences of behavior,
Learning a more adaptive attribution (cause and effect) awareness, and
Learning how to self-reinforce.

The behavioral problem-solving treatment combined self-monitoring, pleasant activity scheduling, and the acquisition of problem-solving skills. In addition, this treatment model, which was less structured, taught children about their feelings and how their behavior affects their social relationships. When compared to a wait-list control group, participants in both active treatments reported significantly less depression. Neither of the active treatment groups appeared superior to the other. These results were maintained at an eight-week follow-up, but the reduction in depressive symptoms did not generalize to the home environment.

Building on the above study, Stark, Rouse, and Livingston (1991) devised a second study of cognitive-behavioral treatment for depressed children. This study was based on the belief that depressive symptoms in children are the result of deficits in coping, self-control, and interpersonal skills and a dysfunctional cognitive style. The treatment model combines behavioral, self-control, and cognitive procedures with the child, with related procedures of structural family therapy. Work with the family occurs alongside the individual treatment and varies depending on the assessment of the family system. The interventions were compared to a traditional counseling condition that was empathic and nondirective, and it was found that children with elevated depressive symptoms in both treatment groups improved significantly more than those in the traditional counseling group.

From these results the researchers identified the key program components: affective education, self-reinforcement, self-monitoring, self-evaluation, activity scheduling, problem solving, social-skills development, relaxation with positive imagery, behavioral assignments, cognitive restructuring, and cognitive modeling and self-instruction. Participants in the self-control and problem-solving groups benefited from education in all of these areas.

Cognitive-Behavioral Intervention for Children and Adolescents

This intervention applies cognitive-behavioral methods to helping clinically depressed children and adolescents resolve their mood problems. It targets their depressive symptoms, social impairments, and negative thoughts (Vostanis, Feehan, Grattan, & Bickerton, 1996). The three main components of the treatment are recognizing and labeling emotions, enhancing social skills, and changing negative cognitive attributions. Each of the nine sessions followed a strict structure, including a review of each day's themes, tasks, practice, and homework assignment (see exhibit 8.2).

This intervention was compared to a control treatment of nonfocused intervention during which participants reviewed their mental states and social activities but the therapist offered no suggestions or interpretations. The results of this study showed that both interventions had positive effects on depression and anxiety, self-esteem, and social functioning. In their

---

Exhibit 8.2:   Cognitive-behavioral intervention for children and adolescents session outline

---

Sessions 1 and 2: education about the meanings of different emotions, distinguishing between different emotional states in the self and others, and linking emotions and moods with behaviors and thoughts

Session 3: education about self-reinforcement and the connection of self-rewards to positive moods and thoughts

Sessions 4 and 5: overview of social problem solving (learning that there are many solutions to problems and ways to approach interpersonal problems and about the link between social relationships and mood)

Sessions 6 and 7: cognitive restructuring, in which the child learns how to distinguish between internal and external effects on mood and how to challenge negative thoughts that lead to depressed moods

Session 8: review of the course

Session 9: children encouraged to apply the principles of the intervention to other areas of their lives

---

summary the authors highlighted the importance of the psychoeducator's empathy, sympathetic listening, and reassurance skills.

Control Enhancement Training

The Primary and Secondary Control Enhancement Training (PASCET) was tested in an empirical study with elementary school children who had mild to moderate depressive symptoms (Weisz, Southam-Gerow, Gordis, & Connor-Smith, 2003). The intervention is based on the theory that skill deficits (i.e., poor problem solving, maladaptive activity selection, poorly developed self-soothing ability, unengaging social style, and inferior performance in school or other valued domains) and negative cognitive habits (i.e., negative cognitions, failure to take others' perspectives, rumination over unhappy thoughts, and perceived lack of control) can produce depressive responses to adverse or stressful life events.

The PASCET intervention utilizes a two-process change model of control and coping. *Primary control* involves the student's efforts to cope by making objective conditions conform to one's wishes when events are modifiable. *Secondary control* involves efforts to cope by adjusting one's beliefs, expectations, and interpretations to fit nonchangeable conditions so as to influence their impact. Primary-control coping strategies address skill deficits, and secondary-control coping strategies address negative habits of thought. The intervention involves ten manualized sessions and five individually tailored sessions with the client, scheduled meetings with the parents, a home visit, and a school visit. The acronyms ACT (for primary control) and THINK (for secondary control) summarize the skills emphasized in the training (see exhibit 8.3). This program demonstrated significant effects in alleviating the participants' symptoms of depression and negative cognitions and increasing their social skills.

Exhibit 8.3:   Summary of skills taught in Control Enhancement Training

ACT

Activities that solve problems (STEPS: say what the problem is, think of solutions, examine each one, pick one and try it out, see if it works)
Activities I enjoy (constructive activity scheduling)

Calm (progressive relaxation and breathing exercises)
Confident (identifying negative and positive social styles and using in vivo experiments and homework to try out positive self-skills)

Talents (identifying skills the children want to enhance and making a practice schedule)

THINK

Think positive (recognizing and reshaping distorted thinking)
Help from a friend (identifying people who can offer helpful perspectives)
Identifying the silver lining if things go poorly
No replaying bad thoughts (combating tendencies to ruminate)
Keep thinking; don't give up (teaching sequential coping because first attempts often fail)

Depression and Suicidal Ideation

Suicide is the tenth leading cause of death in the United States, and depression is a leading factor in suicidal behavior (Strasser & Strasser, 1997). There are numerous factors associated with an increased risk of suicidal behavior in people of all ages:

Women are more likely than men to attempt suicide, but men are more likely to successfully complete suicide.
Elderly people and adolescents are more likely to attempt suicide than those in other age groups.

Separated or divorced people are more likely to attempt suicide than people who are married.

People suffering with serious medical illnesses, such as cancer, are more likely to attempt suicide than healthy people.

People who experience chronic pain are frequently at risk for suicide.

People suffering with chronic mental illness are at an increased risk for suicide.

People who have previously attempted suicide are at greater risk than people with no previous attempts. (James & Gilliland, 2001; Miller & Glinski, 2000)

People who are actively suicidal or at risk for suicidal behavior require more intensive intervention than what psychoeducation alone can provide. However, several programs have been developed for school-age persons as preventive measures or to assist persons who are feeling self-destructive.

Stuart, Waalen, and Haelstromm (2003) believe that training students as "gatekeepers" in schools can help them to identify peers who may be at risk for suicidal thoughts or actions and then report the persons to adults. The authors report that between 25 and 60 percent of teenagers know someone who attempted suicide, yet only 25 percent of this group told an adult about the suicidal peer. The authors trained sixty-five adolescents in their Peer Gatekeeper Training Program and found that the participants gained information about suicide, positive attitudes about suicide intervention, and skills in recognizing suicidal peers and talking to them.

Another group of authors proposes the utilization of youth-nominated support teams to provide supplemental care for suicidal adolescents following a psychiatric hospitalization (King et al., 2002). At discharge, the youths are invited to nominate four persons from their social network who they feel can be helpful in their adjustment to post-hospital life. Instructors provide psychoeducational training for those support persons (if they accept their nominations) so that they are equipped to provide supportive weekly contact to the adolescent. Support persons participate in several sessions with the professional to learn how to understand the youth's depressive disorder and treatment plan, suicide risk factors, strategies for communication, and emergency contact information. The support persons are provided with written materials that provide clear and individualized intervention guidelines. The support persons are asked to maintain weekly contact with the adolescents, discussing daily activities and concerns and encouraging activities that support the adolescent's treatment plan. The professional educators contact the support persons regularly to monitor their interactions with the adolescent. Interestingly, an evaluation of the program indicated that the intervention was effective only for girls with regard to reduced suicide attempts and depressive symptoms. The authors speculate that girls are generally more satisfied with their support networks than boys are and that females tend to spend more time sharing feelings and personal concerns with others.

Summary

A variety of cognitive-behavioral interventions delivered in psychoeducational formats are effective in helping people with depression recover from some of their symptoms and enjoy an improved quality of life through the development of new coping and social skills. As a final note on this topic, it is worth reviewing the work of Paulson and Worth (2002), who wanted to understand from the perspectives of formerly suicidal persons what the most effective aspects of their treatment were. Participants in focus groups reported that the practitioner's being able to acknowledge and address feelings of hopelessness and despair was the most helpful aspect of their intervention. Further, a positive relationship with the practitioner and the facilitation of emotional intensity in conversations were indicators of successful intervention. Conversely, participants identified as ineffective those practitioners who were not accepting or didn't seem to believe their stories of despair. Clients can sense when the practitioner is not comfortable with the topic of depression and suicide and is not able to validate their pain. These findings provide further evidence that persons with depression are looking for a connection with a practitioner (or significant other) that goes beyond the mere provision of information.

Chapter 9

Eating Disorders

The eating disorders are characterized by disturbances in a person's eating behaviors and distorted perceptions of body weight and shape (APA, 2000). Fears of becoming overweight lead people with these disorders to engage in drastic, potentially harmful behaviors that are intended to either cause or maintain weight loss (Garfinkel, 1995). *Anorexia nervosa* and *bulimia nervosa* are the two primary eating disorders. A third diagnostic category, *eating disorder not otherwise specified,* is a residual category at present. It is often used to diagnose persons who engage in chronic overeating and seek help for that problem. It may become identified in the future as binge-eating disorder, but the APA has yet to formally sanction the diagnosis.

Symptoms of the eating disorders can be manifested in clients' thoughts (weight preoccupation, body dissatisfaction, perfectionism, drive for thinness), affect (anxiety, feelings of ineffectiveness, low self-esteem, guilt), and behavior (purging, food restriction, binge eating, counting calories and fat, frequent weighing). Anorexia is distinguished by the refusal to sustain a minimal body weight (85% of what is considered normal for body height and age). Low weight is maintained either by restricting (dieting or exercising excessively) or by binge eating and purging. In bulimia, pathological fears of becoming overweight lead to purging behaviors, such as self-induced vomiting and the misuse of laxatives, diuretics, or other medications. Nonpurging clients rely on fasting or excessive exercise to influence their weight. Binge eating and compensatory behaviors must occur twice weekly for at least three months.

Persons with eating disorders often suffer from serious health complications (Rome & Ammerman, 2003). In bulimia, purging behaviors may lead to enlarged salivary glands and the erosion of dental enamel. Even more seriously, electrolyte imbalances and chronic dehydration increase the likelihood of cardiac arrhythmia and renal failure. Health risks with anorexia include starvation and malnutrition, which affects many bodily systems. Endocrine problems may include amenorrhea (in women) and metabolic abnormalities. Common cardiovascular disturbances include electrolyte imbalances, irregular heart rate, low body temperature, low blood pressure, and heart failure. The client's behaviors may also produce problems in the circulatory system (anemia) and the musculo-cutaneous system (hair covering the body and sensitivity to cold).

The prevalence of anorexia among females is approximately 0.5 percent, and the prevalence for males is one-tenth that rate (Muise, Stein, & Arbess, 2003). In North America bulimia among males is more prevalent than anorexia among females (Yager et al., 2002). Surveys conducted in the United States and England indicate a prevalence rate for bulimia nervosa purging type of 1 to 3 percent of adult females. In the United States, a prevalence rate of 3 percent of high school females has been found (Compas, Haaga, Keefe, Leitenberg, & Williams, 1998). Aside from diagnosable eating disorders, widespread body image dissatisfaction exists among females. One survey found that more than half of ninth- and twelfth-grade girls experienced disordered eating behaviors (Croll, Neumark-Sztainer, Story, & Ireland, 2002). About 30 percent of same-aged males also had engaged in disordered eating.

Because many persons with eating disorders do not acknowledge that they have a problem, engaging them in psychoeducation or any other intervention can be difficult. This fact underscores the importance of prevention, which is the focus of many programs described in this chapter.

Family Factors in Etiology

Families in which eating disorders develop tend to be conflicted, isolated, lacking in cohesion, enmeshed, and less supportive and nurturing (Mizes & Palermo, 1997). Another factor involving families is their transmission of the societal emphasis on weight and appearance. When parents are excessively concerned about their own and their children's shape and size, they may tease or pressure the child to lose weight (Kotler, Cohen, Davies, Pine, & Walsh, 2001; Mizes & Palermo, 1997). A history of sexual abuse is found in 20 to 50 percent of individuals with eating disorders (Yager et al., 2002). Inadequate or abusive parenting and sexual abuse are not specific risk factors for the development of an eating disorder but raise the risk for problems in general (Striegel-Moore & Cachelin, 1999). Conversely, general factors such as good parenting and secure attachment to one caregiver and specific factors such as the absence of parental weight problems or concern are likely to contribute to girls' resilience (Striegel-Moore & Cachelin, 1999).

There is a consensus among practitioners that family involvement should be part of the treatment plan, especially for younger adolescents with anorexia (Robin et al., 1999). Because family factors contribute to the onset of eating disorders, interventions must be conducted with great sensitivity so as not to blame and possibly repel families from participation. Families (usually parents) can participate in either collateral (separate from the client) or conjoint (with the client and/or whole family) sessions. Critical comments from parents need to be brought under control before conjoint family work can take place, however, because these comments are associated with dropout and poor outcome (e.g., Butzlaff & Hooley, 1998).

Psychoeducation and the Eating Disorders

All psychoeducational programs for persons with or at risk for eating disorders include lecture/discussion formats, structured educational materials, and accurate information to challenge misinformation and myths. The therapeutic factors inherent in groups are especially useful for helping participants work through issues related to the eating disorders. The secret, shameful, and chronic nature of an eating disorder contributes to a person's sense of isolation, whereas groups offer peer support, recognition of members' different aspects of competency, and reality testing. They also provide a forum for sharing and challenging some of the participants' distorted beliefs and self-perceptions.

Garner (1997) has identified nine major topics that may be included in effective psychoeducational groups: the multiple causes of eating disorders; cultural context of eating disorders; the physiological regulation of weight; physical complications of eating disorders; effects of starvation on behavior; the negative aspects of vomiting, laxatives, and diuretics for controlling weight; determining a healthy body weight; restoring regular eating patterns; and relapse-prevention techniques.

These groups may be stand-alone interventions or serve as adjuncts to counseling. Eating disorder groups should not include both male and female members, as the mix inhibits member participation (Kalodner & Coughlin, 2002). Groups should also be somewhat homogeneous as to the type and severity of members' disorders. For example, severely bulimic members may become envious of the anorexic members' success in weight control, and the more disturbed members are less likely to be motivated to change. In general, persons with less severe eating disorders who receive psychoeducation (at least five ninety-minute sessions) experience similar gains to those who receive psychotherapy, but gains are less comparable for those with more severe symptoms (Davis, McVey, Heinmaa, Rockert, & Kennedy, 1999).

The positive outcomes of prevention-oriented psychoeducation programs have been documented in a meta-analysis of fifty-seven studies (Fingeret, Warren, Cepeda-Benito, & Gleaves, 2006). The interventions have a positive effect on problematic eating attitudes and behaviors related to the development of eating disorders. (Most studies are conducted with female college students and other special populations of older adolescents and young adults.) A variety of outcome indicators are used in these studies, including knowledge about the disorder, thin-ideal internalization, body dissatisfaction, dieting, and general eating pathology. Small to moderate improvements in general eating pathology and dieting behaviors are evident across a range of intervention strategies both immediately and for some period of time afterward. Further, no harmful effects occur. Studies targeting participants at a relatively high risk of developing an eating disorder have greater benefits than those employing participants not identified as high-risk.

What follows are descriptions of various psychoeducational interventions that have been found effective for persons with or at risk for an eating disorder.

The Self-Enhancement Program for Persons with Bulimia

This seven-week structured group intervention is based on research findings that persons with bulimia suffer from depression, low self-esteem, poor body image, perfectionist tendencies, a high need for approval, difficulty in handling negative emotional states, and setting unrealistic goals for thinness (Weiss, Katzman, & Wolchik, 1985). Another principle of the program is that bulimic women need to refine their existing stress-coping styles and develop new competencies. Most of the focus of this group is on developing new competencies rather than strict behavioral management of the binge-purge cycle. Homework is an integral part of the group experience, as the two leaders provide participants with articles for discussion and written reaction. Participants are asked to reflect on each week's material and make individual plans for how they will implement their learning into their daily lives. Each woman also has two individual counseling sessions during the seven-week program.

The two group leaders screen each interested member in a one-hour session prior to his or her admission to the group. The structure of the group is given in exhibit 9.1.

Exhibit 9.1:   The self-enhancement program schedule

Session 1: education and overview, the nature of the group process, an overview of bulimia

Session 2: eating as coping (developing alternate coping strategies), cues for binge eating, alternative coping responses

Session 3: self-esteem, perfectionism, and depression; perfectionism and bulimia; nourishing ourselves without food; raising self-esteem

Session 4: anger and assertiveness (relationship of anger and assertiveness to bulimia, assertiveness)

Session 5: cultural expectations of thinness for women, societal expectations for thinness, the "perfect woman," the payoffs and price of striving to be perfect, behavior around men

Session 6: enhancing body image, bulimia and body image

Session 7: summing up (where you are now, where you go from here), program summary

Compared to no-treatment controls, women who received this intervention showed significant improvements in their numbers of binges per month, levels of self-esteem, and symptoms of depression. Treatment gains persisted during a ten-week follow-up with each group member.

The Aachen Program

The Aachen Program was developed for the parents of inpatient and outpatient adolescents with eating disorders (Holtkamp, Herpertz-Dahlmann, Vloet, & Hagenah, 2005). The group program is focused on the transmission of information rather than psychotherapy. The leaders believe that providing parents with relevant information about a child's eating disorder during an early treatment phase will help to make their future treatment involvements more successful. The program is limited to five weekly sessions of ninety-minutes (see exhibit 9.2). A child and adolescent psychiatrist, nutritional scientist, and occupational therapist specializing in eating disorders lead the groups. The first two sessions are highly structured with little time allotted for discussion, but the remaining three meetings have a more open format with opportunities to discuss topics generated by the parents. The leaders try to keep the discussion general rather than directly address participants' personal situations, because the latter issues are considered more suitable for individual family therapy.

Exhibit 9.2:   The Aachen Program

Session 1: information about anorexia (psychological and physical consequences, principles of intervention)
Session 2: information about bulimia (symptoms, etiology, principles of intervention)
Session 3: basic principles of a balanced diet
Session 4: components of inpatient treatment (including the perspective of the client and the principles of cognitive-behavioral therapy)
Session 5: relapse prevention and the necessity of long-term treatment; the importance of parents maintaining attention to their own self-care

---

Over a five-year period this program was delivered to 240 participants, representing 153 clients. Mothers participated more often and more regularly, and in 52 percent of cases a family member was present at all five sessions. Pretests indicated that participants experienced a high degree of psychological distress, but an overwhelming majority of parents rated the groups positively with regard to provision of comprehensible information, improved coping strategies for the family member's disorder, and support from other family members.

The Unity Multifamily Therapy Group

The Unity Multifamily Therapy Group (UMFTG) for eating disorders is structured to examine both the impact of family relationships on the eating disorder and the impact of the eating disorder on subsequent family relationships (Tantillo, 2006). The program attempts to increase (through decreasing stress, stigma, and burden) the quality of family life, which has been damaged by the illness, to improve a sense of perceived mutuality in addressing eating-disorder symptoms, and to promote relapse prevention. The groups are facilitated by a single practitioner as a close-ended eight-session group of ninety minutes duration with up to six to eight families (see exhibit 9.3). Group participants are usually drawn from the client's nuclear family, family of origin, or partnership, but others in the client's social network for recovery may also be included.

Exhibit 9.3:　The Unity Multifamily Therapy Group schedule

Session 1: orientation, introductions, discussion of the stages of change and ways of enhancing motivation to change

Session 2: the biopsychosocial factors related to the etiology and course of eating disorders, with an emphasis on family relational influences

Session 3: helping family members to better connect with one another without a focus on the eating disorder, including small-group discussions of these points

Session 4: understanding and establishing family rules, with small-group discussions about rating the importance of major family rules

Session 5: identifying points of tension and disconnection in the family related to the eating disorder and (in small groups) developing strategies to overcome these problems

Session 6: presentation of concrete strategies for repairing family disconnection, putting an emphasis on "we" rather than "I" in the context of family functioning

Sessions 7 and 8: families identify other points of tension and disconnection and engage in joint problem solving; during the final session, the leader helps families make plans for follow-up as needed, and members are encouraged to attend community support groups

---

The UMFTG program is based on two family systems theories. It draws from the family emotional systems perspective (Kerr & Bowen, 1988), as it assumes that certain negative relational patterns exist in a family with a member who has an eating disorder. The program is also based on strategic family therapy, as the eating disorder is conceptualized as something that exists outside the family but that invades the family to create a shared sense of burden that interferes with all members' development. Interestingly, the UMFTG program de-emphasizes problem solving with regard to specific issues and instead promotes the development of mutually supportive relationships within families.

Within UMFTG eating disorders are considered to be diseases of disconnection, because the resulting family interactions serve to emotionally disconnect clients from their own internal experiences as well as from others. Family disconnections also encourage clients to displace their emotional conflicts onto their bodies. The eating disorder distorts one's experience and cognition, but clients stay connected to it in order to avoid external conflicts. The disorder also disconnects clients from their family members through its ability to exhaust and disempower them. They worry that whatever they do or say may worsen the symptoms. The goal of the UMFTG is thus to help members identify sources of disconnection, learn how to embrace difference, and work through disconnection toward more authentic mutual connections.

The UMFTG approach emphasizes the development of a diverse therapeutic social network for the family, with a focus on strategies to improve communication, coping skills, how challenges are addressed, and management of the disorder. Relationships are emphasized because eating disorders occur predominantly in women, for whom relationships are central, and there is a universal experience of disconnections in the etiology and maintenance of eating disorders. An essential assumption of the UMFTG model is that a gender-informed approach to treatment can facilitate psychological change and growth in ways that enhance the healing obtained via traditional family systems, motivational, and cognitive-behavioral approaches.

The UMFTG has not yet been systematically evaluated, although the program developers note that it is based on many elements of McFarlane's (2002) multiple-family groups for schizophrenia, for which there is much empirical support (see chapter 6).

The Udine Prevention Group

At a school for adolescent girls in Italy, researchers have implemented a psychoeducation program for the prevention of eating disorders (Rocco, Ciano, & Balestrieri, 2001). The Udine program is designed to target known risk factors for eating disorders, focusing particularly on relevant adolescent developmental issues, including body shape and weight, social pressures, and achievement orientation. Of the school's 112 students, 86 percent agreed to participate in a randomized study of the monthly nine-session course (covering the academic year) provided by a psychiatrist and psychologist. Each session lasted two hours and alternately focused on three specific disorders (anorexia, bulimia, and disturbance of body image). The information provided included the nature and epidemiology of eating disorders and the importance of early detection of warning signs. The main theme for each session was discussed in the first hour, and then the information was related to specific developmental challenges that can occur in adolescence. The class members were encouraged to take part in discussions with the leaders. The authors reported that the most frequent discussions focused on body-image concerns, problems with self-esteem, and eating attitudes.

At the end of the nine months, all participants in the experimental group scored lower than baseline on measures of eating disorder attitudes, asceticism (denying food to oneself), and feelings of personal ineffectiveness. There was also a decrease in maturity fears among members of the experimental group. The authors admit that they did not perform a longer-term follow-up on their participants.

Student Bodies

Student Bodies is a structured, self-paced eight-week psychoeducational program for college-age women at risk for developing eating disorders that is delivered primarily through the Internet (Celio et al., 2000). The primary goal of the program is to reduce excessive weight concerns and body-image dissatisfaction. The structure of the program is given in exhibit 9.4.

Exhibit 9.4:   Student Bodies program structure

Three face-to-face sessions (weeks 1 and 2: orientation to the program; week 6: group discussion on body-image satisfaction)
Academic reading (one or two articles per week)
Written reflection in response to academic reading (one to two pages)
Online readings about body image, exercise, nutrition, and eating disorders; a cognitive-behavioral exercise
Online body image journal (one or more entries per week)
Discussion group messages (at least two messages per week, one in response to another group member)

The Student Bodies intervention occurs in three phases:

Phase 1 is focused on improved eating behavior. Participants are presented with the treatment rationale and begin to identify personal eating problems, such as excessive dieting and severe food restriction.

Phase 2 is focused on cognitive restructuring around negative thoughts related to the overevaluation of weight and shape, and participants are helped to identify and challenge negative cognitions.

Phase 3 focuses on the consolidation of lessons learned and on relapse-prevention training to encourage maintenance of treatment gains.

Student Bodies is led by a single human services professional who has expertise in eating disorders and their prevention. Face-to-face sessions for up to seventeen participants are held for one to two hours during the first, second, and sixth weeks of the intervention; they are led by the group moderator. These meetings serve to orient participants to the program, develop a sense of cohesion among them, and instruct them on using the program software. To further enhance familiarity among the group members, the online discussion group contains a link to profiles of each member, with an introduction, photograph, and personal statement of goals for the program.

Program participants are required to read one or two articles from a course reader each week on topics such as body image dissatisfaction, weight concerns, dieting, exercise, and nutrition. The purpose of the readings is to encourage participants to consider body image issues from a variety of perspectives. Participants are required to write a one-page critical reflection paper each week on a reading of their choice and send it to the moderator via e-mail. Each reading includes a cognitive-behavioral exercise, such as challenging negative thoughts. Participants are encouraged to post weekly entries in the confidential online body image journal, with the goals of identifying situations that trigger their negative body image ideas and challenging the accompanying distorted beliefs. In the moderated online discussion group, participants are required to post one or two responses to the readings and exercises. They are also asked to post at least one message each week in response to another member's message as a means of promoting supportive discussion. Because the program is offered through the Internet, participants can meet the requirements at any time, night or day, throughout the week.

Student Bodies has shown to be effective in reducing disordered eating attitudes and behaviors and body-image dissatisfaction among college-age women. The strongest results occur at follow-up, with a significant amount of improvement seen on the dependent measures. The Student Bodies intervention does require more personal investment and sustained independent motivation from its participants than some other programs, a factor that may contribute to its positive results among those who complete it.

Another group of researchers has studied the relative effects of two types of communication that occur within the Student Bodies program (Zabinski, Wilfley, Calfas, Winzelberg, & Taylor, 2004). *Asynchronous* communication takes place when members of a group post messages to an electronic bulletin board to be read and responded to by others at their leisure. *Synchronous* communication better mimics face-to-face interactions and is more interactive, as messages are displayed immediately on the screen to be responded to by other participants in real time. These interactions take place in chat rooms or in common areas where participants log on to a particular Internet location to communicate with each other. It was found, as expected, that synchronous communication is more effective over time than asynchronous communication, as participants rated the chat rooms more effective than the message board, possibly because the format is more interactive. Furthermore, the results indicated that programs using synchronous communication might be preferential for some persons at risk for developing eating disorders. For example, participants reported feeling high levels of support from one another during those communications, which was comparable to normative values of support from significant others, family, and friends (Zabinski et al., 2004).

Another study indicated that Student Bodies is effective as a preventive intervention for bulimic behaviors, even without the moderated discussion group feature (Low et al., 2006). This experimental study involved seventy-nine non–eating disordered college women who were randomly assigned to the Student Bodies group, a Student Bodies group without moderated discussion, and a control group. A comparison of the groups indicated that the program helped to prevent the onset of bulimic behaviors in some members and that the reductions persisted at long-term follow-up (nine months), with or without the moderated discussion.

Pros and cons of using the Internet The Internet is a promising method of intervention because it has broad reach, is easily accessible, and ensures anonymity. One major advantage in using computerized interventions is the ability to access the computer at any time. Support is available as needed rather than only during specified group times. On the other hand, with Internet-based educational interventions, issues of confidentiality and privacy can be a concern. For example, in the Student Bodies program participants' photographs were posted on the discussion page (Celio et al., 2000). Further, participants must have a computer and Internet access, be comfortable with computers, and be motivated to persist with a computerized intervention. Other limitations include technology-related problems, such as variable typing speeds and log-in difficulties during high-traffic times.

The Stice Eating Disturbance Program for College Students

Researchers at the University of Texas have piloted an eating disorders seminar to determine the possible effects of such an intervention on students' subsequent attitudes and behaviors around eating (Stice, Orjada, & Tristan, 2006). The intervention consisted of an advanced undergraduate seminar on eating disorders that met twice weekly for one and a half hours each session over a fifteen-week semester. Twenty-five students were enrolled in the course, which was taught by a psychology professor. Classes primarily involved didactic presentations and extended group discussions of the topics outlined in exhibit 9.5. The program also included discussion-based exercises that were intended to be therapeutic, including critical discussions of the thin ideal of feminine beauty, deceptive techniques used to create thin-ideal images in magazines and advertisements, and correcting misperceptions of weight and shape norms. Students were required to complete three essay exams and write a ten-page critical analysis of a course topic of their choice.

Exhibit 9.5:   Topics in the Stice eating disorder prevention course

Descriptive pathology of anorexia, bulimia, binge-eating disorder, and obesity
Epidemiology of eating disorders, body image disorder, and obesity
Sociocultural explanations for body image and eating disorders
Causal models for the eating disorders
Obesity and the energy balance model of weight gain
Risk factors for obesity
Prevention programs for eating disorders and obesity
Treatment interventions for eating disorders and obesity

The results of pre- and posttest data indicated that participants showed significantly greater reductions in thin-ideal internalization, body dissatisfaction, dieting, and eating-disorder symptoms than matched controls. The effects persisted at six-month follow-up and were considered to be medium in magnitude. In a subsequent large-scale follow-up study ($n =$ 125) of the intervention, it was determined that the counter-attitudinal advocacy material (defined as exercises in which participants had to argue against thin-ideal messages) was most essential to the program's effects (Roehrig, Thompson, Brannick, & van den Berg, 2006). Providing this material is not dependent on clinical skills of the class leaders, which means the program can be adapted to classroom-based programs led by teachers or paraprofessionals.

The Cash Program for Body-Image Improvement

Cash and Hrabosky (2003) developed a three-week intervention for college students that utilized the two elements of psychoeducation and participant self-monitoring. In the educational component, participants were provided (by a single leader with a psychology background) with information about problem behaviors related to body image and offered a new understanding of the factors that precipitated and maintained the person's problems. The self-monitoring component entailed helping students to systematically observe and record their behaviors and experiences over time. The program structure entailed one session of psychoeducation and the distribution of written assignments that participants could use to personalize their understanding of body-image issues.

Twenty-nine students from a mid-Atlantic college participated in the intervention, responding to recruiting announcements. At an orientation meeting participants completed the pretest measures and were instructed to meet individually with the researcher briefly once per week in order to return completed materials and discuss any questions they might have about the process. Members were also given a packet containing a summary of their assignments and self-monitoring forms. During week 1, participants were asked to read the assigned materials and complete written help sheets in which they explored their own body-image development, its impact on their lives, and their specific goals for the program. In addition, they were to complete twelve self-monitoring diaries describing recent positive or negative body-image experiences. Participants were also instructed in self-monitoring, a process of observing and recording the activators, beliefs, and consequences of body-image emotions. The subsequent readings provided information on the prevalence of body-image dissatisfaction and its effects on psychosocial functioning, the impact of culture on body-image development, and cognitive-behavioral processes that maintain negative body-image attitudes. Posttest measures were completed at a meeting following the third week of the intervention.

After completion of the intervention, participants reported significantly enhanced evaluations of their appearance and a significant reduction in self-perceived severity of body-image problems. The changes generalized to gains in other life areas, including eating attitudes and behaviors, self-esteem, and decreases in social anxiety. The researchers emphasized that the participant-researcher contact contributed to program compliance.

Psychoeducation and Binge-Eating Disorder

With an interest in the treatment of binge-eating disorder (BED), a group of researchers from the University of Minnesota compared three types of psychoeducation for adult women over eight sessions (Peterson et al., 2001). The program consisted of a manual-based cognitive-behavioral intervention that included both educational materials and homework assignments. The eight-week program included fourteen one-hour sessions held twice weekly and one-hour sessions during each of the final two weeks (see exhibit 9.6).

> **Exhibit 9.6: The binge-eating disorder group schedule**
>
> *Sessions 1–3:* information about BED, nutritional rehabilitation, stimulus-control procedures, and behavioral methods to reduce symptoms
> *Sessions 4–6:* cognitive-restructuring techniques
> *Sessions 7–9:* dealing with impulsivity, mood regulation, self-esteem, body image
> *Sessions 10–11:* stress management, assertiveness, problem solving
> *Session 12:* long-term weight-management techniques
> *Sessions 13–14:* relapse-prevention strategies

Fifty-one females were recruited from physician referrals and newspaper advertisements and assigned to one of three treatment conditions. In one condition, a psychologist provided information for thirty minutes, followed by a thirty-minute group discussion of the material and a discussion of the related homework assignments. In a second condition, participants watched a videotape followed by the psychologist-led discussion and homework review. In the third condition, an educational videotape was shown followed by a discussion led in rotation by members of the group. The videotapes included the psychologist's lecture so as to standardize the conditions.

A total of ten groups were conducted with sizes ranging from four to ten members. Follow-up visits were scheduled at one, six, and twelve months after the intervention. Results indicated that there were no significant differences in outcomes among the three groups, but all participants experienced decreases in binge-eating episodes and time spent binge eating. Thus all three conditions were effective. The promising implication of this study is that persons with BED can be helped with minimal involvement from professionals.

Stepped-Care Approaches

Interventions that are provided sequentially according to client interest or symptom severity are called stepped-care approaches. Participants begin with a first-step service, one that is relatively nonspecific and nonintrusive. These programs are generally psychoeducational in nature, with the goal of normalizing body shape, weight, and eating patterns through didactic instruction. Practitioners who adopt the stepped-care philosophy initially offer persons who experience (or who are at risk of experiencing) an eating disorder a psychoeducational group to help them gain information and then decide what, if anything, they wish to do about their eating concerns. These first-step groups are particularly beneficial to persons whose experience of any disorder (including eating disorders) is characterized by high ambivalence.

In one such group (Feld, Woodside, Kaplan, Olmsted, & Carter, 2001), four hour-long sessions were presented on
    Benefits and costs of having an eating disorder,
    Predicting life in five years with and without the eating disorder,
    Life values and goals in relation to an eating disorder, and
    Assessment of readiness to change.

Even when these group participants did not elect to accept additional interventions, they experienced reduced levels of depression and interpersonal mistrust and increased self-esteem.

Group psychoeducation is used at times as an initial component in the longer-term cognitive-behavioral treatment of bulimia. The first step is particularly valuable because it introduces participants to the rationale for the cognitive and behavioral strategies that compose the later interventions (Davis et al., 1999). Participants in one program attended six ninety-minute meetings held over a four-week period. (A total of ten series of this program were conducted.) Each group included five to eight members. The purposes of the group were to offer self-care strategies, such as meal planning, self-monitoring, and cognitive restructuring, and to assist participants in normalizing their eating behavior through education relevant to bulimia. The structured meetings included the following topics:
    Recovery from eating preoccupations
    The relationship between body and mind
    Making connections with others
    The body's set point for health
    Normal eating practices
    The process of behavioral change
    A state of mind about the body and its care

Two Ph.D.-level psychologists co-led the groups and presented self-care strategies and information in a lecture format, with slides and video material. Group discussion and questions were encouraged, but member self-disclosure was discouraged.

Following the psychoeducational program, participants were randomly assigned to a second step in the treatment process, including sixteen sessions of cognitive-behavioral therapy (CBT). The additional CBT intervention produced improvements in the symptoms of binge eating and purging.

Summary

The eating disorders create serious health and mental health problems for those persons who experience them and also much stress for their families and loved ones. It is universally acknowledged that both prevention and intervention programs can be beneficial for those persons at risk. Educational as well as therapeutic interventions are recommended because persons who experience eating disorders tend to deny or minimize their behavioral and health risks and because of the ways in which they can damage their interpersonal relationships. A variety of interventions have been described in this chapter for all age groups. In addition to their educational aspects, these interventions are organized from the perspectives of cognitive-behavioral theory, interpersonal theory, and several family systems theories. Priorities for future research on these programs need to include longer follow-up evaluations and identification of those patients for whom certain types of psychoeducation are best suited. Future randomized, controlled studies could show whether psychoeducation programs are effective alternatives and adjunctive treatment for various populations.

Chapter 10

Disruptive Behavior Disorders

The *disruptive behavior disorders* involve a child's or adolescent's consistent patterns of behaviors that break the rules of social convention. It is common, of course, for young people to break some rules, and even serious oppositional behavior may be a normal part of those stages of development. Youths who develop disruptive behavior disorders, however, engage in behaviors that create serious and perhaps long-lasting problems for themselves and others. In these circumstances, the children and their caregivers, teachers, and other persons in positions of authority may benefit from an array of intervention, including psychoeducation, so that they can learn ways to help the young people in their care and secure adequate support from others in managing those challenges. The purpose of this chapter is to discuss psychoeducation programs that can be beneficial to participants in correcting the three primary disruptive behavior disorders: oppositional defiant disorder, conduct disorder, and attention deficit hyperactivity disorder.

Oppositional defiant disorder (ODD) is characterized by a pattern of negativism, hostility, and defiance toward authority figures, such as parents and teachers (APA, 2000). These behaviors persist for at least six months and occur more frequently than is typically observed in children of a comparable age and developmental level. The child often loses his or her temper, argues with adults, refuses to comply with adults' requests or rules, deliberately annoys people, blames others for his or her misbehavior, is touchy or easily annoyed, is angry and resentful, and is spiteful or vindictive. The disorder is usually evident before age eight and appears no later than early adolescence. ODD is the most common of the disruptive disorders, with a prevalence rate of 2 to 16 percent in the general population (APA, 2000). The disorder is more prevalent in males than females before puberty, but rates appear equal after puberty (Moffit, Caspi, Rutter, & Silva, 2001).

Conduct disorder (CD) is more serious than ODD, as it involves an entrenched pattern of behavior in which the basic rights of others or major social norms are violated (APA, 2000). This pattern includes four categories of behaviors: aggressive conduct (causing or threatening harm to people or animals), conduct leading to property loss or damage, deceitfulness or theft, and serious rules violations. At least three of sixteen related behaviors must have been present in the year preceding diagnosis, with at least one demonstrated in the previous six months. The two subtypes of CD are childhood onset (at least one criterion is present before age ten) and adolescent onset (an absence of any criterion before age ten).

The distinction between ODD and CD is that children with ODD do not display serious violations of the basic rights of others. In about one-quarter of cases, however, youths with ODD end up developing conduct disorder. Symptom presentation in both disorders involves more confrontational behavior in males than females (Lahey & Waldman, 2003). Females manifest more indirect or relational aggression, such as threats of withdrawal from relationships, alienating, ostracizing, defaming others, and rumor spreading.

Attention deficit hyperactivity disorder (ADHD) is characterized by a persistent pattern (six months or more) of inattention and/or hyperactivity and impulsive behavior that is more frequent and severe than what is typically observed in peers (APA, 2000). It is characterized by a lack of self-control and the inability to sustain direction. The child is distractible, does not often finish what he or she starts, and is irritable and impatient, often interrupting and pestering others. There are three subtypes of ADHD (hyperactive/impulsive, inattentive, and combined); subtype is determined by which symptoms predominate. To qualify for the diagnosis the child must demonstrate symptoms before the age of seven.

For the school-age population, ADHD prevalence rates are estimated at 3 to 9 percent (Gingerich, Turnock, Litfin, & Rosen, 1998). Estimates of the ratios of male to female cases of ADHD vary from 2:1 to 9:1, and girls are less impaired than boys (Cuffe et al., 2001). Two-thirds of such youth continue to meet diagnostic criteria for ADHD in the early to midteen years, and in late adolescence 40 percent may still display some symptoms (Mannuzza & Klein, 1999). Attention problems in adolescents place them at significant risk of driving accidents and other traffic violations (Woodward, Fergusson, & Horwood, 2000). Antisocial behaviors become more common at this time to include 25 to 33 percent of youths with the disorder. Two-thirds have contact with the juvenile justice system, and drug abuse becomes a problem for some (Mannuzza & Klein, 1999).

Risk and Protective Influences for ODD and CD

An early difficult temperament (negative emotionality, intense and reactive responding, and inflexibility) predicts conduct problems in late childhood (Sanson & Prior, 1999). It is not clear, however, whether temperament is biologically based or psychosocial in origin. Low intelligence (IQ) is a risk factor for antisocial behavior, and youth with IQ scores of 85 or less have three times the risk for developing conduct disorder (Wachs, 2000). IQ is also linked to low achievement in school, which is connected to antisocial behavior. Children who are unable to reason verbally may use aggression to manage their social dilemmas. Poor verbal abilities may further interfere with emotional processing in terms of a failure to identify emotions in the self and others. If children cannot reflect on their emotional states, they may react in physical or aggressive ways rather than by engaging in problem-solving activities. A low resting pulse rate has also been related to antisocial behavior (Hill, 2002). Low autonomic reactivity may indicate a suppressed behavioral inhibition system, which in turn may result in difficulty controlling impulses.

Aggressive youths tend to display cognitive distortions, evidenced as an inability to consider a variety of strategies to manage interpersonal problems, difficulty figuring out ways to achieve desired outcomes, difficulty identifying the consequences of particular actions, attributing hostile motivations to the actions of others, and misunderstanding how others feel (Kazdin, 2001). Conduct disorder in females occurs more frequently with internalizing disorders, such as depression (McMahon, 1994). Girls with CD are five times more likely than others to enter a cohabiting relationship by age twenty-one; many of these relationships are with deviant men. By their early twenties, almost half of these girls receive some form of physical violence from a partner (Maughan & Rutter, 2001). Females diagnosed with CD also report higher levels of daily stress paired with fewer active coping strategies and a greater tendency toward self-harm (Burke, Loeber, & Birmaher, 2002).

One major study found that family and social factors predicted the diagnosis of conduct disorder better than characteristics of the child (Dekovic, 1999). Insecure and disorganized attachment styles have been linked to CD in some studies (Burke et al., 2002). Physical abuse within the family is associated with the child's later externalization of problems (Hill, 2002). Abuse may result in children encoding experiences as threatening and attributing hostile intent to others in social situations. Aggression may also be acquired by modeling. Parents may attempt to avoid the strain involved in caregiving for a child with conduct problems, and their avoidance of the child further erodes discipline and supervision (Burke et al., 2002).

Other risk factors include neighborhood characteristics and the youth's socioeconomic status. Negative interactions with the environment often extend into the realm of school and peer groups (Moffitt, 2003). Difficulties with teachers may contribute to poor school performance. Alienation from the norms of the school system may develop, and by the time such children are ten or eleven years old they may bond together in deviant peer groups (McMahon, 1994). If such individuals live in poverty, they have restricted opportunities and are more likely to seek out deviant means to obtain fulfillment and a sense of identity (Miller & Prinz, 1990).

Risk and Protective Influences for ADHD

ADHD is considered a neuropsychological disorder, but its persistence, severity, and long-term outcomes are influenced by psychosocial variables (Langstroem, 2002). Reviews of twin studies conclude varying rates of the extent of genetic factors in accounting for the variance in ADHD, ranging between 30 and 97 percent (Barkley, 2000; Root & Resnick, 2003; Samudra & Cantwell, 1999). The precise genetic mechanisms are not known, but the chances of a family with one ADHD child having more than one child with the disorder are one in three.

Any parenting or family difficulties that contribute to inconsistent, coercive, or decreased efforts at managing the child's behavior may increase problem behaviors in the ADHD child (Weiss & Trokenberg-Hechtman, 1993). Depression in mothers, abuse of substances, increased parenting stress, marital conflict, and increased rates of separation and divorce are present in families with a child diagnosed with ADHD. Parents also suffer from the stress of managing the disorder (Barkley, 2000). Some researchers conclude that attachment patterns between a parent and child contribute to the onset of ADHD. In one study, adopted children with a history of institutional deprivation experienced high rates of inattention and overactivity compared to adopted children without such a history (Kreppner, O'Connor, & Rutter, 2001). Part of this deprivation involved a lack of attachment with consistent caregivers.

Psychoeducation

Psychoeducation is an appropriate intervention for ODD, CD, and ADHD because those disorders bring significant challenges to children and their families in terms of the child's development and family stress levels. The focus on education rather than therapy reflects the assumption that children and their families have strengths and potentials, and as such they may positively contribute to a resolution of the disorder. A combination of strategies—sharing information about the disorders and (at times) medication treatment, teaching parents behavioral management strategies, and using cognitive-behavioral strategies to promote growth—can be incorporated into psychoeducation.

Most psychoeducation programs used with children are behavioral rather than cognitive in origin, due to the cognitive developmental level of those persons (see exhibit 10.1). As with many other issues covered in this book, additional therapeutic interventions may also be utilized by professionals in addressing the child's problems.

Exhibit 10.1: Cognitive-behavioral principles with children and adolescents

Children and adolescents often experience cognitive deficits (lack of information) rather than distortions.
Cognitive procedures can be effective for adolescents but not for children.
Verbal interventions are generally limited in effectiveness prior to adolescence.

Behavioral interventions are effective with children lacking in language ability.
Limited life experience makes generalization difficult for children.
In adolescence there is a sharp decline in the value of adult-mediated reinforcers.
Modeling is a pervasive means of learning for this population.
Children and adolescents respond positively to warmth and nonjudgmental attitudes.

Psychoeducational programs have been available since the 1980s to help children and adolescents change their dysfunctional social behaviors. Early examples include an aggression-replacement training program (including structured learning, anger-control training, and moral education) for institutionalized juvenile delinquents (Glick & Goldstein, 1987), a parent/family intervention training program as part of a day treatment program focused on improving both clinical and academic status (Baenen, 1986), and an elementary school program for child-abuse awareness that focused on child-abuse knowledge and security measures (Volpe, 1984). One model of intervention for children who experienced traumatic childhood abuse (and subsequent behavior problems) was developed for the foster parents of sexually abused children (Barth, Yeaton, & Winterfelt, 1994). The purpose of the group was to increase foster parents' understanding about child sexual abuse, improve the behavior of the child, reduce the number of failed placements, and create a support group for these parents. Another group, called Getting It Together, was developed in a large city juvenile court clinic (Carpenter & Sugrue, 1984). The program combined affective education and social skills training and was focused on family problems, impaired peer relationships, and sexual problems.

What follows are seven detailed examples of psychoeducation for children with disruptive behavior problems.

Parenting-Skills Development

Parenting-skills development represents a major psychoeducational intervention for the parents of children with behavior disorders. In these programs, which can assume a variety of formats, parents are taught various skills, including ways to specify goals for child change, track target behaviors, positively reinforce positive conduct, and learn alternative discipline methods. The educational material is presented through a variety of formats, including didactic instruction, interactive discussion, modeling, and role-play (Miller & Prinz, 1990). Sessions give parents the opportunity to view how techniques can be implemented, practice new methods, and evaluate the progress of newly learned behaviors in the home (Kazdin, 2001). Reviews of parent training have supported its effectiveness, as about two-thirds of children under the age of ten improve (Fonagy et al., 2002). The components of parenting-skills development are listed in exhibit 10.2.

Exhibit 10.2: *Components of parenting-skills development*

Parents select a priority goal concerning the child's behavior.
Goals are broken down into small, observable components.
Goals and tasks are formulated to encourage a presence of positive behavior rather than the absence of negative behavior.
A behavior baseline is determined.
A target behavioral goal is established.
New parenting strategies are introduced and practiced.
Parenting behaviors are utilized in the home setting.
The new behaviors and outcomes are evaluated in terms of the target goal.

As an example, Ms. Bryant elected to participate in parenting-skills development because her son Andy would not do his homework. He also engaged in disruptive behaviors at bedtime. Ms. Bryant worked individually with a practitioner. In order to determine a reasonable target for the desired behaviors, the *baseline,* or current occurrence of the behaviors, must be determined. Its occurrence can be measured in different ways: through its frequency (Ms. Bryant says that Andy never does his homework, so his base-line would be zero) or its duration (Ms. Bryant says that Andy shows appro-priate homework behaviors for only two minutes at a time).

The behavioral term *shaping* means that successive approximations of a desired behavior are reinforced to eventually meet a goal that is initially out of reach for a client. The child must receive clear messages in order to understand the parent's specific behavior expectations. In parenting-skills development, the practitioner may provide parents with a handout on com-mand giving, which includes the following points:

Only use commands that are necessary.
Issue only one command at a time.
Issue clear and specific commands.
Keep commands brief.
Issue statements rather than questions or "Let's" commands (e.g., "Let's go upstairs and put our pajamas on").
Phrase commands as to what the child should do rather than what the child should not do.
Praise compliance to a command.

Reinforcement systems should include high-probability behaviors, social reinforcement, and token economies. *High-probability behaviors* are those in which children frequently engage, such as playing outside, talking on the phone, using the Internet, playing video games, and watching television. Because the child values the activities, he or she will be motivated to maintain them. *Social reinforcements* are interpersonal rewards, such as praise, hugs, pats on the shoulder, a smile, or a thumbs-up sign. *Token economies* are systems in which a parent gives the child points or tokens for desirable behaviors. As they accumulate, the tokens can be traded in for an agreed-upon reward (Barkley, 2000). A token economy involves the use of tangible reinforcers, such as coins, tickets, stickers, or check marks, for desirable behaviors that are then traded in for a reward that might include money, movie tickets, magazines, or anything else the child values.

With Ms. Bryant, the practitioner provided education on the benefits of praising her child. They went down a list of dos and don'ts that demonstrated how Ms. Bryant could enact the principles of praise with Andy. The list of dos included the following:
Describe specifically what Andy does to deserve praise.
Couple verbal praise with eye contact, a smile, or physical affection.
Praise effort and progress as well as achievement.
Praise immediately after the behavior is performed.

The list of don'ts included
Using unlabeled praise or global statements about the child,
Coupling praise and criticism,
Waiting too long after the behavior to praise, and
Taking feelings of awkwardness as a sign to stop praising.

Extinction is a process of no longer reinforcing a negative behavior, which if successful results in a decrease of the behavior. When applying extinction to a particular behavior, one must first examine the function of the behavior. In Ms. Bryant's situation, Andy engaged in disruptive behavior at bedtime to prolong his time awake and to get special attention from his mother. Ms. Bryant was told about the importance of being consistent, ignoring Andy's behaviors every time they occurred. She was also encouraged to make sure Andy got sufficient attention for positive behaviors so that he might not feel a need to misbehave at bedtime. Ms. Bryant was asked to practice in the session after watching the practitioner model appropriate behaviors, such as looking away, maintaining a neutral facial expression, and avoiding any verbal or physical contact, during a tantrum.

Punishment involves the presentation of negative events (e.g., physical discipline, harsh words) or the removal of positive events (privileges) to decrease the occurrence of a response (Kazdin, 2001). These strategies can be effective, although parenting-skills-development experts recommend that positive reinforcements be provided at three times the ratio of punishments, because punishment tends to be demoralizing.

Time-out is a form of punishment that involves physically removing the child from the source of reinforcement for a brief period. The time-out should be structured around a certain amount of time, observing the general guideline of one minute per year of the child's age. Its purposes are to extinguish the negative behavior, help the child calm down, and help the child understand why the behavior is unacceptable. The location for time-out should be free from reinforcement, meaning there should be no activities available.

Ms. Bryant said she could move a stool for Andy to the front hallway of their home for a time-out, although he could see other family members in the living room from there and might call out to them. The practitioner emphasized that Andy's attempts to engage family members in annoying behaviors should be ignored. If Andy's disruptive behaviors escalated there, the time-out period would only end after he got his behavior under control. The time-out should end with the child's being reminded why he was punished. This final step is critical in that the child can learn the reasons for his or her punishment and also reconnect with the parent.

Parents have to be warned that they will initially experience an increase in the undesirable behavior when they begin employing extinction techniques. Ms. Bryant was told to take the inevitable extinction burst as a sign that the technique was working. She was assured that Andy's behavior would improve and that gains would last if she consistently ignored any recurrence of the undesirable behaviors. Ms. Bryant was also reminded to pair her extinction behaviors with positive reinforcement for appropriate behaviors (Kazdin, 2001). If reinforcement of desirable behaviors and ignoring undesirable behaviors failed to stamp out the problems, then they would consider implementing punishments.

For young children the technique of pairing distraction with ignoring negative behaviors can be effective. For instance, if a young child cries because he wants to play with the remote control, the parent could take the remote control away and divert his attention to a brightly colored ball: "Here's something else you can play with. See if you can catch it!" Distraction helps to avoid arguments about a parental command.

Parenting-skills development has been validated primarily for preschool and school-age children; its outcomes are less significant with adolescents, who tend to be more severely impaired (Fonagy et al., 2002). Older children may require adjunctive treatment to parenting-skills development in order to help manage the transactional nature of conduct problems, address child problem-solving deficits, or intervene in other family problems. For school-age children, a problem-solving adjunctive treatment for the children themselves has been offered in addition to parenting-skills development. These programs generally focus on the thought processes children use in approaching interpersonal situations, teaching children a step-by-step approach to solve problems, and fostering prosocial behaviors through modeling and reinforcement (Kazdin, 2001). The combined parent training and problem-solving skills training program for children produced greater impact than either program by itself.

The Strong Families and Making Choices interventions provide good examples of combined parent-training/child-focused programs. These interventions are based on the assumption that children are sometimes unintentionally taught to respond to authority figures with hostility by exposure to parenting styles that feature inconsistent discipline (Fraser, Day, Galinsky, Hodges, & Smokowski, 2004). The Strong Families program comprises fifteen lessons for individual families on child development, parent-child communication, family problem solving, and discipline. Parents are taught skills such as rewarding prosocial behavior and setting limits. The program is delivered in the home setting to compensate for transportation to treatment being a barrier to access. The Making Choices (MC) program teaches social problem-solving skills to children, focusing on the correction of cognitive deficits as they influence aggressive behaviors. MC is provided in groups outside the home and teaches children alternative strategies for perceiving events, formulating goals, and collaborating with others. The children are placed in mixed groups when possible to include some children with more highly developed social skills. This arrangement proves beneficial for all participants in terms of their degree of improvement.

Because children with ADHD have problems with homework completion, other parenting interventions have been designed in addition to providing praise and token reinforcements. These interventions include structuring the home environment (so that the child has a quiet, uncluttered place to work relatively free of distractions, perhaps with a parent sitting nearby), regular teacher verification of satisfactory homework completion, and a home-based reinforcement system featuring regular school-home note exchanges (DuPaul & Power, 2000). In such a system, the teacher evaluates the child once per day on selected target behaviors, such as completing work, attending to instruction, and speaking at appropriate times. Parents review the teacher rating and provide the child with incentives for goal attainment and punishment for failing to make agreed-upon changes.

Many problem behaviors of older children are related to their inability to manage negative emotions in constructive ways. The child experiences cognitive deficits, or a lack of awareness of alternative means of handling anger and frustration. Some psychoeducational groups, like the anger management program described below, seek to help children and adolescents remedy these deficits by acquiring prosocial skills.

The Anger Management Group

The Anger Management (AM) group is an eight-week program for adolescents who lack the ability to make socially appropriate choices when dealing with anger (Feindler & Starr, 2003; Kellner & Bry, 1999). The goals for participants are to learn what causes them to feel angry and act aggressively and to learn and implement skills to reduce their aggression. Most participants are referred by probation officers following a related legal charge.

The AM group is based on cognitive-behavioral theory. One of the hallmarks of this theory is that it accommodates time-limited and educational treatments focusing on specific target problems (Corey, 2005). Behavior theory is helpful in understanding the nature of the problems experienced by group members. Practitioners can understand and help clients understand events that led to the problem behaviors; these events are referred to as cues, antecedents, or triggers. There is then a reaction, the behavior of the client in response to the antecedent, which in the AM group is referred to as the anger button. The client's behaviors are followed by consequences that can be either positive or negative, as illustrated in figure 10.1.

Figure 10.1

A | B | C
An activating event——➤produces a belief or thought——➤that produces an emotion
and behavior

Each AM meeting focuses on a specific topic relating to the concepts of anger and anger management, using education as a primary intervention (see exhibit 10.3). Interventions utilized throughout the program include various forms of skill training (such as self-talk, anger reduction, and communication and assertiveness skills), cognitive restructuring, coping-plan

---

Exhibit 10.3: The Anger Management group schedule

Session 1: orientation, discussion of anger buttons, and description of anger log assignment
Session 2: self-control role models and triggers
Session 3: cues and anger reducers
Sessions 4 and 5: reminders and self-evaluation
Session 6: consequences (from the perspectives of behavior management and self-talk)
Session 7: cognitive distortions and cognitive restructuring
Session 8: review

development, and homework assignments. The criteria used by the leader and the group members to determine the amount of progress being made are decreases in the frequency and intensity of anger and increases in the use of positive means of dealing with anger.

The first session of the AM group begins with an orientation and discussion of rules and goals. To help both the practitioner and participants understand the problems that have brought them to the AM group, there is a lengthy discussion of the ABC model described earlier, with *A* standing for anger button, *B* for behavior, and *C* for consequences. The five domains—social, environmental, emotional, cognitive, and physical—in which behavioral antecedents may occur are presented. Each of these domains and their possible anger triggers are examined, with group members sharing situations in which they become angry. Having the adolescents identify consequences helps both the practitioner and the members get a sense of what is reinforcing about the behavior or of the detrimental consequences that can be used to build the client's motivation to change (Corcoran, 2006). Helping participants recognize the social, emotional, and financial costs of their anger, which is done in part by helping them identify the negative consequences of their behaviors, is a key factor in this intervention (Novaco, 2007).

The weekly homework assignments are also discussed during the first meeting. Every member is expected to fill out an anger log, describing an event during the week which made, or could have made, them angry, how angry they were, what they did, how well they handled the situation, and what they could have done differently.

The second-session topics are self-control role models and triggers. The practitioner uses the behavioral intervention of modeling to engage the group in a discussion of individuals whom they can look to as role models in appropriately dealing with anger-inducing situations. Members are asked to identify individuals who demonstrate good self-control and anger management, either historical figures (such as Martin Luther King Jr.) or people they actually know. Some authors recommend bibliotherapy, or the use of short stories, poems, and films, to help the adolescents model and gain insight into their own feelings and behaviors through identification with fictional characters (Shechtman, 2000). The concept of triggers builds upon the previous session's discussion of anger buttons, or what makes the members angry, including both external events and internal thoughts and feelings. During this portion of the session, cognitive-restructuring concepts are introduced, with the practitioner explaining to the group that people can often change how they feel about a situation by changing the way they think about it. At the end of this session, and every session thereafter, a few individuals share their anger logs with the group, with the practitioner and group members providing them with feedback. The practitioner will often assist the member in viewing a situation in a different manner, or use the opportunity to provide the group with communication-skills training and assertiveness-skills training.

The third-session topics are cues and anger reducers. Cues are defined as physical reactions to anger, such as muscle tension, a pounding heart, or an upset stomach. The practitioner provides the group with information about the physical aspects of anger and helps them identify their cues so they can better recognize when they are getting angry. The anger reducers presented in the group are similar to the relaxation-training interventions of deep breathing and visualization, physical exercise, and a counting technique, where the person starts at a high number and counts backward by multiples of three or seven.

The topics of the fourth and fifth sessions are reminders, things the members can say to themselves to increase their ability to deal with situations in which they are, or could become, angry, and self-evaluation, in which members are taught to look back on situations and judge how they handled themselves, either rewarding themselves for positive behaviors or coaching themselves to find ways that they could have handled the situation better. Reminders and self-evaluation are examples of the self-talk intervention. The practitioner and group members discuss various self-talk phrases that they can utilize in different situations, with the practitioner urging the group members to personalize their reminders. For some problems participants face, many coping skills are required, and thus another intervention is the development of coping plans that incorporate several of these skills. Having participants use self-evaluation assists them in developing effective anger-management plans.

The sixth session of the AM group focuses on consequences, approaching the topic from both behavioral and self-talk perspectives. Group members are encouraged to look at the consequences of their behaviors and identify whether they are the positive consequences they want or the negative consequences they want to avoid. Self-talk interventions are utilized by having clients ask themselves before they act, "If I do [this] now, then [that] will probably happen later."

The seventh session focuses on understanding cognitive distortions and cognitive restructuring. The practitioner presents a number of types of cognitive distortions, which are termed automatic thoughts, such as catastrophizing and overgeneralization. Group members are asked to identify which automatic thoughts they often use. Cognitive-restructuring techniques are then discussed to give group members tools to change their cognitive distortions.

During the final session, the topics discussed throughout the curriculum are reviewed and reinforced. In the most recently completed AM groups, all members reported a decrease in the frequency and intensity of feeling angry and an increase in the constructive use of anger-management skills.

The Support, Empowerment, and Education (SEE) Group

Tapping into the potential leadership strengths of both parents and professionals, a group of New York researchers developed a team model for group intervention with families of youths who have emotional and behavioral problems (Ruffolo, Kuhn, & Evans, 2005, 2006). Through focus groups conducted at two community mental health centers, the researchers learned that parents were frustrated and angry with professionals who were working with their children. Many parents felt labeled as bad by these professionals, and most of them did not view their relationships with professionals as collaborative. Parents identified three major areas of concern in raising a youth with behavior problems: feeling isolated, having difficulties coping, and needing information about how to interact with their child. Following these focus groups, the researchers consulted with several professionals to discuss the issue of joint leadership. These persons noted the positive potential of sharing mutual expertise with parents but also expressed concern about threats to the usual boundaries between professionals and client systems. Following these discussions, a task force of professionals and parents developed a joint training program for group leadership. The trainings involved

> Defining partnership and leadership in groups,
> Addressing the unique roles and contributions of parents and professionals to the model,
> Learning the structured group psychoeducation approach, and
> Developing group skills in joining, problem solving, and empowerment.

The joint training, conducted by two professionals and one parent, took eight hours, and three-hour review sessions were offered every three months during the first year of the program.

The SEE groups operate with an open-group format, twice per month for two hours, with families entering and leaving based on their participation with the mental health center counseling program. Seven families typically participated at one time, for an average duration of six to nine months. The structure was incorporated into a manual as shown in exhibit 10.4.

Exhibit 10.4:　Structure of the SEE group

Chat time
Initial go-round
Problem-solving and solution-finding activities
Educational material
Closing go-round
Final chat time

The SEE format resembles McFarlane's (2002) multifamily group model (see chapter 6). Through problem-solving and knowledge-development activities, the leaders promote the themes of social support, parent education, and parental empowerment. The professional leaders meet individually with the families prior to their group enrollment, and the parent leader's follow-up telephone calls help to initiate therapeutic alliances. Child care is available onsite, and transportation is provided to families if needed. It has been discovered that parents who attend at least two group meetings are likely to stay involved as long as their child remains in the system.

Parent problem-solving skills, coping skills, perceived social support resources, and child behavior are measured at three points in time (baseline, nine months, and eighteen months). Evaluations indicate that youth behavior improves significantly over time, as the parents report improvements in child externalizing and internalizing behavior scores. Participants also identify the parent-professional model as one of the major strengths of the group.

PsychoEducation Responsive to Families

The PsychoEducation Responsive to Families model for children coping with severe emotional and behavioral disorders (C-PERF) is an adaptation of an intervention originally designed for families coping with an adult member who has a severe mental illness (see chapter 6). The curriculum and some features created to enhance family participation, however, are unique to the C-PERF model. Similar to the SEE program, C-PERF values families as having considerable resources to contribute to the intervention process. Because the model also assumes that the difficulties inherent in parenting a behaviorally disordered child are not unique to specific disorders, groups are not restricted to children in certain diagnostic categories.

A psychiatrist or psychiatric nurse and a school social worker, all of whom receive training in the intervention protocol, facilitate the groups. The major study that tested this model included two groups. Each set of members reached consensus about the number and frequency of meetings they would be willing to attend and over what length of time. One group decided to meet eight times (twice monthly) and the other twelve times (ninety minutes weekly). In addition, parents decided to limit participation to caregivers. Child care was provided on site.

In the initial meeting for each family group, the participants were asked to generate a list of concerns they would like to address. The families ranked each problem in order of importance on a list developed by the investigators. The investigators then devised a basic curriculum with modules for all problems identified. Professional project staff (not limited to the leaders) created materials for each topic based on the research and practice literature.

In both groups, sessions were focused on providing members with information, support, and sharing. The protocol included time for check-in and updates, a prepared lecture with a group activity, and group discussions focused on brainstorming solutions for identified problems. Participants received outlines of the lecture notes along with suggestions for further reading.

The researchers surveyed parents at the beginning of the first session and after the final session on the status of their problem issues. An examination of qualitative data from the groups indicated that both psychoeducation groups were a positive experience for the parents. Quantitative findings were also encouraging, as participants demonstrated significant improvement in child attention behaviors. The ability of each group to create a unique curriculum and the high rate of treatment completion (87%) suggests that the families were able to meet a variety of their identified needs.

Recreational Multifamily Therapy

At a day treatment center for children with psychiatric difficulties, it was noted that traditional therapy was not working for youths with behavior disorders because of its overly abstract nature. A new approach was developed to bridge the gap between the life experiences of the clients and the therapeutic aims of the program for children. It was hoped that a recreational environment would be a more effective vehicle for change with the children (Greenfield & Senecal, 1995). The two concurrent groups that were developed incorporated recreational, self-help, and psychoeducation principles.

The psychoeducational program involved a family oriented recreational intervention that included an average of one staff member to five children and their families. The groups were conducted twice monthly on a weekday night for ninety minutes. The evening was devoted predominantly to a recreational event, such as floor hockey, soccer, or volleyball, which involved all family members and ended with a snack. During the first four or five group meetings, the facilitator intervened directly when behavioral difficulties arose, acting as a model for the parents. An atmosphere of mutual coaching evolved, and the parents quickly learned effective ways of setting limits with their children.

The alternating group meetings featured a modified psychoeducational format. Information about behavior theory was presented during the first thirty minutes, followed by a forty-five-minute group discussion and fifteen minutes for refreshments. Presentation topics included ways children express their needs for autonomy at different ages, the role of play and communication in normal development, and the many aspects of aggression during childhood and between family members. Other themes included frustration management and the social isolation of families. Themes raised by single parents during the discussion section included dating, sharing babysitters, and the consequences of economic stress. Questions concerning specific children were referred to the child's team leader before or after group sessions for individual attention.

Another parent-child group at the facility was particularly responsive to the needs of single mothers. Two staff members guided four parent-child dyads in weekly seventy-five-minute meetings held during the day. During the first thirty minutes, the mothers interacted with their children and watched them socialize while the professional staff observed the dyads. Recreational activities addressed fine motor skills (drawing and paper cutting), gross motor skills (throwing balls into a bucket and playing pin-the-tail-on-the-donkey), and skills of a less focused nature, such as listening to music and finger painting. During the second half hour, the parents met separately from the children. The parents discussed their feelings and observations with one staff member, while the children engaged in recreational activities with the other staff member to learn social skills. During the last fifteen minutes, the mother-child dyads formed again and refreshments were served during a discussion of what the children had experienced in the absence of the mothers. The mothers were assigned homework tasks for the next week that involved constructive interactions with their children.

Several factors explain the parents' enthusiasm for these groups. They were learning proper parenting and limit-setting skills and new ways of relating to each other that were fun. The group environment facilitated parents' awareness of the children's strengths, and their sense of isolation was diminished. Likewise, the children gained greater self-confidence and a sense of security within their families.

The following two programs represent school-wide psychoeducational interventions to improve prosocial behaviors among all students.

PeaceBuilders

PeaceBuilders is an elementary school violence-prevention program. It attempts to alter the climate of a school by teaching students and staff simple rules and activities aimed at improving child social competence and reducing aggressive behavior (Flannery et al., 2003). PeaceBuilders is not offered as a set number of sessions or hours per week but includes activities that can be implemented on a daily basis in any classroom by any teacher or staff person. It attempts to increase the daily frequency of prosocial behavior models. In this program all children and staff in a school must learn five simple rules (see exhibit 10.5).

Exhibit 10.5:   PeaceBuilders rules

Praise people.
Avoid put-downs.
Seek wise people as advisers and friends.
Notice and correct hurts we cause.
Right wrongs.

The PeaceBuilders rules are prominently displayed on signs throughout the school. To help students learn them, PeaceBuilders includes daily rituals that are meant to foster a spirit of belonging and to teach cues that can be applied in diverse settings, specific prompts to transfer across behaviors, and strategies to be introduced at times when negative behaviors emerge. For example, both staff and students are encouraged to use praise notes to pay attention to and reinforce positive prosocial behaviors at school. "Peace feet" might be placed on the floors by the drinking fountains to discourage cutting in line. Students are sent to the principal for good deeds as well as for discipline problems. Adults actively monitor hot spots in school where conflicts often arise, such as the lunchrooms and hallways between classes, and they praise prosocial behavior that occurs.

A single program consultant provides teacher training for Peace-Builders, including a pre-intervention orientation for faculty and staff, a half-day training workshop, and extensive site coaching (two hours weekly for the first three to four months and then as needed). Studies of this program have demonstrated school-wide changes with regard to both aggressive and prosocial behavior.

The Olweus Bullying Prevention Program

Another school-based psychoeducational program for child behavior management is the Olweus Bullying Prevention Program (OBPP) (Horne, Stoddard, & Bell, 2007; Kallestad & Olweus, 2003). A premise of this program is that bullying behavior can be checked and redirected into more socially appropriate directions through a restructuring of the school environment. This restructuring is intended to produce changes in the opportunity and reward structures for bullying behavior, resulting in fewer opportunities for bullying and fewer rewards (such as prestige or peer support) for displaying such behavior. The goals of the program are to reduce bullying and victim problems inside and outside the school setting, prevent the development of new bullying and victim problems, and achieve better peer relations at school.

The OBPP is implemented through staff-led groups that include teacher training, classroom presentations, community information sessions at PTA meetings, and family support groups. A prerequisite of the program is that there must be an awareness and involvement of all adults in the school and its stakeholders (parents and community leaders) in the problem of student aggression. (See exhibit 10.6 for a summary of the program structure.)

Exhibit 10.6: ***The Olweus Bullying Prevention Program structure***

School-level interventions: pre-measures (questionnaire and conference day), student supervision during staff breaks, staff discussion groups, and the school coordinating committee
Classroom-level interventions: rules against bullying, class meetings with students, and meetings with parents of the class
Individual-level interventions: serious talks with bullies and students, serious talks with parents of involved children, and development of individual intervention plans

---

The program developers (professional consultants from outside the school) initially conduct an assessment at faculty meetings to determine the extent of the school's bullying problem. Next the program leaders organize a school conference day to address the problem of bullying with all school staff and some student representatives. Once the school overview and orientation is completed, the program is implemented by involving teachers and other school personnel in the creation of a culture of respect and dignity, with a strong focus on effective problem solving and conflict resolution. Several materials are used in the project's implementation. A booklet for teachers and school personnel describes what is known about bullying problems and provides guidelines about what the school can do to counteract those problems. Next a four-page folder with information and advice for parents of victims, bullies, and other children is distributed by the teachers to the families of students. Finally, participating schools are given a videocassette showing episodes from the everyday lives of two bullied children.

As the program is implemented, the school's identified bully prevention coordinator provides ongoing supervision and organizes a coordination group representing all school personnel to ensure that the program is implemented effectively. Meetings among staff and parents occur on a regular basis to ensure that the program is supported within the family system. The school implements class rules against bullying and holds regular class meetings with students about related problems. On the individual level, attention is directed to bullies and victims and talks are held with parents and involved students. The program is evaluated through periodic use of instruments to measure changes in the school climate, teacher attitudes and behaviors, and student behaviors.

Summary

Psychoeducational programs for children and adolescents with behavior problems and their families maintain a focus on behavior and structural family theory, whether or not this is explicitly stated. This focus is maintained because negative child behaviors, whatever their origin, are changeable with the applications of new reinforcers and skill applications from primary caregivers. Adult family members are helped to regain an appropriate sense of authority with regard to expectations for children. Cognitive interventions may be appropriate for adult caregivers but not for children, who have not yet achieved a requisite level of cognitive development for those approaches. Ego psychological interventions, with their emphasis on emotional expression, are less appropriate for problems identified as behavioral, except at times for family members who benefit from venting their frustrations with the challenges of caregiving. Whereas some of the programs described in this chapter are located in mental health centers, others are appropriate for the school setting, where children are often most disruptive to others. In many cases psychoeducation is not sufficient by itself to resolve behavioral problems, but education and support provide children and their caregivers with heightened capabilities to follow through with more socially acceptable and developmentally appropriate means of dealing with their impulses.

Chapter 11

Substance Abuse

Substance use and abuse are both prevalent throughout the world. Among the substances that may abused are alcohol, caffeine, nicotine, sedatives, cocaine, amphetamines, and marijuana. Any adult may legally purchase some substances, whereas others are illegal for most people or are available only by prescription. Although mild or moderate substance use may be harmless and even beneficial to one's health, substance abuse presents a host of health and safety concerns for individuals and society at large (it is associated with crime and traffic accidents, for example). Human services practitioners must be able to assess clients for substance-use disorders and have knowledge of their available treatments. These treatments include psychoeducational interventions, which are especially relevant for those substance abusers who are reluctant to engage in traditional therapies. Alcohol-related disorders are the primary focus of this chapter, although other substances will be addressed as well.

The American Psychiatric Association (2000) provides general criteria for substance abuse and substance dependence, both of which represent mental disorders (see exhibit 11.1). The defining characteristic of abuse involves negative physical and emotional consequences of use, whereas

---

Exhibit 11.1:   *Criteria for substance abuse and dependence*

Abuse

A maladaptive pattern of use with recurrent adverse consequences

Dependence

Tolerance: a need for increased amounts of a substance to become intoxicated, or a diminished effect with the same amount

Withdrawal: the development of maladaptive physical, cognitive, and behavioral changes that are due to stopping or reducing prolonged abuse

Compulsive use: using a substance in larger amounts than intended; being unable to stop or cut down; continued use despite negative emotional or physical symptoms; investing much time in getting, using, or recovering from effects of the substance that interferes with social, work, or recreational activities

dependence refers to compulsive use despite the risk of serious consequences, often accompanied by tolerance and withdrawal.

Prevalence of Substance Abuse

The substance-abuse disorders are the fourth most diagnosed group of disorders in the United States, with a lifetime prevalence of 14.6 percent (Kessler, Chiu, Demler, & Walters, 2005). The prevalence is similar among African Americans and Caucasians but is lower for Hispanic persons (Breslau, Kendler, Su, Kessler, & Gaxiola-Aguilar, 2005; see exhibit 11.2). In older adults, one-month prevalence rates for alcohol-use disorders range from 1 to 2 percent. More than 8 percent (8.46%) of adults meet criteria for a past-year alcohol-use disorder. In 2004, the rate of substance dependence or abuse was 8.8 percent for youths aged twelve to seventeen years (Brown, 2008). Two percent of the population meets criteria for any substance-use disorder.

Exhibit 11.2:   Prevalence of alcohol use and dependence

Substance-dependence rates by age

Children twelve and under: 9.4 percent
Adults: 15 percent

General alcohol-dependence statistics for the United States

Current alcohol users: 51.6 percent
Never used alcohol: 19 percent
Alcohol abusers who meet the criteria for dependence: 30 percent

Alcohol dependence rates by ethnicity

Native Americans: 14.1 percent (highest)
African Americans and Caucasians: 9.5 percent
Hispanics: 10.4 percent
Asian Americans: 4.2 percent (lowest)

Dependence rates by gender

Males abuse alcohol at five times the rate of women.
Women are more likely to engage in prescription-drug abuse.
Women begin drinking later than men but have a more rapid onset
    of addiction and health problems.

People with drug-use disorders are at risk for other mental illnesses (Dumaine, 2003). More than half (51.4%) of adults with substance-use disorders at some point in their lives have another mental disorder. Adolescent abusers have a 60 percent likelihood of being diagnosed with another psychiatric disorder, most frequently depression and the disruptive behavior disorders (Armstrong & Costello, 2002). Unfortunately, substance use in people with mental disorders may lead to an exacerbation of their symptoms, and it is associated with poor health and risk-taking behavior. Significant medical consequences are also associated with the substance-use disorders. Substance dependence (excluding nicotine) in the United States annually accounts for 40 percent of all hospital admissions and 25 percent of deaths (Santora & Hutton, 2008). Common medical problems related to drinking include gastrointestinal (gastritis, ulcers, liver problems, and pancreatitis) and cardiovascular (hypertension and cholesterol and subsequent heart disease) conditions (Mirin et al., 2002).

Risk and Resilience Influences for Substance Abuse

The substance-use disorders usually begin in late adolescence or early adulthood (Crum et al., 2008). Risk mechanisms specific to substance abuse and dependence for adolescents include the early onset of drinking (before age fourteen), the exhibition of serious behavioral problems, and the presence of adverse family conditions (Hingson, Heeren, & Winter, 2006). Problematic alcohol use seems to be moderately heritable for adolescents (Young, Rhee, Stallings, Corley, & Hewitt, 2006). Family risk is particularly related to a lack of positive parental monitoring (Siebenbruner, Englund, Egeland, & Hudson, 2006). Protective mechanisms include parental warnings about alcohol and having abstinent friends. At the community level, the availability of drugs and alcohol offers risk whereas community prohibitions against such use are protective.

For substance-use disorders that begin in adulthood, heritability is low, although stronger for males (Walters, 2002). Other disorders that often precede substance use are depression in females and antisocial personality disorder in males (Lynch, Roth, & Carrol, 2002). Many females with substance-use problems have a history of physical or sexual abuse (Orwin, Maranda, & Brady, 2001). At the social level, peers who use substances place an individual at risk.

Some characteristics of people and their environments influence the course of alcohol abuse and dependence (Conner, Sorensen, & Leonard, 2005). Most generally, high levels of pretreatment use and substance use during treatment present risks for relapse. Having a concurrent mental disorder is a risk influence against recovery. In particular, persons with depression tend to be slower to benefit from professional intervention (Conner et al., 2005). Socially, a lack of family support, having substance-abusing peers, low socioeconomic status, and life stresses that include physical or sexual victimization are risk influences. Protective mechanisms for the course of substance-related disorders include the person's motivation not to use, an absence of other mental disorders, family support, non-substance-using peers, the ability to develop new relationships, and Alcoholics Anonymous (AA) attendance. (The risk mechanisms for substance abuse are summarized in exhibit 11.3.)

Exhibit 11.3:   Risk influences on substance-use disorders

Biological

Neurochemical irregularities (dopamine and serotonin levels) have been implicated in substance-use problems.

Family histories of use support genetic factors, although such patterns could be socially learned.

People who can tolerate larger amounts of alcohol tend to have a greater genetic predisposition to alcoholism.

Psychological

Alcohol and other drugs may fulfill an unmet psychological need.

Self-medication for stress accounts for use in at least 15 to 20 percent of addicts.

People can learn and become conditioned to substance use through environmental reinforcement.

The person has addiction-prone personality traits, including tendencies toward denial, minimizing, rationalizing, projection, grandiosity, and selective attention.

The family may play a role in teaching substance-use behaviors and also serve as motivators or sustainers during a client's recovery.

Social

Culture and peer-group influences may encourage use.

The person's drinking styles, behaviors, and comportment when intoxicated suggest a lack of judgment.

The person's beliefs about substance use feature expectations of rewards, social expectations for use, and an absence of perceived negative sanctions.

Social networks include a high number of substance abusers.

Economic loss contributes to behavior.

The inner-city economy of crack cocaine presents such residents with opportunities to use.

Substance Abuse Intervention Principles

Permanent abstinence is usually the goal of substance-abuse intervention. Whether adult clients can manage controlled drinking is a controversial topic (Bukstein et al., 1997). Some programs are designed for special populations, such as adolescents, pregnant or postpartum women, and women with young children. Many people receive intervention from locations that are not specialized for the treatment of these disorders, including self-help groups, private physicians, emergency rooms, and prisons or jails (Booth, Shields, & Chandler, 2009). Regardless of the treatment site or modalities utilized, positive outcomes are associated with the frequency, intensity, and duration of treatment participation (Mirin et al., 2002).

The Alcoholics Anonymous model of recovery has tended to dominate the substance-abuse intervention field (Kelly, Myers, & Brown, 2002). In AA self-help groups, the participant reaches and maintains abstinence by moving through a series of twelve steps with the assistance of a support group and sponsor. AA and NA (Narcotics Anonymous) groups have been shown to increase abstinence, self-efficacy, and social functioning for those who attend, especially when they engage in outside activities with people they meet at AA (Bond, Kaskutas, & Weisner, 2003). Self-help groups should not act as a substitute for other interventions for persons who are mandated to attend treatment, however, as they tend to stop drinking only while attending those groups (Kownacki & Shadish, 1999).

Cognitive-behavioral psychoeducation interventions can be targeted at substance-use problems (McCrady, 2000). These interventions focus on altering thought processes that lead to maladaptive use, altering the behavioral chain of events that lead to use, helping clients deal with craving, and promoting the development of social skills compatible with remaining sober.

The Role of Families in Intervention

Families have tremendous potential impact on either perpetuating or ameliorating the substance-abuse problems of a member, including influence on the abuser's willingness to comply with intervention (Mirin et al., 2002). Studies have consistently found higher rates of improvement when families are involved in treatment. In addition, most family interventions are superior to alternate conditions in terms of the client's length in treatment and reduced drug use (Stanton & Shadish, 1997). For these reasons, many psychoeducational programs are intended for, or include, the abuser's family members.

Before reviewing psychoeducation programs, it is important to first consider the treatment challenge of the substance abuser's denial of his or her problem, using the perspective of the Trans-theoretical Stages of Change model.

The Trans-theoretical Stages of Change in Substance Abuse

The Trans-theoretical Stages of Change (TSOC) model has been a major positive influence on substance-abuse intervention, with implications for psychoeducation (Connors, Donovan, & DiClemente, 2001). This assessment model was developed to help providers address the reluctance of many people with substance-use disorders to change their behaviors. It is particularly useful in matching interventions to clients at different stages of change. Within the TSOC model are the six stages of change explained in exhibit 11.4. One attractive feature of the TSOC model is that intervention techniques from any theoretical orientation (ego psychological, cognitive-behavioral, etc.) can be used when addressing the relevant stage of change.

Exhibit 11.4: *The Trans-theoretical Stages of Change model*

Precontemplation: the person is not yet considering change, does not see him- or herself as having a problem

Contemplation: high ambivalence; the person both considers and rejects change, vacillates between reasons to change and reasons to stay the same

Preparation: the person accepts the need to change, to do something about the problem; at this point he or she may enter into action or slip back into contemplation

Action: the person engages in specific actions to bring about change in the problem areas

Maintenance: the person attempts to maintain the changed behavior and avoid the problem behavior; the challenge is to sustain the change accomplished by the previous actions

Relapse: revision back to the problem behavior; relapse is quite possible when the person is trying to change long-standing behavior patterns

---

Within the TSOC model, the practitioner must take particular care to identify substance abusers who are either in precontemplation, denying that a change is needed, or in contemplation, when the problem is recognized but they are only considering change. Intervention challenges for persons in these categories can be summarized as follows:

Motivation to change must be elicited from the client, not imposed from the outside.

A client's motivation for enacting change relative to some problem behavior is often impeded by his or her ambivalence.

It is the client's task to articulate and eventually resolve his or her ambivalence.

A person's readiness to change is a product of interpersonal interaction, and thus the practitioner's attitudes toward the client may facilitate or impede the process.

Direct persuasion is not an effective method for resolving ambivalence.

References to the TSOC model occur in the later discussion of specific psychoeducational programs.

Psychoeducation

An important ingredient in most substance-abuse intervention services is the use of client and family education about addiction-related topics (Fals-Stewart, Birchler, & Kelley, 2006). Central among the issues taught to substance abusers and their significant others during the course of any treatment are the following:

Brain chemistry and the process of addiction
Understanding conditioned cues and craving and identifying high-risk situations for use or relapse
The effects of drugs and alcohol on biological, psychological, and social functioning
Addiction and the family
The need to make lifestyle changes when battling addiction
Relationships between substance abuse and other disorders

Other topics for education in substance-abuse treatment that are more skills-focused may include developing new coping skills, increasing the sense of self-efficacy, dealing with relapse, and drug and alcohol monitoring (Rawson, Obert, McCann, & Marinelli-Casey, 1993a).

Psychoeducational material may be presented in a variety of formats, including classroom settings, small-group discussions, single or time-limited family meetings, and as a part of regular counseling sessions. Through discussion and perhaps homework assignments, clients are helped to learn about the specific conditions that have the greatest association with their drug or alcohol use, as shown in exhibit 11.5. Following is a review of a variety of program examples.

Exhibit 11.5: Conditions that have high associations with substance use

High-risk states: times of the day, being around drug-using friends, visiting bars, having money, having idle time
Behavioral warning signs: compulsive and impulsive behavior, time spent with drug users, stopping recovery activities, returning to secondary drug use
Cognitive warning signs: euphoric recall of drug use, relapse justification, drug dreams, rationalizations to discontinue recovery behaviors
Affective warning signs: emotions associated with drug use

Motivational Interviewing and Enhancement Interventions

Motivational interviewing (MI) is a method for enhancing motivation to change by exploring and resolving a client's ambivalence about an alleged problem (Miller & Rollnick, 2002). MI is a demonstrably effective means of engaging clients who are either resistant or unmotivated to address substance-abuse issues. A brief intervention, motivational interviewing is used both as a stand-alone treatment that relies heavily on client education and as an initial step toward engaging clients in other more intensive intervention approaches.

Within the Trans-theoretical Stages of Change model, motivational interviewing is primarily designed to work with those persons who are in the stage of either precontemplation, denying that any change is needed on their part, or contemplation, believing they might have a problem but only considering change. MI works to resolve the client's ambivalence by providing information about substance use, the advantages and disadvantages of use, and the advantages and disadvantages of changing. The practitioner seeks to create dissonance between a person's goals (in terms of health, future well-being, success, and relationships) and problem behaviors, so that the desire to change is bolstered. A client's perception of the alleged problem is thus the focus of the practitioner's efforts.

The specific models of intervention that have been developed from the MI approach are called Motivational Enhancement Intervention (MEI). These models are highly educational in nature, as shown in the following examples.

One group of researchers developed an MEI program to investigate the potential for reducing marijuana use among ninety-seven high school–age adolescents in two schools (Walker, Roffman, Stephens, Berghuis, & Kim, 2006). The program consisted of two weekly sessions of thirty to sixty minutes each, provided at the school during the day. The practitioners (two master's level and one bachelor's level clinicians) solicited information about the student's marijuana use and, after doing so, provided feedback that was educational in nature. This feedback consisted of the following information:

Normative comparisons of the person's marijuana use
Patterns of marijuana use
Positive and negative aspects of marijuana use
The person's expectations related to marijuana use
Problems related to use
The quantity and frequency of alcohol and any other drug use
The status of the person's available social support
The person's life goals and their relationship to marijuana use
Costs and benefits of reducing use
The sense of self-efficacy for resisting use

The confidential program was advertised as a free service to adolescents who wanted information about their marijuana use. Most participants were assessed at the precontemplation or contemplation stages of change. At the end of the intervention, students who requested additional information about their drug use were given a skills booklet that included exercises for goal setting, trigger identification, and quitting strategies.

The researchers defined meaningful change as a 50 percent reduction in baseline marijuana use at sixty-day follow-up. In fact, the participants reduced their marijuana use by only 16 percent over the sixty days. The researchers concluded that this level of drug-use reduction was modest and might be unlikely to affect the negative consequences of participants' drug use. Participants who were in the preparation or action stages of change did experience a significant reduction in use, although this reduction was mild.

Another group of researchers developed the Marijuana Treatment Project for general populations of clients who express interest in eliminating their perceived dependence on the drug. The first two sessions of this nine-session three-stage intervention feature psychoeducation as a first step in preparing the participant for behavior change (Steinberg et al., 2002). In this motivational enhancement component, leaders met with participants one or two times to help them identify treatment goals and build self-efficacy for making desired changes. The counselor assisted the participants in observing discrepancies between their life goals and current status, maintained a positive emphasis toward change, minimized arguing or challenging the participant, and communicated empathy. Following the interview, the practitioners provided a personal feedback form to all participants. This form included the participants' average number of days of use per month compared to national averages, frequency of use compared to adults who sought treatment, and his or her total number of marijuana-related problems experienced in the past ninety days compared to adults who seek treatment. Participants were then invited to enter phases 2 and 3 of the program, which included problem solving (with a focus on other life problems) and skills building. As in the previous study, those participants who made changes in their drug use were more likely to have been preparing for change before enrolling in the program.

Two other motivational enhancement programs focus on alcohol use. The first is the Drinker's Check-Up (DCU) intervention (Hester, Squires, & Delaney, 2005). This intervention is a free assessment and feedback service for persons who want to find out if alcohol is harming them. The DCU is advertised as being not a treatment program but a confidential consultation. Master's level clinicians provide two sessions with individual participants, with an emphasis on assessing their alcohol use for evidence of abuse and dependence. Practitioners also provide normative and risk-related feedback. It has been found in several studies of this program that participants reduced alcohol use significantly and maintained their gains after eighteen months. The DCU participants were assessed as similar to persons in formal treatment programs on measures of alcohol use and related problems. The DCU is thus a promising intervention for persons who would not otherwise seek help for their problems.

A second MEI program for alcohol users is a two-stage program for college students referred to a university alcohol incident referral program after committing alcohol-related offenses for the first time (Borsari, Tevyaw, Barnett, Kahler, & Monti, 2007). Forty-three mandated students participated in the program study. The first part of the program was a minimal intervention consisting of a ten- to fifteen-minute discussion with a peer counselor about the events leading up to the alcohol incident, the reactions of the person's friends and family, and any changes the student has made to his or her drinking as a result. At the end of the conversation, the counselor provided the student with a twelve-page booklet containing information on what constitutes standard drinking, guidelines for sensible drinking, indicators of risky drinking, information on what to expect should one decide to make a change in drinking, and strategies to cut down on drinking.

Four weeks after the baseline assessment and minimal intervention, participants completed an Internet follow-up questionnaire to see if they met criteria for risky drinking. If so, they were referred to part 2 of the intervention, called brief motivational intervention (BMI). Eighty-eight percent of the program participants were referred to BMI, which consisted of a single one-hour meeting with an alcoholism counselor who provided the student with personalized feedback on his or her reports at baseline and follow-up. The pair then engaged in a discussion of the normative quantity and frequency of drinking, blood alcohol content and tolerance, alcohol-related consequences, the influence of settings on drinking behavior, and expectations of alcohol use. The participant was also provided with information related to his or her personal experiences and introduced to harm-reduction strategies.

In a follow-up study after ten weeks, there were no significant differences in alcohol use and related problems among persons who completed the program and those who were in a control group. The program did have a positive impact, however, on participants who were relatively light drinkers.

Motivational Enhancement Groups

Motivational enhancement interventions that focus on education are often provided in group formats (Ingersoll, Warner, & Gharib, 2002). One, called a core motivational group, uses a ten-session semi-structured format. The leader covers each of ten specific topics (see exhibit 11.6) in ninety-minute sessions while encouraging discussion among participants. The topics are ordered to follow the stages of change, but it is not necessary that they be

Exhibit 11.6:   The core motivational enhancement group topics

Topic 1: introduction to the group and an exploration of lifestyles
Topic 2: the stages of change
Topic 3: awareness (the good and not-so-good things about alcohol use)
Topic 4: looking forward
Topic 5: decisional balance (pros and cons of changing and of staying the same)
Topic 6: exploring values
Topic 7: supporting self-efficacy and change success stories
Topic 8: supporting self-efficacy by exploring strengths
Topic 9: planning for change
Topic 10: the importance of confidence and desire for change

addressed in order. That is, the leader can adapt the sequencing of topics to the interests of the members. Various written exercises are available to use in these groups, but some leaders prefer to explore topics through discussion only. The group can be run with either an open or a closed format. In an open group, new members may be added at any time, and though they will have missed the earlier material, they can be served immediately after requesting services. In a closed group, members cannot join after the second session. The benefits of a closed format are a more cohesive group, with more opportunities for risk taking as members learn to trust one another.

The single-session motivational interviewing group is suitable for serving substance users who can not or will not make a larger time commitment to an intervention. The purpose of the group is to discuss health habits and lifestyles that might be causing problems for the participants. This group is also semi-structured. It is not expected that the leader will cover all eight topics (see exhibit 11.7), however, as he or she should focus on the needs of the group members.

Exhibit 11.7:   Topics for the single-session motivational interviewing group

Topic 1: lifestyles, stress, and substance use
Topic 2: health and substance use
Topic 3: a typical day
Topic 4: the good things and the less-good things
Topic 5: providing information
Topic 6: the future and the present
Topic 7: exploring concerns
Topic 8: helping with decision making

In this model, members sit in a circle with an easel chart or blackboard nearby. The leader introduces him- or herself and invites each member to provide his or her first name and the reason he or she has come to the group. The leader asks the group to share information about lifestyles and daily habits and then encourages members to discuss these issues. At key points the leader summarizes a topic and then asks another question to move into another topic area. This procedure continues with each topic taking five to fifteen minutes. Members are encouraged to provide support and feedback to one another as they consider their issues that may require change.

Parenting with Love and Limits

The Parenting with Love and Limits (PLL) program has been designed for adolescents with co-occurring substance-abuse and behavioral problems and their parents (Smith, Sells, Rodman, Coalitions, & Reynolds, 2003). The program is designed to address three perceived gaps in the practice literature regarding adolescent substance abusers. First, there is a growing body of evidence that links adolescent substance abuse to dysfunctional family dynamics. Thomas and Corcoran (2001) reported that family support was often cited by teens as being most helpful in quitting drugs and maintaining sobriety. Second, the majority of substance-abusing teens in treatment also exhibit other problems, such as truancy, fighting, and defiance. In these cases, family-based treatments are found to be effective not only in reducing substance use but also in alleviating associated symptomatic behaviors (Kumpfer, Alvarado, Tait, & Whiteside, 2007). Finally, researchers have found the psychoeducational component of family substance-abuse treatment to be effective in reducing the teen's drug use as well as heightening parental functioning. One problem with traditional parenting groups, however, is the significant dropout rates of both parents and teens.

PLL was developed to address these deficits. The goals of the program are to assess whether or not active parent involvement and the concurrent treatment of severe behavior problems will reduce teen substance use and to determine if these changes can be maintained over a twelve-month follow-up period. The follow-up is critical because teen substance-abuse and conduct-disorder relapse rates are typically high, sometimes as high as 75 percent (Kraft, Schubert, Pond, & Aguirre-Molina, 2006).

Three questions were examined in a major study to evaluate the PLL program:

1. Will active parent involvement and the concurrent treatment of severe behavior problems reduce teen substance abuse?
2. Will reductions in substance-abuse behavior be maintained at the twelve-month follow-up?
3. Will adolescents relapse within a twelve-month period as measured by rearrest rates through juvenile court records?

Ninety-three parents and 102 adolescents attended a six-week Parenting with Love and Limits program. The adolescents ranged in age from nine to eighteen years. Each participant was diagnosed with substance abuse and a comorbid diagnosis of either oppositional defiant or conduct disorder. In addition, the adolescents committed a wide variety of concurrent offenses, with the most commonly occurring offense being shoplifting (22.5%). The majority of the adolescents were Caucasian, and the other participants were African American or Mexican American. Both males and females were present in the sample. All adolescents were court ordered and drug tested to determine a baseline rate of substance abuse.

The six-week PLL psychoeducational program utilized the principles of structural family therapy (see exhibit 11.8). It provided parents with a step-by-step approach for stopping both their teenagers' substance abuse and behavior problems. In this way, parents would be helped to resume their positions of authority in the family system. Two group facilitators led small groups of parents, caregivers, and their teenagers (no more than four to six families or fifteen total people in each group) in six classes of two hours length. Two co-facilitators were needed to manage the breakout groups.

Exhibit 11.8:   Parenting with Love and Limits program schedule

Session 1: understanding why your teen misbehaves (parents learn why the teen initiates behaviors like substance use, disrespect, running away, or violence to defeat parents every time they try to regain control of the household); parents and teens go into breakout groups to vent their feelings and frustrations about these issues

Session 2: hot buttons (parents learn how their teen pushes their hot buttons [whining, disgusted looks, swearing, etc.], and teens learn about how parents push their buttons [lecturing, criticizing, nagging])

Session 3: contracting (parents learn how and why their old methods of contracting have failed and how to put together a contract with rewards and consequences; teens meet in their breakout groups to write their own contracts)

Session 4: troubleshooting (parents learn how teens have a special ability called enhanced social perception to think two steps ahead and derail even the best-laid contract)

Session 5: stopping the hidden aces (parents choose from a menu of creative consequences to stop the teen's seven "big guns": disrespect, ditching or failing school, running away, drugs or alcohol, sexual promiscuity, violence, and threats of suicide)

Session 6: reclaiming lost love (participants are helped to understand how years of conflict have drained the softness out of the parent-child relationship and learn strategies to reclaim this lost love)

Parents and teens usually met together, but there were times in which each group met separately to address certain issues. The PLL program provided parents with a treatment manual on curtailing their teenagers' substance-abuse and behavior problems. Each facilitator went through a two-day training on how to conduct the program.

The Adolescent Substance Abuse Subtle Screening Inventory was administered to the adolescents before and after each PLL course (Feldstein & Miller, 2007). It measures five areas: self-perception of alcohol abuse, self-perception of other drug abuse, overt attitudes toward drug use, subtle attitudes toward drug use, and defensiveness about drug use. Recidivism or relapse rates for all adolescents who completed the program were measured through juvenile court records for each adolescent.

The high completion rate (85% of adolescents and 94% of parents for all six weeks) indicates that the study was a credible investigation into the program's effects. The subscales measuring adolescents' judgments on whether or not they have substance problems were significantly lower following their participation in the program. No significant differences were found on the other subscales. Of the adolescents who completed the PLL program, only 15 percent relapsed or re-offended over a twelve-month period. This evidence suggests that group-oriented family psychoeducation can be effective in helping parents reassert their authority and reduce or curtail adolescents' behavior problems and substance abuse. The researchers asserted that the key ingredient in the current study was parental involvement and providing parents with skills to address their adolescents' behavioral problems.

The Matrix Neurobehavioral Model for Psychoeducation

The Matrix Neurobehavioral Model is a cognitive-behavioral program that assumes addicts can experience a biological recovery from chronic stimulant abuse through sequenced stages of recovery (Rawson, Obert, McCann, & Marinelli-Casey, 1993b). Along with the cognitive-behavioral emphasis, there is a significant amount of family participation in educational sessions. The program includes one forty-five-minute individual session and three ninety-minute group sessions per week for four months, three group sessions and two individual sessions for an additional two months, and one group per week during months seven through twelve. During the first six months, there are three conjoint sessions with the client and family member. The program unfolds as follows:

Individual sessions focus on topics sequenced to address the emergence of issues in stimulant recovery, including triggers, dealing with craving, leisure activities, time management, following a recovery plan, coping with emotions, drug-using friends, lifestyle changes, and the neurochemistry of cocaine withdrawal. Three conjoint sessions with family members focus on positive relationship changes.

A family education group includes six sessions covering the topics of addiction and the brain, drug use and AIDS, the effects of addiction on relationships, effects of stimulants, types of treatment, and an introduction to twelve-step programs.

A relapse-prevention group addresses the topics of addict behavior, relapse justification, relapse and fatigue, relapse and holidays, secondary drug use, leisure activities, sex and recovery, and emotional building. Relapse analysis clarifies the antecedents of relapse and reframes such episodes in order to avoid an abstinence violation effect.

The Matrix Neurobehavioral Model has been formalized into a treatment manual and has been successfully tested for effectiveness in a variety of studies since 1985.

Summary

Many of the substance-abuse disorders are considered to be addictive, with a biological basis. For this reason, and also because of the prevailing conceptualization of alcoholism as a disease, professional intervention that includes psychoeducation is highly appropriate. There is a great deal of information available on the biological, psychological, and social causes and effects of substance abuse, and it is important for persons experiencing these problems and their significant others to have access to this information. A particular problem for substance abusers is their denial of the problem, and such information can provide sufficient evidence of the risks involved in substance abuse that they may break through this denial. The importance of mutual support is dramatically demonstrated in Alcoholics Anonymous and related programs, and such support can be integrated into any group or multifamily intervention. Finally, the Trans-theoretical Stages of Change model, which was developed specifically for use in the substance-abuse treatment field, is useful in helping practitioners determine what types of treatment and information are helpful to different types of consumers.

A number of stepped-care models of intervention were reviewed in this chapter. This approach is used with persons exhibiting different levels of risk and treatment response. Persons not responding to a less-intensive level of treatment are then provided with more intensive treatment (Sobell & Sobell, 2000). These models are particularly well suited for persons who are ambivalent about what kinds of intervention they want to engage in, if any.

Chapter 12

Alzheimer's Disease

Alzheimer's disease (AD) is the most common form of dementia that afflicts (mostly) older adults. Formally termed Dementia of the Alzheimer's Type, it is characterized by cognitive deficits that result from an atrophy (wasting away) of tissue in several areas of the brain (Cummings & Cole, 2002). Memory impairment is always required to make a diagnosis of dementia. Other prominent symptoms may include *aphasia* (loss of the ability to use words appropriately), *apraxia* (loss of the ability to use common objects correctly), *agnosia* (loss of the ability to understand sound and visual input), and the *loss of executive functioning* (the inability to plan, organize, follow sequences, and think abstractly). A physician is required to diagnose this disorder because identifiable medical conditions that may cause the symptoms must be ruled out.

Alzheimer's disease has a gradual onset and progresses through a slow, steady decline in the person's cognitive functioning, ending in death. The duration of its course is unpredictable, although five to ten years is common. Its causes are not yet known and there is no cure, but medical treatments may help to slow its course. AD may occur with *early onset* (before age sixty-five) or with *late onset*. A minority of AD patients develop the disorder between ages forty and fifty, and an earlier onset implies a more rapid course (McMurtray, Ringman, & Chao, 2006). Prevalence estimates range from 1.5 percent for persons aged sixty-five to sixty-nine years to 16 to 25 percent for persons more than eighty-five years old (APA, 2000). The average age of diagnosis is eighty years, although memory loss unrelated to the disorder affects nearly 50 percent of persons over the age of eighty-five with various levels of severity. Approximately 5 million Americans were diagnosed with AD in 2001, and the number may rise to 15 million (34 million worldwide) by 2050 if effective forms of prevention and treatment are not found.

In people with AD, brain cells in the cortex and hippocampus (areas that are responsible for learning, reasoning, and memory) die after they become clogged with two abnormal structures: neurofibrillary tangles (twisted masses of protein fibers) and plaques (deposits of a protein called amyloid) (Meeks, Ropacki, & Jeste, 2006). Symptoms begin with changes to amyloid, which is part of a larger molecule that extends from a neuron's outer membrane (Ziabreva, Perry, & Perry, 2006). Normally this molecule dissolves after use, but in AD enzymes cleave the molecule in the wrong places, leaving behind insoluble amyloid fragments. These fragments bind to one another, forming fibrils that make them even harder for the body to clear. These fibrils in turn bind with each other to form plaques, and when they reach a certain threshold the brain can no longer function efficiently. Brain neurons slowly die.

Behavioral problems are the leading reason family members seek medical intervention on behalf of a person with dementia (Finkel, 2001). Exhibit 12.1 lists the range of problem behaviors evidenced by persons with dementia. Not all people exhibit all of these behaviors, and they occur with varying degrees of severity.

Exhibit 12.1: Problem behaviors that may be exhibited by persons with dementia

Perceptual disturbances (including delusions [false beliefs], hallucinations [false sense perceptions], and misidentifying people)
Mood disturbances (depression and apathy)
Wandering and other dangerous behaviors
Agitation or rage (including restlessness)
Sleep disturbances
Distressing repetitive behavior
Inappropriate sexual behavior (fondling, touching, masturbation, and verbal remarks)
Incontinence
Refusal to eat

Risk and Resilience Mechanisms for Alzheimer's Disease

Risks for Alzheimer's disease are heavily weighted toward genetic and biological processes. There is between a 58 and 79 percent biological heritability for AD for both men and women (Gatz et al., 2006). Specific information about genetic processes in Alzheimer's disease is lacking, but mutations in any of four genes are associated with its development (Nowotny, Smemo, & Goate, 2005). Some biological risk influences for AD are associated with gender and race. There is a gender difference in AD but only after age ninety, when it becomes higher among women (Ruitenberg, Ott, van Swieten, Hofman, & Breteler, 2001). A particular gene (APOE-4) appears to increase the risk of AD for persons in some ethnic groups, but more consistently for Caucasians (Papassotriopoulos, Fountoulakis, Dunckley, Stephan, & Reiman, 2006). Persons with Down's syndrome have an increased risk of AD, and mothers who deliver such children prior to age thirty-five also have an increased risk. Several biological protective influences have been identified with Alzheimer's disease, including regular exercise, maintenance of low cholesterol, and absence of head trauma (Jedrziewskia, Lee, & Trojanowskia, 2007).

There are no known psychological causes of Alzheimer's disease. Depression has been identified as a small but significant risk influence (Ownby, Crocco, Acevedo, John, & Loewenstein, 2006). Sometimes depressive symptoms are an early symptom of AD (Gatz, Tyas, St. John, & Montgomery, 2005). When people begin to experience the symptoms of AD, however, depression and anxiety become common. People exhibit mood swings, become distrustful of others, and show increased stubbornness. Those emotions and behaviors may be in response to frustration and changes in self-image, but biological reasons have also been offered to explain why depression is often present with AD (Bonavita, Iavarone, & Sorrentino, 2001). The characteristic neurofibrillary tangles are more pronounced in cerebral areas where the pathogenesis of depression occurs, and thus the two disorders may share a biological association.

Lifestyle factors may contribute to negative health conditions that put some people at greater risk for AD, although the role of these influences is speculative (Lyketsos et al., 2000). Possible contributing factors include infections, nutritional deficiencies, brain injury, endocrine conditions, cerebrovascular diseases, seizure disorders, substance abuse, and brain tumors. Persons with higher risks of these types generally have relatively low educational backgrounds and occupational status. They consume high-fat foods, have low blood levels of folic acid and vitamin B-12, and have elevated levels of an amino acid that has been linked to circulatory problems. Their lifestyles may include poor exercise habits, a greater likelihood of smoking cigarettes, and the ingestion of environmental toxins, such as water pollutants and aluminum.

Protective risk influences for Alzheimer's disease include a high education level, being employed, and regular engagement in activities that utilize cognitive functions (Jedrziewskia et al., 2007).

Effects of Alzheimer's Disease on the Family

Family members of persons with Alzheimer's disease often experience severe problems in their own social functioning and their relationships with the ill relative. Only one-third of persons with dementia in the United States live in nursing homes (Hoe, Hancock, & Livingston, 2006), which means that families are the primary caregivers for most of these individuals. Though the symptoms of Alzheimer's disease are distressing for the affected person, the situation is equally stressful for the caregivers (Phillipe, Lalloue, & Preux, 2006). The primary caregiver is often required to take the lead in organizing interventions. He or she is challenged to monitor the client's changing levels of dependence as the disease progresses. The caregiver faces ongoing challenges in balancing his or her own limits on time, energy, and patience. The stresses experienced by family caregivers may be heightened by their fears of loss, guilt over not being an adequate caregiver, ambivalence about the caregiver role, and fears about their own mortality. Support availability is significantly associated with less stress (Morano, 2003).

Predictors of caregiver burden include the patient's behavioral disturbances (especially at night) and hallucinations (Allegri et al., 2006). Caregivers may develop some degree of resentment toward the client, especially when it is perceived that the care recipient's negative behaviors are willful (Martin-Cook, Remakel-Davis, Svetlick, Hynan, & Weiner, 2003). Such intensive caregiving carries a high cost in terms of psychological, physical, and financial resources. Caregivers are vulnerable to marked declines in mental health (particularly depression and anxiety), physical health, and social activities, as well as disrupted household routines and relationships (Gallagher-Thompson et al., 2000).

The presence of Alzheimer's disease also produces family conflicts. One group of researchers analyzed fifty families to explore conflicts that can arise when a member has dementia (Peisah, Brodaty, & Quadrio, 2006). They found that family conflict most often involved children of the person with dementia and that it most often derived from accusations of inadequate care, financial exploitation, or isolation of the person with dementia.

Positive associations have consistently been found between caregiver coping and patient quality of life (McClendon, Smyth, & Neundorfer, 2004). Caregivers with proactive problem-solving strategies are less stressed than those with avoidance coping strategies (Aschbacher et al., 2005). One study of persons with Alzheimer's disease living in the community found a positive association between caregiver coping and patient survival time (McClendon et al., 2004). Conversely, the caregiver's internal (vs. shared) coping style was related to shorter recipient survival time. The authors speculate that the more withdrawn/internal caregivers are less psychologically available to the person with dementia and may provide less person-centered care. Another study of caregivers, representing all stages of the disease, found that the availability of emotional support has a mediating effect on depression, somatic complaints, and life satisfaction (Cooper, Katone, Orrell, & Livingston, 2004).

There are some differences among caregivers of older adults (not limited to Alzheimer's disease) from different ethnic groups with regard to stress, resource availability, and psychological outcomes. Minority caregivers are younger, less likely to be a spouse, and more likely to receive informal support from persons outside the family (Pinquant & Sorensen, 2006). They provide more care than Caucasian caregivers and feel stronger obligations to do so. Asian American caregivers use less formal support than Caucasian caregivers and along with Hispanic caregivers are more depressed than their Caucasian counterparts. Asian American families are slower to seek professional interventions than Western families, being more likely to rely on cultural traditions of family caregiving (Jones, Chow, & Getz, 2005).

Other differences among ethnic groups have been noted. Hispanic caregivers experience less depression, lower levels of role captivity (being constrained from managing other life roles), and higher amounts of self-acceptance than non-Hispanic caregivers (Morano & Sanders, 2006). Further, for Hispanic caregivers the subjective sense of burden mediates the effects of stress on somatic complaints and depression (Morano, 2003). African American caregivers experienced lower levels of caregiver burden than Caucasian caregivers. All ethnic minority caregivers reported worse physical health than Caucasian caregivers, however.

Caregiver and family stresses due to having a loved one with Alzheimer's disease are universally acknowledged. Fortunately, psychoeducation represents an intervention with much practical value for members of that population.

Psychoeducation

Overview

Psychoeducation for Alzheimer's disease features techniques to help caregivers understand the process of dementia and cope with their negative emotional reactions. Caregivers can benefit from planned respite care, information about dementia, services, benefits, and recognition for their hard work. In addition, they need help in recognizing and dealing with the warning signs of caregiver stress: denial, anger, social withdrawal, anxiety, depression, exhaustion, sleeplessness, irritability, and an inability to concentrate.

Psychoeducation is used with groups of families or individual families and tends to be structured (Depp et al., 2003). Length of treatment ranges from four to twenty sessions. Groups should take into account the determinants of burden, stage of the illness, and stage of mourning of the caregiver, as these factors suggest specific caregiver needs (Walker, Pomeroy, McNeil, & Franklin, 1994). Many psychoeducational interventions for dementia are cognitive-behavioral in nature, guided by two major assumptions. The first assumption is that caregivers' beliefs about the nature of the caregiving role (e.g., perceptions of role burden) will influence their ongoing mood and, in turn, the types of behaviors they exhibit (i.e., use of positive reinforcement vs. punishment) when providing care to the ill relative. The second assumption is that changing behaviors and thoughts can lead to alterations in caregiver mood and affect. By identifying and challenging ineffective thoughts and by increasing pleasant daily activities, the negative emotional experiences of caregivers can be substantially reduced (Burgio, Solano, Fisher, Stevens, & Gallagher-Thompson, 2003). The primary goals of cognitive-behavioral intervention for dementia caregivers are thus to reduce psychological distress through the practice of relaxation skills, encourage positive lifestyle modifications by increasing the number of pleasant daily events, and enhance effectiveness in managing the demands of daily care activities through improved problem-solving skills.

Brodaty, Green, and Koschera (2003) conducted a meta-analysis of thirty studies to review outcomes (primarily perceived burden and depression) of caregiver interventions. Caregiver coping skills, social support, knowledge of dementia, and mood of the care receiver were also measured in some studies. The studies included predominantly female spouses. Overall the interventions were found to significantly reduce caregiver depression, but the effects of increases in knowledge, coping skills, and social support were only moderate and the interventions were not found to significantly reduce caregiver burden. Including the care receiver was found to be important to the success of a program. In the following, several programs are reviewed in detail.

General Approaches

Gallagher-Thompson and her associates (Gallagher-Thompson et al., 2003; Gallagher-Thompson & DeVries, 1994) have conducted the majority of studies on cognitive-behavioral interventions for caregiver depression. Their interventions typically consist of twelve to sixteen ninety-minute sessions conducted over a period of six months. In their National Collaborative Resources for Enhancing Alzheimer's Caregiver Health (REACH) intervention, they compared the effects of cognitive-behavioral intervention alone (featuring coping-skills development) to the same intervention with the added feature of a peer support group on the psychological functioning of Mexican American and Caucasian dementia caregivers. Dementia caregivers in the experimental group reported significant reductions in symptoms of depression and increased use of adaptive coping strategies from pre- to posttreatment, whereas the support group participants showed little or no change on those measures. No differences in this pattern were observed across ethnic groups.

Caregiver interventions often include the two components of behavior management and coping-skills development. One study with more than 300 participants found that caregivers receiving both training components scored far better with regard to their mood and sense of well-being than caregivers receiving only skills training (Burns, Nichols, Martindale-Adams, Graney, & Lummus, 2003). Another study of forty-five caregivers of persons in the early stages of Alzheimer's disease found that five weekly educational seminars about the disease and its caregiving aspects substantially improved participants' knowledge (Kuhn & Fulton, 2004). Their self-efficacy and reactions to the patient's impairments improved moderately, although their levels of depression showed no improvement. Another experimental study of thirty-eight anxious caregivers found that a nine-week group program using cognitive-behavioral interventions significantly reduced their anxiety symptoms (Akkerman & Ostwald, 2004). A four-year longitudinal study of 406

caregivers concluded that counseling and support together reduced negative caregiver reactions to the clients' troubling behaviors (Mittleman, Roth,
Haley, & Zarit, 2004).

One program included a four-session caregiver-training program in
which participants watched professionals administering to loved ones and
then progressed to helping their loved ones on their own. Control-group
comparisons were made at seven and seventeen weeks on caregiver estimates of independent living, measures of cognition, function, quality of
relationship, caregiver mood, and feelings of self-efficacy. The only significant finding was in the expected inverse relationship between caregiver
sense of self-efficacy and depression (Martin-Cook, Davis, Hynan, & Weiner,
2005). On a related topic, Teri, McCurry, Logsdon, and Gibbons (2005)
found that community consultants could be successfully trained to provide
caregivers with support and education, to an extent that ninety-five caregivers in an experimental condition experienced less depression, less sense
of burden, and diminished reactivity to client behavior.

Specific Program Examples

The Caregiver Support Group   The Caregiver Support Group is designed for any family members who provide care for frail elderly members
(Toseland & Rivas, 2006). Led by a professional social worker, it illustrates a
blend of a structured group format with unstructured follow-up meetings.
The structured portion of the program involves eight weekly two-hour
meetings focused on education, coping-skills development, and problem-
solving skills development, as shown in exhibit 12.2.

Exhibit 12.2:   The Caregiver Support Group components

Educational Component

One week is devoted to each of the following topics:
   Introduction
   Caregivers' emotional reactions to the illness
   Care receivers' reactions to the illness
   How providers can care for themselves while caring for the frail
      relative
   Communication between the caregiver, care receiver, and other
      family members
   Community resources awareness
   Medical needs, pharmacology issues, nursing home placement
      process
   Home management techniques and resources for environmental
      modification

Coping-Skills Component

These five topics are flexibly incorporated into each group meeting
as needed:
Didactic teaching
Relaxation training
Cognitive restructuring
Self-monitoring
Self-instruction

Problem-Solving Component

These topics are featured toward the end of the program and are
based on specific issues that participants are experiencing at home:
Educate the client about the problem-solving process
Define the problem in concrete terms
Compile a list of uncensored alternatives
Evaluate each response alternative
Implement the preferred alternative
Evaluate, *or* return to an earlier step

The monthly follow-up meetings are less structured and focus on providing support and assistance as needed to members based on whatever
practical problems transpire between meetings. This program has not been
formally evaluated, but it has been adopted as a practical intervention by a
number of service providers.

Although specific time is set aside during each meeting to cover the
three components described in exhibit 12.2, leaders always provide support
interventions as well. These interventions include member opportunities to
ventilate about stressful experiences, leader and peer validation of similar
caregiving experiences, affirmation of members' abilities to cope, praise for
providing good care, support and understanding, a sense of hopefulness
about the future, and mutual aid.

The structure of the coping-skills element of the program follows:

Session 1: The leader assures members that their reactions to the ill
relative's health problems are normal; formally acquaints members with
the concepts of stress, appraisal, and coping (Lazarus, 2007); and offers
members an opportunity to discuss their reactions to the ill relative's
behaviors, their beliefs about the sources of the ill relative's behavior,
and the coping strategies they have been using.

Session 2: The leader helps members identify and label their emotional and bodily coping responses to the relative's physical and mental condition and to their own role as caregiver; reinforces effective
coping skills; encourages members to work toward changing ineffective coping skills; teaches members to better recognize signs of stress

and their typical cognitive appraisal and coping reactions; and asks members to keep a diary to record their experienced stresses and their reactions to them.

Sessions 3–4: Two relaxation techniques (deep breathing and progressive muscle relaxation) for the participants are introduced and practiced to counteract the effects of strain associated with caregiving.

Sessions 5–8: The leader teaches and practices cognitive-restructuring strategies, including self-talk, taking the perspective of other persons, and self-instruction; promotes the identification of early stress cues as signals to activate effective appraisals and coping strategies; emphasizes the use of inner dialogue to plan coping strategies; and introduces the concept of coping imagery as a means of identifying preferred coping strategies.

During session 7, members are given the option of meeting monthly as an ongoing support group, and they are further invited to maintain regular telephone contact with each other if desired. The ongoing meetings are not a mandatory element of the program, but many members welcome them, even though they may gradually drop out of the process over time (hopefully because they have received sufficient help to manage their family situations).

The spouse-caregiver intervention   The spouse-caregiver intervention provides a good example of a structured model of care that incorporates both psychotherapy and psychoeducation components (Campbell, 1997; Mittleman, Ferris, Shulman, Steinberg, & Levin, 1996). The primary goal of the intervention is to allow spouse caregivers to postpone or delay institutionalization of their ill relatives while minimizing negative consequences to themselves. The intervention comprises the three components shown in exhibit 12.3.

Exhibit 12.3:   Components of the spouse-caregiver intervention

Component 1: individual and family education and counseling, including two individual and four family counseling sessions over a four-month period
Component 2: a weekly support group
Component 3: continuous availability of family counselors to help with crises or ongoing problems

---

The initial counseling session takes place immediately after an intake evaluation. The counseling focuses on how the caregiver can prevent and deal with patient problem behaviors in ways that allow him or her to have more control over the environment. The four family sessions, lasting sixty to ninety minutes each, focus on problems that are uncovered during the assessment. Participating family members are encouraged to provide emotional and instrumental support in a variety of ways to the primary caregiver. At the end of four months, the caregiver is encouraged to join an Alzheimer's disease caregiver support group that meets weekly for eight months to provide ongoing support, education, and an extended social network for each member. The third component of the program is the provision of counselors to help with crises or ongoing problems whenever needed, by phone or in person, including evenings and weekends. The counselors help the caregivers to deal with stressful situations and problems as they arise, encouraging the caregivers to take care of themselves and seek support from others in their families and social networks.

This program was tested experimentally as 205 spouses of Alzheimer's disease patients living at home were recruited and enrolled in the program over a period of three years. The participants were randomly assigned to the experimental and control (usual agency counseling) conditions. Caregiver depression (which had been significant but not different between the experimental and control groups) was assessed at baseline and every four months for the first year. The most depressed participants were female and those with the more severely ill relatives, but at eight months caregivers in the treatment group were significantly less depressed, due in part to increases in family cohesion and social support. After eight years of follow-up, it was found that the patients in the treatment group had stayed at home an average of 329 days longer than those in the control group. It was concluded that the intervention resulted in less caregiver depression and improved coping, which delayed nursing home placement for patients with mild to moderate, but not severe, dementia.

The next few examples include programs that utilize the telephone and computer as a means of providing education and support to caregivers who cannot easily take time away from their homes.

Structural Ecosystems Therapy Structural Ecosystems Therapy (SET) is a technology-assisted intervention designed to reduce depressive symptoms in family caregivers of persons with Alzheimer's disease. It is used at the Miami site of the Resources for Enhancing Alzheimer's Caregiver Health (REACH) (Eisdorfer et al., 2003; Mitrani & Czaja, 2000). SET is a combination of structural family therapy and the ecological perspective, designed to improve caregiver interaction with the social environment, so that emotional, social, and instrumental needs can be met. At the REACH site participants attend weekly sessions of SET for four months, followed by biweekly sessions for the next two months, and monthly sessions for the final six months, for a total of twelve months of participation. Initial assessments of the family's structure, developmental stage, personal boundaries, and conflict-resolution style are conducted. The practitioner seeks to identify both maladaptive patterns that lead to distress and adaptive patterns that relieve burden. The process of family interactions rather than its content is the primary focus of the intervention.

Technology services offered in the SET program include

> The invitation to place regular conference calls with up to six other people,
>
> The opportunity to participate in telephone conferences with professionals,
>
> Provision of voice-mail boxes so that members can leave messages for each other, and
>
> Linkage to the contents of the Alzheimer's Association Resource Guide.

In one study of this program, 225 participants were recruited from the Miami site of the REACH project. Participants were randomly assigned to one of three groups: SET intervention, SET plus computer-telephone integrated system intervention, or minimal support control. At six-month follow-up the SET plus computer-telephone integrated system group participants showed a decrease in depression. The other two groups did not show reductions in depression.

Telehealth   Health care delivery via the telephone provides a particularly good vehicle for meeting the special education and support needs of rural family caregivers. Researchers initiated a series of studies examining the impact of a telephone-based education and support network, known as the Alzheimer's Rural Care Healthline (ARCH), for rural dementia caregivers and their health care providers (Glueckauf et al., 2005). The program consists of the seven components listed in exhibit 12.4.

Exhibit 12.4:   Seven program components of Telehealth

Overview of the characteristics of progressive dementia
Relaxation-skills development
Effective thinking about the challenges of caregiving
Incorporation of pleasant daily activities as a guard against emotional distress
Assertive communication in caregiving situations and with other family members
Development of problem-solving skills through personal goal setting
The importance of a social support network and of continuing to refine coping skills

The cognitive-behavioral intervention consists of twelve weekly goal-setting and implementation sessions with caregivers. Seven are telephone-based group sessions, and five are telephone-based individual sessions. The schedule of telephone-based classes is as follows:

> *Sessions 1–6:* Each caregiver meets online in groups of three for forty-five-minute classes.
>
> *Sessions 7–11:* Each caregiver receives four one-hour individual telephone sessions focusing on goal setting and implementation. Each caregiver is encouraged to identify and put into effect two personal caregiving goals. Caregivers are instructed to conduct a basic behavior analysis of identified target problems, followed by the selection and practice of alternative cognitive-behavioral strategies. Each participant is asked to monitor and report the extent of change in the severity and frequency of problem occurrences from week 7 to one-week posttreatment.
>
> *Session 12:* Caregivers are taught additional techniques for maintaining their gains.

Posttesting occurs one week following the conclusion of classes. Primary outcomes include improvements in depressive symptoms, caregiver burden, caregiver self-efficacy, and identified caregiver problems.

Project CARE   Project CARE is a behavioral intervention designed to reduce caregiver distress related to symptoms of AD and overall caregiver burden (Gonyea, O'Connor, & Boyle, 2006). Structured interventions are conducted over the course of five weeks (see exhibit 12.5). The behavioral and psychological symptoms of dementia in care recipients, such as anxiety and aggression, are measured as outcomes, and it is hypothesized that the severity of these symptoms will decrease after participation in Project CARE.

Exhibit 12.5:   *Project CARE program topics*

Session 1: overview of group goals and guidelines
Session 2: increasing pleasant events and improving communication
Session 3: increasing pleasant events and understanding behavior
Session 4: understanding and changing difficult behaviors
Session 5: final review

Eighty caregivers in a major study of the program were randomly assigned to the intervention group or a psychoeducational control group. The control group was provided with basic information about Alzheimer's disease, safety and communication tips, and support. Following the intervention, the CARE group participants reported less posttreatment stress related to client behaviors than the control group. The two groups did not show a significant posttreatment reduction in caregiver burden, and the severity of the symptoms of dementia of the care recipients did not improve significantly.

The caregiver role-training group   The role-training intervention is designed to enable family caregivers to adopt a more clinical attitude (a perspective that encourages a healthy level of emotional detachment) about caregiving, thereby decreasing some of the negative consequences of that role, such as burden and depression (Hepburn, Tornatore, Center, & Ostwald, 2001). The intervention includes five distinct components (see exhibit 12.6).

Exhibit 12.6:   The caregiver role-training group components

Information provision
Strategies for managing the behavior and changing expectations of
   the recipient and understanding the kinds of information they
   should provide to that individual
Role clarification (responsibilities and limits)
Belief clarification, to develop a clinical attitude about caregiving,
   and strengthening recognition of the importance of self-care
Mastery-focused coaching to reinforce problem-solving skills

In one study, ninety-four caregivers (who were invited to bring additional family members to the group) were enrolled. The researchers used an experimental design and continuous recruitment over two and one-half years for a total of sixteen seven-session workshops. Five months after intake caregivers in the treatment group reported less burden and depression and were less bothered by the behaviors of the ill relative than members of the control group.

The end-of-life booklets   One educational program provides end-of-life educational booklets on caregivers' sense of self-efficacy with dementia patients who are nearing death (Braun, Karel, & Zir, 2006). A rationale for this intervention is that there is a need for more caregiver-targeted end-of-life (EOL) education but that few resources are available. The authors developed and tested five twenty-page educational booklets on the topics of advanced care planning, funeral and memorial services, care for the dying, what to do when a loved one dies, and help for the bereaved. A convenience sample of family caregivers included 570 white, Asian, and Pacific Island caregivers who reported reading at least one of the booklets. Results showed improvements in EOL knowledge, advance directive completion, and willingness to consider hospice or home-based death. Ethnic differences included higher dropout rates and lower rates of familiarity with advanced directive and hospice among Pacific Islanders. The authors suggest that cultural variations about willingness to discuss EOL issues are reflective of socioeconomic status. For example, Pacific Islanders have relatively low life expectancy due to lower rates of health insurance and higher rates of mortality, obesity, and poverty. EOL planning may not be considered a high priority in light of these factors. Significant increases in receptivity to hospice care were observed in all ethnic groups, however. The researchers suggest the need to promote EOL planning in less interested citizens, as those who dropped out were more likely not to have positive attitudes.

Summary

Psychoeducational programs for the caregivers of persons with Alzheimer's disease are an effective means of providing education and support and of helping them to enhance their coping mechanism for this time-consuming and emotionally draining role. There is a consensus in the literature that such programs have a variety of benefits for those involved. This chapter reviewed the nature of stresses that caregivers experience, how they tend to be eager for support and to acquire new coping strategies, and a variety of programs that exist for members of the population. Interestingly, few psychoeducational programs are available for persons with Alzheimer's disease, although some efforts have been made to work with persons in the early stages of the illness, when their cognitive faculties are still relatively intact (Davis, 2005).

Chapter 13

Physical Health Conditions

The previous chapters in this book have been concerned with psychoeducation for a range of mental, emotional, and behavioral problems. This chapter is unique in that it is concerned with how such programs can be of assistance to persons with serious physical conditions and their families. Persons who experience chronic and debilitating health conditions are subject to emotional and family stress and are often in need of information to cope with these conditions more effectively. Psychoeducational programs have been shown to help ameliorate the negative effects of health conditions among participants. These programs often emphasize increased knowledge, empowerment, and support in the context of the illness or disability. Programs offer participants opportunities for obtaining health-related resources, learning from peers, minimizing isolation through mutual connection, and problem-solving skills development. They frequently involve cognitive strategies to build participants' sense of self-efficacy.

This chapter reviews a range of psychoeducational programs developed to deal with the physical and emotional challenges brought on by cancer, HIV/ AIDS, traumatic brain injury, sickle-cell disease, and other somatic disorders.

Cancer

Cancer is a class of diseases in which a group of cells display uncontrolled growth and intrusion on and destruction of adjacent tissues and often spread to other parts of the body through the lymph nodes or blood. Cancer comes in many forms, such as breast, lung, prostate, pancreatic, liver, mouth, and throat, and affects people of all ages, although the risk for most types of cancer increases with age. Cancer causes about 13 percent of all deaths, and 7.6 million people died from cancer worldwide during 2007 (American Cancer Society, 2009).

Cancer profoundly affects the body, the person, and the family. Illnesses such as cancer are sometimes called emotional crucibles because they create an emotional roller-coaster ride for persons involved that is draining but also potentially empowering. The degree of physical limitation imposed by the cancer and the outlook for survival provide a context for problems the individual and family may experience. During the early phase of the disease the person and family must decide what the cancer means to them in terms of how they will relate to one another. This period requires role changes and shifts in the patterns of family life. If the cancer becomes terminal, the person and family enter periods of mourning and bereavement. Several reviews have shown that psychoeducational interventions can be effective in improving the emotional functioning of cancer patients and their families. Five such programs are reviewed next.

Interactive Psychoeducation

In a qualitative case analysis study of two families regarding the shared experience of cancer, a trio of researchers found that the participants found interactive psychoeducation to be critically important (Robinson, Carroll, & Watson, 2005). The researchers conducted interviews to learn about the personal perspectives of family members who were participating in a treatment for cancer. The intervention consisted of therapists helping families to understand the illness and to find ways to cope with the stresses it brought into their families. The family members expressed that one of their main reasons for seeking help was that they needed to know whether the mix of emotions they were experiencing was unusual. As the families made these requests, the therapists introduced short interactive psychoeducational segments to provide them with the information needed, either during or after a regular family session. By integrating this information into the therapy process, practitioners were able to help alleviate the common fears of families that they are "doing it wrong" or "not coping correctly." Sharing information with the families helped them organize and normalize their experiences. The researchers recommend that practitioners working with families have at least a general understanding of common cancer-related issues that occur in these families.

Psychoeducation and Breast Cancer

A six-week psychoeducational program has been developed for women who do not necessarily have cancer but have tested positive for breast cancer gene mutations (McDaniel & Speice, 2001). Women who test positive for the gene often feel abandoned and frightened when the physical investigation is over, so this group represented an effort to assist these women in proactively dealing with their new health concerns. The group was composed of nine Caucasian women ranging in age from thirty-two to sixty years, and six of them already had cancer. The women chose to come to the group alone rather than with partners or other family members.

The group was semi-structured. The first fifteen minutes of each meeting were spent with the medical team answering questions and communicating information about the gene, the disease, and its treatment. The next seventy-five minutes were spent on the topics developed by the women during the first session (see exhibit 13.1).

> **Exhibit 13.1:   Group for women with breast cancer gene mutations schedule**
>
> *Session 1:* family reactions to testing (including reactions from part-
> ners, children, and extended family)
> *Session 2:* disclosure (who in the women's families is also at high
> risk, who to tell about the risk, and when)
> *Session 3:* confidentiality with insurers and the workplace
> *Session 4:* the women's own emotional reactions and coping strategies
> *Session 5:* body-image concerns
> *Session 6:* relationships with health professionals

This program was evaluated qualitatively through interviews with the members. The authors report that the sessions were emotionally intense and that the women bonded quickly after an initial period of hesitation. Following the intervention, all of the women said they had underestimated what it would mean to them to know that they were positive for the mutations, and they agreed that knowing about their genetic status was better than not knowing it. All agreed that their reactions, and the reactions of those close to them, had been far more complicated and difficult than they had foreseen. They acknowledged that the group provided a safe environment in which they could discuss these painful topics.

Breast Cancer Psychoeducation for African American Women

The effectiveness of psychoeducation has been demonstrated more often among Caucasian than minority patients. In a study designed to address this limitation in the research literature, seventy-three African American women with non-metastatic breast cancer were randomly assigned to an eight-week psychoeducational group intervention or an assessment-only control condition (Taylor et al., 2003). The participants included women who had undergone breast cancer surgery within the previous ten months at two hospitals. All women who met the above criteria were invited to participate in the study. Six cohorts of consecutively enrolled participants took part in the study. The researchers predicted that the intervention group would acquire greater knowledge about breast cancer and report better psychological adjustment. Further, there would be a larger effect among those with greater baseline psychological distress, poorer baseline physical functioning, lower incomes, and lower education levels. Outcome indicators included measures of general psychological distress, cancer-related distress, and knowledge.

Intervention participants attended eight weekly semi-structured meetings held at the university or a nearby hospital. Each meeting lasted two hours, and each group included eight members. The study psychologist and a psychiatrist facilitated the first two cohorts and individually facilitated the other four cohorts. There were four major topics covered:

1. Relaxation training
2. The role of spirituality and religion in coping with breast cancer
3. Coping with fears of cancer resurgence
4. Ways of using and maintaining social support to help cope with breast cancer

Four outside speakers were included: a nurse or physician who discussed cancer education, a physical therapist who demonstrated arm exercises and ways of managing possible side effects of treatment, an African American breast cancer survivor, and a nutritionist. Before each meeting began, all participants engaged in a relaxation exercise and were asked to offer other topics for that day's discussion. Participants were all given a relaxation audiotape and a tape recorder for use at home between sessions.

Study results at twelve months indicated that participants in the experimental group had more knowledge of breast cancer and related issues than members of the control group. They reported less general distress, and overall the intervention resulted in improved mood relative to the control condition. Women with greater baseline distress and lower income were able to achieve higher levels of functioning. In terms of cancer-related distress, the intervention resulted in a significant improvement among those with high baseline distress but not among those with low baseline distress. Although the most unique element of this program was the inclusion of spirituality and religious concerns, that variable was not measured in the evaluation.

Psychoeducation for Men with Prostate Cancer

This program was designed to positively affect the general and prostate-specific quality of life for men with prostate cancer (Helgeson, Lepore, & Eton, 2006). The researchers were interested in studying whether the variables, including self-esteem, self-efficacy, and depression would be affected among men who participated in a psychoeducational group. The study was based on the findings of previous research suggesting that the effects of psychoeducation on quality of life for persons with cancer are mixed.

The 250 men selected for this study, referred by physicians from eleven radiation and oncology groups, were randomly assigned to one of three conditions: group education, group education with peer discussion, or usual care. The educational intervention provided the men with information to enhance their understanding and control of the illness experience. The men were taught how to make healthy lifestyle changes; how to communicate with family, friends, and health care professionals; and how to cope with the negative side effects of medical interventions. The facilitated peer discussion component focused on the educational topics and discussions of how the material might be personally relevant to the men. Patients in the control condition received nothing beyond their standard medical care.

Eight groups of men, with ten to twelve members each, were created for each of the three conditions. The educational intervention consisted of six weekly one-hour lectures given by experts in the areas of prostate cancer biology and epidemiology, side effects of treatment, nutrition, stress and coping, relationships and sexuality, and follow-up care. Patients were encouraged to attend the lectures with a family member or friend. The education plus discussion intervention consisted of the same lecture series with forty-five additional minutes of group discussion led by a male clinical psychologist. Female family members convened in a separate room for their own discussions, facilitated by a female oncology nurse. The average time between treatment and the baseline interview was two months. Follow-up assessment occurred at two weeks, six months, and twelve months after the intervention.

The researchers assumed that men with a higher level of baseline distress would benefit most from a psychological intervention. A second assumption was that persons who were low in certain internal resources relevant to quality of life would benefit from interventions that accentuated those resources. Outcome indicators included measures of physical functioning, mental functioning, depressive symptoms, and prostate-specific functioning. It was found that men who began the study with lower levels of global self-esteem, lower levels of prostate-specific self-efficacy (less certain that they could control the side effects of prostate cancer), and higher depressive symptoms benefited most from the interventions. The findings were consistent across outcomes and across time. General self-esteem, unrelated to the specific cancer situation, appeared to be the most powerful mediating variable. The findings were not unique to one of the two active interventions in this study, suggesting that the education was the primary significant program ingredient.

Psychoeducation for Colorectal Cancer via Mail

Colorectal cancer is the second most common cause of cancer death in the United Kingdom, but if detected at the localized stage, survival rates reach beyond 80 percent (Wardle et al., 2003). Although preventive screening procedures are useful, their effectiveness depends on participation among high-risk persons. Predictors of nonparticipation with screenings include an absence of current health problems or symptoms, constraints related to time and travel, worries about pain involved in testing, and not wanting to know about possible health problems. To address these issues, a group of British researchers developed and tested a psychoeducational intervention designed to modify negative attitudes about colorectal cancer screenings with the use of an intervention brochure (Wardle et. al., 2003). The study was designed to evaluate the efficacy of a written, mailed intervention that, in addition to presenting basic factual information about colorectal cancer and screenings, addressed psychological barriers to screening.

The sampling frame included all persons ages fifty-five to sixty-four who had visited general practitioners in fourteen centers in England and had been recommended for routine colon cancer screenings ($n = 400,000$). Personnel at the screening center sent invitations to these persons and asked if they would definitely or probably attend a screening. For this study, only persons who indicated they would probably attend were chosen, as they represented a comparatively hard-to-engage group. Six thousand subjects were randomized into the treatment (booklet) and control (usual information) conditions. After being sent a demographic and attitudinal questionnaire, 3,000 persons responded and were randomized for the study.

The information booklet was designed to address perceived barriers to the screening exam and increase the reader's positive expectations, and thereby improve attendance. It addressed potential barriers to the test, possible coping strategies, and alternative views of the screening process. It provided a review of the benefits of screening, directed attention to the positive emotional impact of the process, and provided normative social information by featuring a range of people who had accepted the screening invitation. The format of the booklet was conversational narratives consisting of short paragraphs to stimulate reading. It presented questions and answers in the form of conversations between friends and family members in a cartoon-strip fashion. Each conversation addressed a particular barrier to screening. Quotations from already-screened participants were included. All study participants were sent appointments for their screening and were asked to suggest another appointment time if the one offered was not convenient. Attendance any time over the following three months was included in the study data.

Study variables included attitudes toward screening, self-efficacy for seeking social support, adherence to social norms, anticipated affective reactions, anxiety, and screening intention. The sample was 50 percent male with a mean age of 60.4 years. It was found at the end of the study that attendance was significantly higher in the intervention group than the control group (53.5% vs. 49.9%), and attendance was higher among males in both groups combined (55% vs. 49%). The intervention was as effective in lower socioeconomic groups, which had been a concern of the researchers. The overall results of the study indicated that the intervention successfully modified all of the targeted variables. Compared with the control group, members of the intervention group had less negative attitudes toward screening, had higher self-efficacy for seeking social support, and anticipated feeling better if they went through with the test, whatever the result.

HIV/AIDS

Approximately 1.5 million people in the United States are infected with human immunodeficiency virus (HIV), which causes acquired immunodeficiency syndrome (AIDS) (Hall et al., 2008). People with AIDS often turn to their families of origin for support, and the caregiving role can be extremely stressful. The stigma of AIDS and the fear of contagion, the financial burden, and the emotional trauma of losing a loved one can often lead to alienation, social isolation, shame, and secrecy on the part of the family.

With advances in medicine during the last twenty years, HIV-positive status has evolved from a death sentence into a controllable medical condition. Still, while HIV-positive persons are living longer, the prevalence of infection in the United States continues to rise. The mental health issues that can arise from peoples' experiences with HIV-positive status are significant. Since the late 1980s, research has focused on enhancing the effectiveness of psychoeducation for treatment and prevention of HIV/AIDS through the creation of groups that target specific populations and common experiences.

The caregivers of persons with HIV/AIDS typically experience anticipatory grief, but the duration of the illness, its stigma, and the multiple losses associated with the disease (due to the loved one's continually changing physical appearance, mental acuity, and experience of many illnesses) often impede their ability to engage effectively in the grief process (Walker et al., 1994). A summary of the caregiver's needs with regard to grieving is provided in exhibit 13.2. Fortunately, the programs described in this chapter address these caregiver needs.

Exhibit 13.2:   Anticipatory grief needs of the caregivers of persons with HIV/AIDS

Medical and resource information
Information about the normalcy of their and their loved one's feelings
Opportunities to express the full range of emotions
Assistance with identifying emotions associated with losses
Support through feelings of disenfranchisement (no socially sanctioned place to mourn losses)
Complete unfinished business with the dying person
Open family communication (as much as possible)
Participation in the loved one's treatment plan
Acceptance of one's own needs and possible new roles following the death of the loved one
The ability and opportunity to say good-bye

The HIV/AIDS Caregiver Support Group

HIV/AIDS professionals recognize the need to provide support services to caregivers of this client population. Toward this end, researchers in Texas developed and evaluated an eight-week caregiver psychoeducational program using a quasi-experimental design (Pomeroy, Rubin, & Walker, 1995). Outcome variables included perceived stress, anxiety, depression, social support, and stigma related to the caregiver role. Participants for the program were drawn from referrals to an AIDS service agency in Austin. Three experimental and one quasi-experimental groups were used in the study with eight, eleven, ten, and six members, respectively. Thirty-three family members, with an average age of thirty-one years, completed the study. Measures were taken at pretest, posttest, and two months following (see exhibit 13.3).

Exhibit 13.3:   The HIV/AIDS caregiver support group schedule

Session 1: discuss the course of the illness, including behavior and psychological changes; discuss stigma; telephone one other group member during the week for support

Session 2: discuss infections and medical treatments; discuss anger; find and practice a new outlet for anger

Session 3: discuss resources, referrals, and stresses; engage in stress-reduction activities

Session 4: discuss hospitalization and the medical system; discuss feelings of powerlessness and helplessness; engage in exercises to feel more in control of life situations

Session 5: discuss respite and home health care; discuss fears and uncertainties; write a worry list and worry only at specified times

Session 6: discuss medical and nutritional needs; discuss social isolation and support systems; engage in one leisurely activity

Session 7: discuss financial issues; discuss anticipatory grief; talk or read about living wills

Session 8: discuss plans for the future; discuss termination issues; consider monthly follow-up meetings

---

The eight weekly ninety-minute sessions were led by licensed social workers. The first part of each session (thirty minutes) featured a presentation and discussion of an educational topic relevant to the family members' concerns, and the second part focused on supportive group processes using a task-centered approach. The educational component included information about the medical aspects of HIV/AIDS, home health care, local agencies providing relevant services, the medical system, financial concerns, and the grieving process. The support component of the group focused on managing stigma, dealing with feelings of anger toward the person with AIDS, society and the medical system, coping with stress, overcoming anxieties and fears that arise because of uncertainties associated with the illness, the importance of a supportive network of friends and professionals, and coping with the anticipatory grief that often accompanies the diagnosis.

Results were statistically significant for stress, stigma, depression, and anxiety, with the most powerful effect on depression. Only the variable of social support showed no change over time, possibly because the participants had already formed effective networks. All of the positive effects persisted at the two-month follow-up. The authors stressed that the task-centered model is compatible with psychoeducation in that it focuses on practical problems of daily living.

AIDS Psychoeducation for Jail Inmates

The growth rate for HIV/AIDS among incarcerated people is nearly six times the rate of the United States population, but programs addressing the topic have been slow to develop. A group of researchers concerned about this issue implemented and evaluated a ten-session psychoeducational group intervention for male inmates in a large southwestern jail facility (Pomeroy, Kiam, & Green, 2000). They believed that combining emotional support and education would help inmates feel less emotionally distressed in general and better able to process the HIV/AIDS information they received. The program shares some of the organizing principles described in the previous study.

The county jail inmates participating in the program were nonviolent offenders who responded to the open invitation of a social worker. The men were screened by one of the co-facilitators. Each group was capped at twelve participants; three experimental groups were filled to capacity, for a total of thirty-six participants, although only twenty-five inmates completed the program due to transfers. Twenty-eight men composed a control group that received no psychoeducation. In order to accommodate the anticipated high turnover rate in the jail, the ten-session program was offered twice weekly for ninety minutes. A facilitator with a master's degree in social work led the groups with the assistance of two graduate social work students.

The intervention consisted of three components: HIV education, support with general emotional concerns, and a task-oriented component for skill building. The task component included homework assignments so that the participants could address their emotional concerns between meetings. The first part of each session lasted forty-five minutes and consisted of a presentation and discussion of an educational topic related to HIV/AIDS, as well as a discussion of the homework assignment from the previous session. The second part of the session focused on supportive group processes using cognitive-behavioral and task-centered techniques. Some of these topics included how to cope with depression and anxiety, how to reduce stress, the importance of social support, self-esteem, anger management, and coping skills. An outline of each week's agenda appears in exhibit 13.4.

Exhibit 13.4: *AIDS psychoeducational group for inmates schedule*

Session 1: overview of HIV/AIDS (with the "I am" exercise)
Session 2: opportunistic infections (automatic thoughts exercise)
Session 3: preventing the transmission of HIV (changing negative thoughts)
Session 4: safer sex practices; healthy versus unhealthy relationships (stress-reduction exercise)
Session 5: safer sex continued (stress-reduction exercise)
Session 6: drug use and HIV (anger management)
Session 7: staying healthy (anger management)
Session 8: financial issues; building confidence (goal-setting exercise)
Session 9: planning for the future; recognizing personal resources (strengths exercise)
Session 10: termination (moving out and moving on)

The dependent variables in this study were anxiety, depression, trauma symptoms, and knowledge of HIV/AIDS. Based on the pretest and posttest data, statistically significant differences between the groups were observed in all four variables. The researchers concluded that expanded use of this program could help social service professionals reach large numbers of persons who do not have ready access to such services and provide them with opportunities to process their feelings and change their behaviors while educating them on a topic of great relevance to their physical well-being.

The Making Positive Changes Program

As the number of persons with HIV has grown, parents with the virus face challenges in organizing their child-rearing practices. The four-session Making Positive Changes Program (MPCP) was developed to promote well-being in families with HIV-positive parents (Mason & Vazquez, 2007). The three objectives of the group were to increase participants' knowledge about the impact of HIV on families, increase access to resources and social support, and provide opportunities to learn and practice skills that contribute to family well-being. The major topics covered fall into the two broad categories of parenting and self-care, with two sessions devoted to each of these topics (see exhibit 13.5). Each session is three hours in length.

Exhibit 13.5:   The Making Positive Changes Program

Parenting (two sessions): setting appropriate expectations for children; developing rules and family communication; helping teens learn to handle peer pressure; deciding when and how to disclose HIV status

Self-care (two sessions): goals for personal health and well-being; financial goals; employment, benefits, and legal rights

---

Group participants are recruited through flyers posted at area agencies serving persons with HIV. All participants in the original Chicago program were HIV-positive parents of young children, and the majority were African American females. Two experienced social workers co-facilitated the sessions. Additionally, two nonprofessional HIV-positive peer facilitators, referred by area professionals, participated in the program. They facilitated group discussions and turned out to be essential in the recruiting process. Meetings were held at a university student union, both for convenience and also as a means of insuring participant anonymity.

The first half of each MPCP session is focused on the presentation of a topic for the day, sometimes utilizing guest presenters. The second half consists of discussion of topics of interest to the participants (they are invited to make suggestions throughout the program) along with lunch. Each participant is encouraged to set one related personal goal for the following week. Group sessions are open, with an average of nine people attending each group.

At the end of the program, participants complete evaluation forms designed by the researchers. Feedback is uniformly positive, with participants noting what they learned from the group and not suggesting any major changes to the group design. The results of this study further suggest that specifying psychoeducational groups for HIV-positive persons based on common experiences—in this case parenthood—may increase the potential effectiveness of the intervention. The intervention also points to the benefit of having HIV-positive peer facilitators working in conjunction with professionals.

Physical Disabilities

The next three program examples illustrate the utility of psychoeducation for persons with physical disabilities rather than illnesses.

The Wellness Workshop for Women with Disabilities

Psychoeducation researchers sometimes assert that certain types of programs may be most beneficial to women. For example, some feminist theorists propose that health promotion groups conducted exclusively for women can break down gender-related feelings of social isolation by allowing participants to freely share common experiences, connect with one another, learn about their uniqueness as women, and process topics that may be difficult to address in mixed groups. With these assumptions in mind, researchers at the Baylor College of Medicine in Houston developed a weekly seven-session program for improving the physical, psychological, and social health status of women with a range of physical disabilities (Hughes, Nosek, Howland, Groff, & Mullen, 2003). Called the Wellness Workshop for Women with Disabilities, the program was also intended to raise the participants' levels of self-efficacy for health-promoting behaviors. The researchers hypothesized that the workshop would result in improved scores on measures of self-efficacy, health status, social support, autonomy, and coping.

Persons sought for this program were to be eighteen years of age with a self-reported physical disability that resulted in limitations to their mobility or self-care. The women who participated in the program responded to a mailed written announcement sent through the researchers' access to a local database. Sixteen women eventually completed the study, representing a range of disabilities, including joint and connective tissue diseases, neuromuscular disorders, cerebral palsy, amputation, and post-polio conditions. Pretest measures were taken to gauge levels of self-efficacy, health status, social support, autonomy preferences, and coping styles.

The topics included in the workshop are outlined in exhibit 13.6. Two sections of the seven-week program were held on different days to accommodate the women's scheduling needs. Two women with physical disabilities (not among those who joined the program) were trained to serve as facilitators. Group activities included action planning (setting weekly goals and stating one's level of confidence in achieving them) and problem solving (reporting on successes or failures in meeting goals and generating new plans of action). The women were encouraged to share disability and health-related experiences in order to maximize their mutual connection. A program handbook included handouts, charts, resources, and references.

Exhibit 13.6:   The Wellness Workshop for Women with Disabilities schedule

Session 1: orientation; introduction to the buddy system, the concept of wellness, and the action-planning format

Session 2: teaching and applying cognitive-behavioral skills; describing the benefits, strategies, and guidelines for physical activity

Session 3: developing an understanding of emotional wellness; providing facts about depression and its prevention and management; introducing the concept of self-esteem from a feminist perspective

Session 4: offering tips for effective communication and assertive behavior; introducing the concept of the participating patient; discussing personal rights and safety planning

Session 5: information and strategies for healthy sleep and rest; discussion of healthy eating and diet strategies; sharing resources for diet and nutrition

Session 6: information related to the well-woman examination in the context of disability; teaching facts and sharing resources related to problem behaviors

Session 7: discussing sexual awareness and sexual rights in the context of disability; introducing relaxation scripts related to body image and appreciation; processing workshop experience and sharing plans for maintaining health-behavior changes

At the end of the programs, significant changes were noted in the participants' self-efficacy for diet, medical decision making, social support (the availability of others with whom to relax), physical functioning, perceived role limitations due to physical problems, and vitality. Further, all of the women reported high levels of satisfaction with the experience. The results confirm the effectiveness of group interventions for improving the health and well-being of women with chronic illnesses and other physical disabilities. The results further indicated that in the area of health promotion for persons with physical disabilities, women are willing to participate in workshops of this type, and peers can effectively serve as facilitators.

Traumatic Brain Injury

Examinations of the patient–health care provider relationship have traditionally been oriented around the two models of shared decision making and patient-centered medicine (Pegg et al., 2005). In general, providing patients with enhanced information to increase their sense of cognitive control is said to produce better health outcomes. The interpersonal manner in which information is conveyed also has an impact on patient outcomes.

A group of researchers at a veteran's hospital were interested in evaluating the effects on traumatic brain injury (TBI) patients of personalized information about their injuries, acute care treatment, and rehabilitation progress (Pegg et al., 2005). This study was the first to explore the effectiveness of an informational intervention for a TBI population designed to enhance patient perception of involvement in care and to assess the role of patient–health care provider interactions. Twenty-eight patients from a TBI unit of a Veterans Affairs medical center were randomly assigned to one of two information intervention groups. The experimental patients received detailed, personally tailored intervention about their condition and the treatments that were being administered. A control group was provided with only general information about TBI and the acute and long-term stages of treatment. Twenty-five men and three women participated in the study, with injuries due to motor vehicle accidents, falls, assaults, and stroke. Their rehabilitation programs included both cognitive and speech therapy.

The researchers hypothesized that the experimental patients would experience better outcomes regarding their effort in treatment, their progress, and their treatment satisfaction. Further, because one of the intended effects of the experiment was an increase in patients' sense of empowerment and participation in decision making, it was expected that staff would see these patients as more interpersonally active in their rehabilitation. That is, the best patient outcomes would occur when the relationship between patients and health care providers approached a complimentary dimension.

All of the intervention meetings consisted of structured discussions in which patients were encouraged to seek information of interest to them. No written materials were provided. The general information sessions provided to the control group were limited to the topics of brain injury, rehabilitation, and the rehabilitation process, through the use of videotapes.

The personal information intervention consisted of three sixty-minute meetings, scheduled at intervals that were consistent with the stages of the patient's rehabilitation. All interventions were provided by one of two members of the hospital rehabilitation team. The first session occurred after the first three days of the patient's program and presented an opportunity to share information with the patient about his or her condition and treatment plan. Patients had an opportunity to review their records and see how the interventions were organized into a systematic sequence. The second intervention was provided at the midpoint of the patient's intervention, typically after five weeks of therapy, and focused the patient's progress. The patient's gains received emphasis, based on a review of treatment plan reports and progress notes from individual therapists. The third and final intervention was delivered in the days before discharge and was timed to occur at the completion of therapies and final physical testing. It featured a progress update of the cognitive and speech therapies, a discussion of lingering deficits and how they may affect the patient, and information about the client's ongoing treatment plan.

At the end of the study, it was found that patients who were provided with the personalized information exerted greater effort in their subsequent therapies that required physical activity. Their effort ratings in speech therapy, however, were unchanged. The researchers speculate that this may be because speech therapy requires participation with a directive therapist. Patients in the experimental group also made greater strides in achieving overall functional independence, especially in the area of cognitive functioning. The program had the largest positive impact on patient reports of satisfaction with their rehabilitation treatment, which itself was positively associated with therapist ratings of patient effort in therapy. The authors concluded that personalized psychoeducation provided along with physical rehabilitation has significantly positive effects on patients and contributes to a better experience in treatment and an improved quality of life.

Pediatric Sickle-Cell Disease

Sickle-cell disease (SCD) is the most prevalent genetic disorder in the world, occurring in 1 of every 400 to 500 African American births and in 1 of every 1,000 to 14,000 Latino births (Kaslow et al., 2000). The disorder is characterized by chronic tissue damage related to the blockage of blood flow produced by abnormally shaped red cells. Commonly reported health problems include infections, acute chest syndrome, lung disease, renal dysfunction or failure, retinopathy or retinal detachment, leg ulcers, gallstones, severe fatigue, retarded growth, delayed puberty, jaundice, and organ damage. Youths with the disease develop behavior problems, cognitive deficits, social difficulties, and maladaptive coping styles.

Family interventions are the treatment of choice for pediatric SCD. Children's health care utilization is attributable to the role of caregivers, and family therapies have shown to be effective in treating chronic childhood illness. The more positive outcomes are found in families with significant knowledge about the disease, better child psychological adjustment, and positive family and friend support. Pediatric patients report less anxiety and better psychological adjustment when they are provided with information about their upcoming medical procedures, and such knowledge leads to better health practices, increased treatment compliance, and improved perceptions of illness control.

For these reasons, a group of researchers developed a six-week family psychoeducation intervention to enhance disease knowledge and improve the psychological and social functioning of youths with SCD and their primary caregivers (Kaslow et al., 2000). Thirty-nine seven- to sixteen-year-old males (fifteen) and females (twenty-four) with SCD and their families were randomly assigned to participate in either the experimental program or a treatment-as-usual condition. All of the youths were receiving medical treatment at a large university hospital serving predominantly low-income African American patients. The intervention staff, all of whom worked at the facility, comprised eight supervised undergraduate and graduate students in psychology, and all but one was African American. The sessions lasted for one hour, and participants were paid ten dollars per session for their participation. Although all family members were encouraged to participate with a child, most families included only a female caregiver and child. Baseline child measures included disease knowledge, psychological adjustment, family and social functioning and support, and process measures (views about the intervention). Caregiver measures included the same variables.

The six-session family psychoeducational intervention was highly structured. The first two sessions addressed the primary stressor of sickle-cell disease. Sessions 3 through 6 were focused on enhancing coping processes for managing the stressor, which were expected to be associated with improved adjustment. The patient's goals and weekly activities were reviewed at each session. Meetings included an educational presentation, activities (role-plays and games), and the assignment of homework. Materials used included culturally relevant audiovisual aids and handouts, behavior charts, and a workbook for each family member. Details of the six sessions are given in exhibit 13.7.

Exhibit 13.7:   The pediatric sickle-cell anemia support group schedule

Session 1: goals of the intervention; introduction to the stress-coping-adjustment model; factual information about SCD

Session 2: preventive health care strategies (including recognizing warning signs of disease-related complications and determining steps to follow when symptoms occur); identifying strategies to decrease disease-related complications

Session 3: age-appropriate pain-management techniques (relaxation, guided imagery); parents helped to develop active problem-solving strategies

Session 4: active listening techniques; adaptive ways of explaining the causes of positive and negative events; expressing feelings more directly

Session 5: interpersonal relationships; the association between positive family relationships, peer relationships, and child's effective coping; appropriate separation-individual processes and the value of social support

Session 6: review of program topics; program evaluation; troubleshooting for possible problem areas; referrals for ongoing care and support

---

The study findings revealed that the family intervention yielded more improvements in child and primary caregiver disease knowledge than did treatment as usual, and the children maintained this disease knowledge at six-month follow-up. No other finding achieved statistical significance, although the researchers suggested that psychosocial improvements not readily evident from the qualitative measures also occurred. These improvements included initiatives to seek additional information about SCD, improved communication between parent and child, an increase in child autonomy, improved relationships with medical providers, more consistent school attendance, better coping with the disease, improved perceptions of quality of life, and more frequent utilization of resources and social support.

Somatization

Somatization disorders are those in which persons experience their emotional problems physically. The disorders are characterized by unexplained physical symptoms or bodily preoccupations. Such persons tend to have long, complicated medical histories that lack systematic presentations. Their experience of physical symptoms is *not* under their voluntary control but is linked to unconscious psychological factors. Persons with these disorders are challenging to health care providers because in spite of the absence of diagnosable health problems, they engage in excessive medical help-seeking behavior. The person rarely goes one year without seeking medical attention. It is estimated that 5 to 10 percent of general practice medical patients have somatization disorders, and most are women. They experience chronic pain and vague physical complaints (usually including gastrointestinal, sexual, or neurological symptoms) and are reluctant to consider referrals to mental health providers. The somatization disorders are associated with anxiety, depression, and significant impairment in functioning. In an effort to reduce the prevalence of this disorder, some health care professionals have developed education groups that teach such persons to more rationally monitor their health status.

The Wellness Group

The Wellness Group is a six-week multifamily group for distressed women who are high utilizers of health care services (McDaniel & Speice, 2001). The program is co-led by a family therapist and family physician or nurse practitioner and is offered on a rotating cycle so that patients and family members can join at any time and stay until they complete the six sessions. Local physicians refer participants to the group, and 75 percent of those who attend are women. They often come alone, demonstrating their lack of family support. Classes are held in the evenings and include dinner. The ninety-minute weekly format includes a fifteen-minute medically focused discussion led by the physician or nurse practitioner, thirty minutes of relaxation and stress-reduction activities, and forty-five minutes of discussion focused on a topic related to having a chronic health condition.

Discussion topics range from communicating with physicians and dealing with stress and how it affects health to learning how to maintain a consistent health care regimen. Educational videos on depression, anxiety, panic, and other mental illness are included in the intervention. Outcomes of the group have been positive, according to posttest surveys provided to participants. One significant finding in support of the group is that persons who attend admit that they would have been far less likely to accept a referral to psychotherapy without the intervention. Still, many of the participants continue to seek biological explanations for their distress after the group ends.

It's Not All in Your Head

In an effort to promote self-psychoeducation for somatization issues, Asmundson and Taylor (2005) wrote the book *It's Not All in Your Head: How Worrying about Your Health Could Be Making You Sick—And What You Can Do about It*. This book presents a fourteen-week self-help program for people who have the awareness, or the suspicion, that they suffer from health anxiety. Organized into three sections—understanding health anxiety (four chapters), breaking the health anxiety cycle (three chapters), and maintaining gains (three chapters)—the book emulates the intervention processes of psychoeducation, skills training, and relapse prevention. Chapters include the topics outlined in exhibit 13.8.

Exhibit 13.8:   *The* It's Not All in Your Head *self-help program*

Section 1: Understanding health anxiety

Introduction to the health anxiety cycle
Bodily noise, or those unwanted physical sensations
Links between health anxiety and co-occurring anxiety disorders
Links between health anxiety and mood disorders

Section 2: Breaking the health anxiety cycle

How to relax: tense-release, release-only, and rapid relaxation exercises (three sessions)
Behaviors that may exacerbate stress levels and contribute to
  health anxiety, including retraining breathing patterns, enhancing
  problem-solving skills, and managing time more effectively (four
  sessions)
Cognitive distortions related to attending to body noise
The evidence for and against the accuracy of disease-related thoughts
  and challenging these anxiety-producing cognitions (two sessions)
How certain behaviors can affect the health anxiety cycle (two sessions)
Eliminating anxiety-feeding behaviors and confronting feared sensations and situations through exposure (two sessions)

Section 3: Maintaining your gains

Relationships with primary care physicians
Enlisting the help of friends in breaking the health anxiety cycle
Developing a personalized health anxiety relapse-prevention program

---

The book includes worksheets for carrying out the exercises described, as well as case vignettes that illustrate types of illness situations and responses. Although a publication of this type is not amenable to systematic effectiveness evaluation, it does represent an interesting type of self-guided psychoeducation.

Summary

The programs described in this chapter affirm the effectiveness of psychoeducation as an adjunct to the medical treatment of chronic physical conditions and illnesses. It appears that specific targeting of common concerns among afflicted persons improves the effectiveness of these groups in alleviating mental health issues. Groups that include nonprofessional peer facilitators are also effective, as members can identify with facilitators who share their experiences. Cognitive-behavioral intervention and task-centered homework assignments are utilized in many of these programs. These kinds of interventions seem especially appropriate for psychoeducation, given their proven effectiveness for alleviating mental health symptoms within a short time period. The outcomes of several of the studies noted in this chapter point to the importance of balancing therapeutic and educational aspects of treatment in order to improve psychological well-being while enhancing positive health behaviors.

Chapter 14

Bereavement

This ending chapter of the book will cover an endings topic. *Bereavement* is the state of having lost a close friend or relative to death. It is a universal experience, a process that affects more people than any other subject in this book. Ten million people are bereaved each year in the United States (Hansson & Stroebe, 2007). Five percent of children lose one or both parents before age fifteen, and by age sixty-five more than half of women have been widowed at least once. Although bereavement is a normal process, psychoeducation can help survivors to make constructive life adjustments.

Grief refers to the psychological and physiological responses to bereavement. These responses may include sleep disruption, loss of appetite, sadness, guilt, anger, anxiety, and despair. *Mourning* refers to the behavioral and social manifestations of grief. Grief is healthy, and in fact minimal or absent grief is considered unhealthy for one's overall social functioning. The work of acute grief is letting go; it tends to follow a predictable pattern and usually ends by two years (or less) after the loss (see exhibit 14.1).

Exhibit 14.1: The stages of grief

Denial is experienced as numbness, avoidance, isolation, or direct denial of the event and its implications. The loss does not seem real.

Anger may be directed at the deceased person or toward significant others. Feeling helpless, the mourner wants to take the negative feelings out on something or someone else or to express anger in familiar ways.

Bargaining is the mourner's process of trying to get back what was lost. Common thoughts include "If only I had just . . ."; "I wish we could have . . ."; and "Maybe if I do this . . ." In the case of a lost relationship, the mourner might bargain with the other person in an effort to get them back: "If I change my behavior, will you come back?"

Depression is a time of sadness that follows denial, anger, and bargaining when the mourner recognizes the reality of the loss and its implications. It may include crying, withdrawal, or other expressions of sadness.

> *Acceptance* is the stage at which a mourner begins to reorganize his or her thinking to incorporate the loss and move on with life. The sadness becomes a part of the mourner but does not keep him or her from functioning normally most of the time. The intensity of the sadness diminishes but never entirely goes away.
>
> *(Kubler-Ross, 1997)*

There are positive emotions associated with grieving, although these may not be evident in the beginning. They include enjoyment in recalling happy times, taking pride in honoring the deceased person, feelings of warmth in recalling closeness, and relief from the burden or pain associated with the deceased person's final days.

Uncomplicated, or normal, bereavement is not associated with enduring negative consequences for most people. Still, psychoeducation may help individuals and families make positive life adjustments during the grief and mourning process by providing them with information and access to supportive others. Further, interventions for bereaved persons at risk for ongoing depression help to prevent or reduce the more serious symptoms.

The Grief Process

Natural grief takes two forms: *primary grief,* which persists for up to several months, and *abiding grief,* which is longer-term. In the former phase there is shock, preoccupation with thoughts and memories of the deceased, withdrawal, and the experience of painful emotions. In the latter phase the person experiences acceptance, less of a preoccupation with related thoughts and memories, greater engagement with life activities, more positive emotions, and a sense of personal growth. When grief works, primary grief evolves into abiding grief. The symptoms of grief decrease over time, although some symptoms may remain fairly intense after one year. Caregivers report high levels of depression prior to and two months following the death, but at seven months after the death the symptoms tend to subside (Underwood, 2004). The perception of being unprepared for the death puts a person at risk for possible difficulties in eventually accepting the loss and may be an indicator of complicated bereavement.

Self-blame and blame of the deceased play roles in post-loss adjustment. Both are predictive of a maladaptive adjustment. The extent to which the person uses continuing interpersonal bonds may be more important to one's adjustment than the type of emotions expressed openly. That is, the outward expression of distress may not be a critical aspect of adjustment following bereavement. Persons seem to make sense of their loss by seeking to understand the event in terms of their existing worldviews.

Complicated grief refers to situations in which a person's painful emotions are so long lasting and severe that he or she has trouble accepting the death over time and resuming his or her own life. It is characterized by preoccupation with the person who died, a yearning for contact with the deceased, disbelief and an inability to emotionally comprehend the death, avoidance of reminders of the person who died, and feelings of anger, bitterness, and envy. Complicated grief occurs among 10 to 20 percent of bereaved persons (APA, 2000).

There is clearly an overlap between the symptoms of bereavement and major depression. The latter is considered abnormal after a grieving period of approximately two months and represents one kind of complicated bereavement. Bereavement-related depression occurs among 25 percent of bereaved persons two to seven months after the loss, 15 percent at thirteen months, and 10 to 15 percent at two years (Underwood, 2004). Forty-seven percent of widowed persons become depressed during the first year, and during that time there is an increased risk of medical illness, death, and suicide.

Symptoms that are not characteristic of normal grief, and that may be indicative of a depressive disorder, include the following:

> Guilt about things other than actions taken or not taken by the survivor
>
> Thoughts of death other than the survivor feeling that he or she would be better off dead or should have died with the deceased person
>
> Preoccupation with worthlessness
>
> Marked psychomotor retardation
>
> Prolonged and marked functional impairment
>
> Hallucinatory experiences other than thinking that he or she hears the voice of, or transiently sees images of, the deceased person (APA, 2000)

The goals of complicated-grief intervention, which should include therapeutic strategies in addition to psychoeducation, are acceptance of the death, resumption of personal goal setting, reduction of painful feelings through the emotional processing of the loss, social re-engagement, and the development of new coping skills.

Assessing Bereavement

Many agencies that offer services related to death and dying issues assess persons for their level of risk for bereavement complications. As one example, risk can be identified at one of three levels: low, moderate, or high (L. Barker, Bon Secours Hospice social worker, personal communication, July 2009; see exhibit 14.2). The implications of this assessment for intervention will be discussed later.

Exhibit 14.2:   Three levels of risk in bereavement

Low: normal grief, good support availability, a capacity for open expression of feelings
Moderate: grief is normal but severe; the person experiences depression, somatic distress, low support, history of difficulty with loss, unresolved conflict with the deceased
High: history of mental illness, suicidal ideation, depression, substance abuse, excessive guilt or anger, multiple losses, unresolved losses, other life crises

---

Families and Bereavement

When one family member dies, the entire system is affected and the family system may be a source of support or stress. The Bowen (1978) family systems and structural theories, detailed in chapter 3, provide useful frameworks for family assessment.

Bowen's (1978) family systems theory asserts that no life event stirs more emotionally directed thinking in the individual, and more emotional reactivity in those around him or her, than death. The family experiences an emotional shock wave, a network of underground aftershocks that can occur anywhere in the extended family system in the months following the death. Open (communicative) families experience less disruption and cope more effectively with the loss. In more differentiated families, members realize that grief affects each person differently and they can support one another to allow each to grieve in his or her own way. Emotional cutoff can lead to pathological grieving if extended family members are not available during a loss.

In family systems theory the processes that family members use to cope with grief can be functional or dysfunctional. To decrease vulnerability to triangulation, interpersonal boundaries need to be flexible enough to allow support from outside the family. Differential grief is a family emotional systems concept with relevance to this point (Gilbert, 1996). It involves each person's construction of meaning about the death. The more central the lost relationship was to one's own life, the greater the sense of loss. The levels of differentiation that members share may contribute to differences among family members' ability to grieve. Lower levels of differentiation move members toward togetherness, which can help relieve anxiety. Extreme fusion, however, may lead to cutoff as a means to deal with the discomfort of intense closeness.

Strategies for resolving grief within the Bowen family systems context include recognizing the loss, acknowledging the unique grief experienced by each member, and reinvesting all members into the "new" family. Intervention may include the use of grief rituals (including funerals) to foster openness in the family so each member can share his or her own perception of the loss. The practitioner helps the family form new alliances that promote differentiation and healthy functioning between and among family members.

In structural theory, the loss of a family member through death necessitates a structural adaptation. The death may initiate changes in the family's executive authority, locus of power (especially as minors may find themselves thrust into positions of power), and intra-family alliances. These structural changes may or may not be adaptive. A practitioner must assess the family subsystems (which may become cross-generational), boundaries (permeable or impermeable), and roles (flexible or rigid). The practitioner needs to assess what roles the deceased person occupied prior to death and how well the family will be able to reorganize its subsystems to accommodate them. Intervention with the structural approach includes helping the family construct or maintain healthy or appropriate subsystems, alliances, and boundaries after the death of a family member.

Several studies have explored the impact of bereavement on family systems. One study focused on children and surviving parents within forty-one families who had recently suffered the loss of a parent, either suddenly or through long-term illness (Saldinger, Cain, Kalter, & Lohnes, 1999). The authors hoped to determine the effects of anticipatory death on the postmortem adjustment of surviving children. As hypothesized, anticipated death was associated with a more difficult adjustment period in children, though this outcome was not true for adults. Children interpreted and responded to terminal illness in a variety of ways. Some of them realized that loss is imminent and could begin adapting to it, whereas others found the illness merely frightening. Another research group used qualitative accounts of the surviving parent to understand the process of a child's retaining an attachment to a dying parent both before and after death (Saldinger, Cain, Porterfield, & Lohnes, 2004). They interviewed fifty-eight families and found that children benefited from maintaining these connections, but they struggled with this process after death. Encouraging children to stay connected to the parent, educating the child about possible emotional and physical changes in the parent related to illness, and encouraging the dying parent to leave the child a tangible legacy all contributed positively to this attachment process. The authors warned against trying to construct a well-orchestrated good-bye in a patient's last moments, however, and instead encouraged trying to achieve finality at an earlier time.

Another author has outlined stages in the counseling process of parentally bereaved children with a surviving parent or other close relative (Warmbrod, 1986). Stressing the value of working with the surviving family as a unit, the author explains that each family member, because of differences in age, roles, and relationships to the deceased, will grieve differently. The author suggests dividing family counseling into three stages: first focusing on the death and funeral, then on the past and memories, and finally on the future and continued ways to cope. This structure speaks to the need to honor the grieving process in a supportive way, something that can be difficult for surviving parents who are struggling with grief as well as the desire to protect children from additional sadness. Working through grief together in a supportive, therapeutic environment can allow each family member opportunities to safely confront feelings of loss.

This chapter has considered the normal and abnormal grief processes that follow bereavement and the family dynamics that can influence those processes. All of this information should be included in psychoeducation so that the survivor's experience can be normalized.

Psychoeducation and Bereavement

Bereavement interventions can be conceptualized as primary, secondary, and tertiary in nature (see exhibit 14.3). Psychoeducation may be appropriate for persons targeted for primary and secondary prevention, but tertiary prevention activities require additional therapeutic interventions, because those persons are experiencing a significant emotional disorder.

Exhibit 14.3:   *Three levels of prevention in grief management*

Primary: support services for persons experiencing normal bereavement

Secondary: interventions for people who are at risk for complications of bereavement (e.g., those who have dealt with a suicide or homicide)

Tertiary: interventions for people who are experiencing bereavement-related complications

---

A literature review by Zisook and Shuchter (2001) summarizes the benefits of psychoeducation for persons experiencing bereavement (see exhibit 14.4). Psychoeducation services typically provide information about grief and opportunities for expressing and understanding feelings, remembering and commemorating the death, and facilitating open family communication. In all grief interventions the practitioner should

Offer direct expressions of sympathy,

Acknowledge that he or she does not know exactly what the bereaved person is going through,

Refer to the deceased person by name,

Inquire about and refer to the circumstances of the death, and

Encourage expressions of feeling.

Exhibit 14.4:   Benefits of psychoeducation for bereaved persons

Access to other people who understand (catharsis)
Discovery of the universality of one's experience (uniqueness of
  one's loss is respected)
Celebration or honoring of the person's life
Information about social security, other benefits
Social and recreational activities may help to restructure one's life
Social-skills exercise
Beginning to create a new identity
(Zisook & Shuchter, 2001)

The practitioner should *not* be casual or passive, imply that the death was for
the best, convey to the bereaved person that he or she is strong and will get
over it, or avoid discussion about the person who has died. These sorts of
responses indicate a lack of empathy with the grieving person's experiences.

Margaret Underwood (2004) has conducted a literature review and
developed a set of principles for bereavement support groups. She recom-
mends that groups include the goals listed in exhibit 14.5.

Exhibit 14.5:   Goals for bereavement support groups

Provide members with safety and support, feelings that are often
  damaged by loss events
Educate about the processes of grief
Normalize and validate reactions to the loss event and subsequent
  life changes
Anticipate and prepare members for future challenges related to the
  loss
Facilitate problem solving related to the loss experience

Closed groups are more effective than open groups, even though they
are not always practical. Constantly admitting new members can compro-
mise the development of cohesiveness, and the presence of new members
may prevent some emotionally challenging material from emerging. Groups
should also be time-limited, as participants usually have a limited amount of
emotional and physical energy to invest in such an experience. Along the
same lines, sessions should be limited to one to two hours in order to provide an optimal time to process emotional material.

To help them understand where individuals are in the grieving process,
group leaders should collect information about prospective members prior
to their participation. The topic areas listed in exhibit 14.6 should be
explored in a pre-group assessment interview.

Exhibit 14.6:   Issues for pre-group assessment with bereaved persons
Circumstances of the loss
Relationship history with the deceased person
Life since the loss (including any concurrent stressors)
Actual and potential support systems
The person's loss history (how he or she has managed losses in the past)

With general principles of support-group development considered, the chapter turns to reviews of several examples of such programs. The reviews begin with descriptions of programs available to adults and follow with programs focused on children and adolescents. The effects of early loss on children have been studied extensively, but interventions designed to address childhood grief are documented less often.

For Adults

Hospice bereavement services   Like most hospice programs, Bon Secours Hospice includes bereavement services (L. Barker, Bon Secours Hospice social worker, personal communication, July 10, 2009). In helping survivors through this process, staff follow Kubler-Ross's (1997) five-stage death and dying model (see exhibit 14.1). Part of the intervention is psychoeducational in nature.

When a client and family are enrolled in the hospice program, a pre-bereavement assessment is done to determine what the survivor's needs will likely be following the death of the loved one. The client is placed into one of the three risk categories described in exhibit 14.2. Bereavement services begin at the death of the patient and continue for thirteen months. The assigned bereavement counselor attends the memorial service and offers to meet with the person or family to begin counseling services at their convenience. Additionally, a volunteer (who receives twenty hours of training from the agency) calls the survivor on the day of the death and remains available throughout the bereavement period to provide respite care and friendly listening. The bereavement counselor, at a minimum, sends information to the client at one, three, nine, and twelve months after the death. The first of these mailings is a sizeable bereavement packet that includes information about the grieving process and the agency's services.

The psychoeducational portion of the bereavement services consists of a variety of regularly scheduled support groups to which all survivors are invited. The purposes of the groups are to provide members with a forum to learn about the grief process, to process their grief experiences, and to

learn about practical matters related to adjusting to the loss of a loved one. Meetings are held monthly at a specially designated, comfortable site at the hospice offices. Topics of the meetings are as follows:
Coping with loneliness in grief
"Aren't you over it yet?"—myths about grief
Loss of a parent
Asking questions, finding comfort: faith and loss
"Do you ever feel like you're going crazy?"—how grief affects us

Both daytime and evening groups are offered to accommodate the schedules of participants. Two staff members lead the open-ended groups, and typically ten to fifteen people attend each one.

In addition to these monthly seminars, other support groups are offered to specific target audiences. There are groups that focus on the loss of a parent or grandparent, the loss of a sibling, and the loss of an adult child. Programs are offered to children and teens as well, some of which use the mediums of art and music to help the participants learn about grief.

The format of the Bon Secours groups is consistent with the theoretical perspective of ego psychology, as participants are encouraged to vent their feelings and reflect on their emotional status and needs. People who attend the bereavement support group tend to be emotionally raw. It is important that the facilitators respect the needs of participants rather than structure the meetings too rigidly in advance. Thus, the leaders plan a special topic for each meeting that is advertised in advance, such as loss and the holidays or practical matters such as financial planning. The meetings begin with open-ended conversation, as the leaders assess the mood of the group. This conversation is followed by an introduction of the month's topic, but the direction of each meeting is unpredictable. Actual topics of conversation vary depending on the participants who are present and what their concerns are at the time.

The major skills required of the group leaders are the capability to assess the mood of each group and the member abilities to be mutually supportive, to provide clear and useful information (including handouts), and to manage a group process (including all members, controlling dominant members, encouraging silent members). The experience of the Bon Secours facilitators is that most people who decide to attend the bereavement support group do so for up to twelve months. The program is not formally evaluated, but participant feedback is actively requested during each session and when the overall bereavement services are concluded.

The funeral home setting   Recently some funeral homes have begun to expand their traditional services by offering psychoeducational bereavement services to their customers as well as to the general public (Lensing,

2001). This expansion of services represents an effort by those organizations to expand their advertising and clientele and to engage in longer-term relationships with families. Although the content of these programs, generally provided via open-ended educational groups that meet on an occasional basis, is similar to that of the hospice program described earlier, they have a different tone in that the professional provider (often a social worker) does not know the families well and the funeral service is operating as a for-profit endeavor. As this represents a new trend, there is no data available on the effectiveness of these services on the family bereavement process.

For Children and Adolescents (with Adults)

The Parent Guidance intervention   The Parent Guidance program assumes that surviving parents play the central role in fostering their children's healthy development. The program seeks to enhance parents' self-esteem, functioning, and confidence as a way of promoting the well-being of the child (Horsley & Patterson, 2006). The role of the professional is to clarify issues, set goals, offer support, and help parents anticipate problems and identify solutions. Intervention focuses on the conditions that can influence adaptation to the loss. The most important conditions are the quality of the surviving parent-child relationship, the parenting the child receives following the loss, and the stability of the child's environment. By maintaining as much stability and consistency as possible, surviving parents can enhance their children's sense of control and mastery over the environment.

The focus of the Parent Guidance psychoeducational program is children who are losing a parent to cancer. Professional staff perceive parents as colleagues, as it is important to reassure parents of their own competence in meeting their children's needs. By working with the parents to enhance their knowledge of childhood bereavement, their awareness of their children's special needs, and their own parenting skills, the likelihood is enhanced that ongoing help will be available to their children. Another purpose of the intervention is to increase parents' understanding of the nature of bereavement reactions in children at different developmental stages. A realistic appraisal of the normality of their children's behavior alleviates some of the anxiety they experience when confronted with an unfamiliar situation. This understanding can forestall inappropriate hurt or anger when children do not express their grief as overtly as parents expect.

This Parent Guidance program uses a format of individual family rather than group meetings. It is initiated approximately six months prior to the projected death and persists for four to six months after the death. The program's pre-death and post-death components each consist of approximately eight sessions, spaced two to three weeks apart, in which a practitioner meets with various family members. Within each component, five meetings are conducted with the well parent alone; one or two meetings include each of the children alone, as needed for a comprehensive assessment; and one meeting is held with the well parent and children together. In the pre-death phase, the ill parent may be included in some sessions as requested by the family.

When the sick parent approaches the terminal phase, parents become most receptive to hearing and acting on the information provided by the intervention. Denial becomes increasingly difficult to sustain, and the need to deal with the death and its impact on the family cannot be avoided. The period approaching the terminal phase of the illness and continuing for several months after the death is the one in which families experience the greatest distress and children feel their own care to be most adequate. Failure to be honest with the child about the gravity of the illness can profoundly diminish the child's trust in the surviving parent later, when the ill parent dies.

Parent Guidance program staff believe that it is unreasonable to ask family members to anticipate and grapple with post-death issues beforehand. The practitioner tries to schedule the first post-death session within the three to four weeks after the death to allow family members time to react to the event, sort out some of their confusion, and begin their resumption of normal activities. The social support available to surviving family members frequently begins to decline about a month after the death. The program's supportive dimension focuses on the well parents' dealing with their own grief and resuming their parental functions. Addressing the grief that accompanies such a loss is a means of facilitating the children's adjustment. Supporting the well parents in their functioning, affirming their competence, and providing reassurance that they can adequately meet their children's needs are important aspects of the program.

A pilot study of the Parent Guidance program demonstrated that a large majority of parents and children found the intervention helpful in enabling them to cope with the stresses of the terminal phase of the illness and the acute grief period (Horsley & Patterson, 2006).

Other Programs for Children

Bereaved Children and Their Surviving Parents This program is a twelve-week group intervention also designed for parentally bereaved children and their surviving parents (Schoeman & Kreitzman, 1997). The structure of the intervention included the four themes of normalizing, educating, teaching coping techniques, and cognitive restructuring. The support group design consisted of separate but parallel group sessions for children and their adult caregivers, with topics often complementing one another. For instance, one week the children focus on how to express feelings of grief while the adults learn how to support children in expressing their grief. During the last four group sessions, children and adults meet together to discuss their feelings of grief, develop ways to cope with grief, and move forward in their new family structure. The authors reported success with this group program in addressing its four themes but did not evaluate it over time.

Support for Parentally Bereaved Children   This program was designed to serve parentally bereaved children alone (Masterman & Reams, 1988). The program developers introduced formats for two age groups: preschool and school age. Both included eight structured sessions, but the group for the younger children employed mostly play techniques. Though the topics covered are similar to other models of bereavement groups (reaction to the death, the funeral, and the future), this group followed the same structure every week, which included time for greetings, discussion, play, and a summary. Child interventions contained elements of bibliotherapy (books about death), play, and game playing, all of which help to elicit feelings (Zambelli & DeRosa, 1992). This group was always led by two facilitators, one male and one female, so that each child would be able to relate to someone of the same gender as the deceased parent. Each child was also given homework assignments that were related to each week's topic and were discussed during subsequent meetings. The success of this group was described but never formally evaluated.

Summary

Bereavement is a ubiquitous, natural process that should not be considered dysfunctional or disordered in most instances. People who are grieving are likely to pass through the five stages of grief with the assistance of their natural support systems, and there is limited evidence that professional intervention makes a difference in the process. Some bereaved people and families, however, seek out and may experience relief by receiving information about grief and experiencing the support provided. Some persons experience complicated grief, which if not addressed can lead to serious and long-term depression. Finally, children benefit from interventions in which their grieving is addressed directly by parents in a way that facilitates their expressions of emotion. For all of these situations, psychoeducation is an intervention modality that can have beneficial effects.

Afterword

Psychoeducation seems to be everywhere in the human services today. This book represents an effort to summarize how psychoeducation is used to help people with many problems in living who come to the attention of professionals and consumer organizations. It makes no claims to comprehensiveness, however. From the list of current uses of psychoeducation in chapter 1, for example, the following applications were not covered: women who have experienced sexual assault, human services professionals who experience vicarious trauma, adolescent girls who experience negative social pressures, children of divorce, separation resilience groups for couples who spend much time apart, minority persons who are adjusting to college or are in need of greater psychosocial competence, and school-age children who desire to develop their racial identities. The focus of this book has been on psychoeducation with persons and their significant others who have mental, emotional, and behavioral problems; people with physical health disadvantages; and people experiencing bereavement. The literature includes information about the other applications listed here, and the interested reader is encouraged to search for them. The author's hope is that the material in this book has stimulated a greater interest among readers in the scope of the modality.

Although the versatility of psychoeducation is clear, this book closes with a consideration of some remaining questions about the future of the modality.

Consumer- versus Professional-Led Programs

Among the first psychoeducators were the lay leaders of advocacy organizations who wanted to take intervention out of the hands of the professionals who they perceived as remote, difficult to comprehend, and stigmatizing. Examples of these programs were included in chapter 6, in the National Alliance for the Mentally Ill's consumer-run and peer-to-peer groups. Since NAMI's early years, however, many professionals (including this author) have established partnerships with the organization and begun providing groups of their own, with similar structures and goals. Most of the programs described in this book are in fact led (or co-led) by professionals. Sometimes these persons work along with consumers, but more often they do not. The experts have access to up-to-date information about the challenges in living on which their programs are based, but they often bring a psychotherapy perspective to the work, with a deficits rather than a strengths focus. As a result, some psychoeducation programs risk losing the practicality of the original interventions.

I believe that the field of mental health intervention was greatly enhanced by the consumer organization's taking the lead in providing education and support for their members. My hope is that psychoeducation will not lose the perspective of the consumer, which features a well-rounded appreciation for the complexities of the lived experiences of persons who are affected by the related problems in living.

Psychoeducation and Psychotherapy: Merging Interventions?

On the other hand, professional therapists, some of whom integrate psychoeducation into their overall activities, have enhanced their effectiveness by doing so. There are many examples included in this book of professionals who have creatively integrated education and support into their other intervention modalities. The essential nature of psychoeducation can be preserved in their programs that are structured and topics-focused. Another way that productive integration can be implemented is though stepped-care approaches, in which psychoeducation is offered as a first step in a longer-range intervention process.

Specifying Target Populations

Some psychoeducators believe that regardless of the issue being addressed the intervention can have greater impact if leaders more carefully specify their target audiences. For example, this book showed how a program for depression was limited to women, with the assumption that their experiences were unique and could be addressed more specifically if men were not included. Another group focused on a health care issue that included only African American women, as this population was found to be underserved in other programs of the type. In my family education and support group, I learned, to my dismay, that groups including parents, spouses, and siblings were not well received or evaluated by the minority participants (spouses and siblings), because their concerns did not match well with the concerns of the parents.

Most programs are not so selective in their inclusion criteria, however, and it may not often be feasible to set strict admission criteria due to the limited numbers of potential participants and the desire not to exclude other persons in need of the service. Still, there is a need for more research in this area to determine how topics might more successfully address the needs of the audiences.

A Word about Evidence-Based Practice

The available evidence has been presented about the demonstrated effectiveness of every program in this book. Some psychoeducation programs have been evaluated through relatively sophisticated experimental designs, whereas others only report satisfaction surveys completed by their participants. In this writer's opinion, the more primitive, less generalizable research methods deserve to be respected, because it is difficult to make generalizations about any interventions that rely in large part on the interpersonal skills and relationship-development qualities of the leaders. These variables are difficult to capture and thus are rarely taken into account in evaluation research. Still, the proponents of evidence-based practice sometimes argue that this point is insignificant.

Evidence-based practice (EBP) in the human services means that outcome studies should justify that an intervention is effective for a particular problem issue. It refers to the process of utilizing the available empirical research to guide interventions (Vandiver, 2002). Put simply, the practitioner must answer the question, "What evidence do you have that your proposed intervention will be effective with your client?"

There are three recommended approaches to operationalizing EBP in practice, including (in order of preference) the practitioner's use of formal practice guidelines supported by research studies, expert consensus guidelines, and when appropriate guidelines are not available, a self-directed approach (Rosen & Proctor, 2002). This movement among the human service professions toward evidence-based practice is related to their desire for increased accountability to clients and third-party payers and to further the knowledge base of the professions.

All practitioners want to use interventions that are effective, but efforts to identify evidence-based practice models are controversial for a number of reasons (Rosenthal, 2004). Most research methodologies have not been able to examine the leadership and relationship factors in psychoeducation. Likewise, the personal characteristics of service providers are often overlooked, such as their experience with particular problem areas and overall competence in carrying out a particular intervention. Further, with regard to the existing research there is a bias toward cognitive and behavioral strategies. A majority of the demonstrably effective interventions to date are cognitive or behavioral, but this fact is due in part to an underrepresentation of other interventions in research studies. Qualitative researchers, for example, are distrustful of efforts to generalize intervention outcomes because of the complexities involved in every instance of clinical intervention (O'Connor, 2002). The use of intervention manuals (formal written directives used and recommended in many programs) may limit the natural responsiveness of psychoeducators to unique situations that arise in a program. It is not always clear how closely practitioners follow these procedures, as they may respond differentially to challenges that emerge in the course of intervention.

Evidence-based practice has been adapted from the medical model of care, but in the social sciences practitioners must be very cautious in assuming that two clients or groups are alike, even when they share similar problems. Variables such as a person's social support, socioeconomic status, distress level, motivation, and intelligence may be more important predictors of program response.

So what is the appropriate relationship between psychoeducation and evidence-based practice? Some argue that practitioners need to be concerned only with what interventions are most likely to provide desired outcomes as demonstrated by empirical research. Others emphasize that EBP is reductionistic, simplifying the personality of the service recipient, the skill level of the practitioner, and the range of interventions that a practitioner actually provides in a given program. I close, then, with a finding from Sparks, Duncan, and Miller (2008) that the two most important elements of effective practice are the working alliance that develops between the practitioner and recipient and the practitioner's ongoing attention to the client's reactions to the intervention process. The presence of shared goals, a consensus on methods used, and the emotional bond are most predictive of positive clinical outcomes. As a part of this process, the psychoeducator should regularly solicit feedback and input from participants about how well the intervention is working for them. With these practices in place, the intervention should succeed.

I wish you the best of luck in your psychoeducation efforts!

References

Akkerman, R. L., & Ostwald, S. K. (2004). Reducing anxiety in Alzheimer's disease family caregivers: The effectiveness of a nine-week cognitive-behavioral intervention. *American Journal of Alzheimer's Disease and Other Dementias, 19*(2), 117–123.

Allegri, R. F., Sarasola, D., Serrano, C. M., Taragano, F. E., Arizana, R. L., Butman, J., et al. (2006). Neuropsychiatric symptoms as a predictor of caregiver burden in Alzheimer's disease. *Neuropsychiatric Disease and Treatment, 2*(1), 105–110.

American Cancer Society. (2009). *Cancer statistics 2009: A presentation from the American Cancer Society.* Retrieved July 24, 2009, from www.cancer.org/docroot/PRO/content/PRO_1_1_Cancer_Statistics_2009_Presentation.asp

American Psychiatric Association. (2000). *Diagnostic and statistical manual of mental disorders* (4th ed., text rev.). Washington, DC: Author.

Anderson, C. M., Hogarty, G. E., & Reiss, D. J. (1980). Family treatment of adult schizophrenic patients: A research-based psychoeducational approach. *Schizophrenia Bulletin, 4,* 512–520.

Anderson, C. M., Reiss, D. J., & Hogarty, G. (1986). *Schizophrenia and the family.* New York: Guilford.

Anderson, J. (1997). *Social work with groups: A process model.* White Plains, NY: Longman.

Antonuccio, D. O., Lewisohn, P. M., & Steinmetz, J. L. (1982). Identification of therapist differences in a group treatment for depression. *Journal of Consulting and Clinical Psychology, 50*(3), 433–435.

Armstrong, T., & Costello, J. (2002). Community studies on adolescent substance use, abuse, or dependence and psychiatric comorbidity. *Journal of Consulting and Clinical Psychology, 70,* 1224–1239.

Aschbacher, K., Patterson, T., von Känel, R., Dimsdale, J. E., Mills, P. J., Adler, K. A., et al. (2005). Coping processes and hemostatic reactivity to acute stress in dementia caregivers. *Psychosomatic Medicine, 67*(6), 964–971.

Ascher-Svanum, H., & Whitesel, J. (1999). A randomized controlled study of two styles of group patient education about schizophrenia. *Psychiatric Services, 50*(7), 926–930.

Asmundson, G. J., & Taylor, S. (2005). *It's not all in your head: How worrying about your health could be making you sick—and what you can do about it.* New York: Guilford.

Authier, J. (1977). The psychoeducational model: Definition, contemporary roots, and content. *Canadian Counselor, 12*(1), 15–22.

Baenen, R. S. (1986). Predictors of child and family outcome in a psychoeducational day school program. *Behavioral Disorders, 11*(4), 272–279.

Bandura, A. (1997). *Self-efficacy: The exercise of control.* New York: W. H. Freeman.

Bandura, A. (2001). Social cognitive theory: An agentic perspective. *Annual Review of Psychology, 52,* 1–26.

Barkley, R. A. (2000). *Taking charge of ADHD* (Rev. ed.). New York: Guilford.

Barkow, K., Maier, W., Ustun, T. B., Gansicke, M., Wittchen, H. U., & Heun, R. (2003). Risk factors for depression at 12-month follow-up in adult primary health care patients with major depression: An international prospective study. *Journal of Affective Disorders, 76*(2), 157–169.

Barnett, S. M., Sirey, J., Bruce, M., Hamilton, M., Raue, P., Friedman, S., et al. (2002). Predictors of early recovery from major depression among persons admitted to community-based clinics. *Archives of General Psychiatry, 59,* 729–735.

Barth, R. P., Yeaton, J., & Winterfelt, N. (1994). Psychoeducational groups with foster parents of sexually abused children. *Child and Adolescent Social Work Journal, 11*(5), 405–424.

Bateson, G., Jackson, D. D., Haley, J., & Weakland, J. (1956). Toward a theory of schizophrenia. *Behavioral Science, 1,* 251–264.

Beardslee, W., Versage, E., & Gladstone, T. (1998). Children of affectively ill parents: A review of the past 10 years. *Journal of the American Academy of Child and Adolescent Psychiatry, 37*(11), 1134–1141.

Beck, A. T. (1967). *Depression: Clinical, experimental, and theoretical aspects.* New York: Hoeber.

Benioff, L. (1995). What is it like to have schizophrenia? In S. Vinogradov (Ed.), *Treating schizophrenia* (pp. 81–107). San Francisco: Jossey-Bass.

Berlin, S. B. (2002). *Clinical social work practice: A cognitive-integrative perspective.* New York: Oxford University Press.

Bidart, C., & Lavenu, D. (2005). Evolutions of personal networks and life events. *Social Networks, 27*(4), 359–376.

Bloom, B. S. (1976). *Human characteristics and school learning.* New York: McGraw-Hill.

Bonavita, V., Iavarone, A., & Sorrentino, G. (2001). Depression in neurological diseases: A review. *Archives of General Psychiatry* (Suppl. 7), 49–66.

Bond, J., Kaskutas, L. A., & Weisner, C. (2003). The persistent influence of social networks and Alcoholics Anonymous on abstinence. *Quarterly Journal of Studies on Alcohol, 64,* 579–588.

Booth, B. M., Shields, J. J., & Chandler, R. K. (2009). Recent achievements in alcohol and drug abuse health services research. *The Journal of Behavioral Health Services and Research, 36*(1), 5–10.

Borsari, B., Tevyaw, T. O., Barnett, N. P., Kahler, C. W., & Monti, P. M. (2007). Stepped care for mandated college students: A pilot study. *The American Journal on Addictions, 16,* 131–137.

Botsford, A. L., & Rule, D. (2004). Evaluation of a group intervention to assist aging patients with permanency planning for an adult offspring with special needs. *Social Work, 49*(3), 423–431.

Bowen, M. (1960). A family concept of schizophrenia. In D. D. Jackson (Ed.), *The etiology of schizophrenia* (pp. 346–372). New York: Basic Books.

Bowen, M. (1978). *Family therapy in clinical practice.* New York: Jason Aronson.

Braun, K., Karel, H., & Zir, A. (2006). Family response to end-of-life education: Differences by ethnicity and stage of caregiving. *American Journal of Hospice and Palliative Medicine, 23*(4), 269–276.

Brennan, J. W. (1995). A short-term psychoeducational multiple-family group for bipolar patients and their families. *Social Work, 40*(6), 737–743.

Breslau, J., Kendler, K. S., Su, M., Kessler, R. C., & Gaxiola-Aguilar, S. (2005). Lifetime risk and persistence of psychiatric disorders across ethnic groups in the United States. *Psychological Medicine, 35*(3), 317–327.

Brodaty, H., Green, A., & Koschera, A. (2003). Meta-analysis of psychosocial interventions for caregivers of people with dementia. *Journal of the American Geriatrics Society, 51*(5), 657–664.

Brown, G. W., & Harris, T. O. (2008). Depression and the serotonin transporter 5-HTTLPR polymorphism: A review and a hypothesis concerning gene-environment interaction. *Journal of Affective Disorders, 111*(1), 1–12.

Brown, J., Cohen, P., Johnson, J. G., & Smailes, E. M. (1999). Childhood abuse and neglect: Specificity of effects on adolescent and young adult depression and suicidality. *Journal of the American Academy of Child and Adolescent Psychiatry, 38*(12), 1490–1496.

Brown, S. A. (2008). Prevalence of alcohol and drug involvement during childhood and adolescence. In T. P. Beauchaine & S. P. Hinshaw (Eds.), *Child and adolescent psychopathology* (pp. 405–444). Hoboken, NJ: John Wiley and Sons.

Bukstein, O., Dunne, J., Ayres, W., Arnold, V., Benedek, E., Bensenn, R., et al. (1997). Practice parameters for the assessment and treatment of children and adolescents with substance use disorders. *Journal of the American Academy of Child and Adolescent Psychiatry, 36*(1), 140–157.

Burgio, L. D., Solano, N., Fisher, S. E., Stevens, A., & Gallagher-Thompson, D. (2003). Skill-building: Psychoeducational strategies. In D. W. Coon, D. Gallagher-Thompson, & L. W. Thompson (Eds.), *Innovative interventions to reduce dementia caregiver distress* (pp. 119–138). New York: Springer.

Burke, J., Loeber, R., & Birmaher, B. (2002). Oppositional defiant disorder and conduct disorder: A review of the past 10 years, part II. *Journal of the American Academy of Child and Adolescent Psychiatry, 41,* 1275–1294.

Burns, D. (1999). *Feeling good: The new mood therapy.* New York: Avon.

Burns, R., Nichols, L., Martindale-Adams, J., Graney, M. J., & Lummus, A. (2003). Primary care interventions for dementia caregivers: Two-year outcomes from the REACH study. *The Gerontologist, 43*(4), 547–555.

Butzlaff, R. L., & Hooley, J. M. (1998). Expressed emotion and psychiatric relapse. *Archives of General Psychiatry, 55,* 547–552.

Byalin, K., Jed, J., & Lehman, S. (1985). Designing and evaluating intervention strategies for deinstitutionalized mental patients. *International Review of Applied Psychology, 34*(3), 381–390.

Campbell, T. L. (1997). Family intervention in Alzheimer's disease. *Families, Systems, and Health, 15*(2), 227–233.

Candelario, N., & Huber, H. (2002). A school-based group experience on racial identity and race relations. *Smith College Studies in Social Work, 73*(1), 51–72.

Caplan, G. (1990). Loss, stress, and mental health. *Community Mental Health Journal, 26*(1), 27–48.

Carlson, G. A. (2002). Bipolar disorder in children and adolescents: A critical review. In D. Shaffer & B. D. Waslick (Eds.), *The many faces of depression in children and adolescents* (pp. 105–123). Washington, DC: American Psychiatric Association.

Carpenter, P., & Sugrue, D. P. (1984). Psychoeducation in an outpatient setting: Designing a heterogenous format for a heterogenous population of juvenile delinquents. *Adolescence, 19*(3), 113–122.

Cash, T. F., & Hrabosky, J. I. (2003). The effects of psychoeducation and self-monitoring in a cognitive-behavioral program for body-image improvement. *Eating Disorders, 11,* 255–270.

Celio, A. A., Winzelberg, A. J., Wilfley, D. E., Eppstein-Herald, D., Springer, E. A., Dev, P., et al. (2000). Reducing risk factors for eating disorders: Comparison of an internet- and a classroom-delivered psychoeducational program. *Journal of Consulting and Clinical Psychology, 68*(4), 650–657.

Chambless, D. L., Bryan, A. D., Aiken, L. S., Steketee, G., & Hooley, J. M. (1999). The structure of expressed emotion: A three-construct representation. *Psychological Assessment, 11*(1), 67–76.

Clarkin, J. F., Glick, I. D., Haas, G. L., Spencer, J. H., Lewis, A. B., Peyser, F., et al. (1990). A randomized clinical trial of inpatient family intervention: V. Results for affective disorders. *Journal of Affective Disorders, 18*(1), 17–28.

Clemens, S. E. (2004). Recognizing vicarious traumatization: A single session group model for trauma workers. *Social Work with Groups, 27*(2–3), 55–74.

Cole, M., & Dendukuri, N. (2003). Risk factors for depression among elderly community studies: A systematic review and meta-analysis. *American Journal of Psychiatry, 160,* 1147–1156.

Colom, F., & Lam, D. (2005). Psychoeducation: Improving outcomes in bipolar disorder. *European Psychiatry, 20,* 359–364.

Colom, F., & Vieta, E. (2004). A perspective on the use of psychoeducation, cognitive-behavioral therapy and interpersonal therapy for bipolar patients. *Bipolar Disorders, 6*(6), 480–486.

Colom, F., Vieta, E., Reinares, M., Martinez-Aran, A., Torrent, C., Goikolea, J. M., et al. (2003). Psychoeducation efficacy in bipolar disorders: Beyond compliance enhancement. *Journal of Clinical Psychiatry, 64,* 1101–1105.

Compas, B., Haaga, D., Keefe, F., Leitenberg, H., & Williams, D. (1998). Sampling of empirically supported psychological treatments from health psychology: Smoking, chronic pain, cancer, and bulimia nervosa. *Journal of Consulting and Clinical Psychology, 66*(1), 89–112.

Conner, K. R., Sorensen, S., & Leonard, K. E. (2005). Initial depression and subsequent drinking during alcoholism treatment. *Journal of Studies on Alcohol, 66*(3), 401–406.

Connors, G., Donovan, D., & DiClemente, C. (2001). *Substance abuse treatment and the stages of change: Selecting and planning interventions.* New York: Guilford.

Constas, M. A., & Sternberg, R. J. (2006). *Translating theory and research into educational practice: Developments in content domains, large-scale reform, and intellectual capacity.* Mahwah, NJ: Lawrence Erlbaum Associates.

Conus, P., Cotton, S., Abdel-Baki, A., Lambert, M., Berk, M., & McGorry, P. D. (2006). Symptomatic and functional outcome 12 months after a first episode of psychotic mania: Barriers to recovery in a catchment area sample. *Bipolar Disorders, 8*(3), 221–231.

Cooper, C., Katone, C., Orrell, M., & Livingston, G. (2004). Coping strategies and anxiety in caregivers of people with Alzheimer's disease: The LASER-AD study. *Journal of Affective Disorders, 90*(1), 15–20.

Corcoran, J. (2006). *Cognitive-behavioral methods for social workers: A workbook.* Boston: Allyn and Bacon.

Corey, G. (2005). *Theory and practice of counseling and psychotherapy* (7th ed.). Pacific Grove, CA: Brooks/Cole.

Corsini, R. J., & Wedding, D. (Eds.). (2000). *Current psychotherapies* (6th ed.). Itasca, IL: F. E. Peacock.

Cottrell, D., Fonagy, P., Kurtz, Z., Phillips, J., & Target, M. (2002). What works for whom? A critical review of treatments for children and adolescents. In *Depressive disorders* (pp. 89–105). New York: Guilford.

Croll, J., Neumark-Sztainer, D., Story, M., & Ireland, M. (2002). Prevalence and risk and protective factors related to disordered eating behaviors among adolescents: Relationship to gender and ethnicity. *Journal of Adolescent Health, 31,* 166–175.

Crum, R. M., Green, K. M., Storr, C. L., Ialongo, N., Anthony, J. C., Stuart, E. A., et al. (2008). Depressed mood in childhood and subsequent alcohol use through adolescence and young adulthood. *Archives of General Psychiatry, 65,* 702–712.

Cuffe, S. P., McKeown, R. E., Jackson, K. L., Addy, C. L., Abramson, R., & Garrison, C. Z. (2001). Prevalence of attention-deficit/hyperactivity disorder in a community sample of older adolescents. *Journal of the American Academy of Child and Adolescent Psychiatry, 40*(9), 1037–1044.

Cuijpers, P., van Straten, A., Smit, F., & Andersson, G. (2009). Is psychotherapy for depression equally effective in younger and older adults? A meta-regression analysis. *International Psychogeriatrics, 21*(1), 16–24.

Cummings, C. M., & Fristad, M. A. (2007). Medications prescribed for children with mood disorders: Effects of a family-based psychoeducational program. *Experimental and Clinical Psychopharmacology, 15*(6), 555–562.

Cummings, L. J., & Cole, G. (2002). Alzheimer's disease. *Journal of the American Medical Association, 287,* 2335–2339.

Davis, L. (2005). Educating individuals with dementia: Perspectives for rehabilitation professionals. *Topics in Geriatric Rehabilitation, 21*(4), 304–314.

Davis, R., McVey, G., Heinmaa, M., Rockert, W., & Kennedy, S. (1999). Sequencing of cognitive-behavioral treatments for bulimia nervosa. *International Journal of Eating Disorders, 25*(4), 361–374.

Dekovic, M. (1999). Risk and protective factors in the development of problem behavior during adolescence. *Journal of Youth and Adolescence, 28,* 667–685.

Depp, C., Krisztal, E., Cardenas, V., Oportot, M., Mausbach, B., Ambler, C., et al. (2003). Treatment options for improving wellbeing in dementia family caregivers: The case for psychoeducational interventions. *Clinical Psychologist, 7*(1), 21–31.

Dincin, J., Selleck, V., & Streicker, S. (1978). Restructuring parental attitudes: Working with parents of the adult mentally ill. *Schizophrenia Bulletin, 4,* 597–608.

Dixon, L., McFarlane, W. R., Lefley, H., Lucksted, A., Cohen, M., Falloon, I., et al. (2001). Evidence-based practices for services to families of people with psychiatric disabilities. *Psychiatric Services, 52*(7), 903–910.

Dore, M. N., Nelson-Zlupko, L., & Kaufmann, E. (1999). "Friends in need": Designing and implementing a psychoeducational group for school children from drug-involved families. *Social Work, 44*(2), 179–190.

Duggal, S., Carlson, E. A., Sroufe, L. A., & Egeland, B. (2001). Depressive symptomatology in childhood and adolescence. *Development and Psychopathology, 13*(1), 143–164.

Dumaine, M. (2003). Meta-analysis of interventions with co-occurring disorders of severe mental illness and substance abuse: Implications for social work practice. *Research on Social Work Practice, 13,* 142–165.

DuPaul, G. J., & Power, T. J., (2000). Educational interventions for students with attention-deficit disorders. In T. Brown (Ed.), *Attention-deficit disorders and comorbidities in children, adolescents, and adults* (pp. 607–634). Washington, DC: American Psychiatric Press.

Eisdorfer, C., Czaja, S. J., Lowenstein, D. A., Rubert, M. P., Arguelles, S., Mitrani, V. B., et al. (2003). The effect of a family therapy and technology-based intervention on caregiver depression. *The Gerontologist, 43*(4), 521–531.

Emer, D., McLarney, A., Goodwin, M., & Keller, P. (2002). Which group teaching styles best promote information gain for adults with mental disorders? *Journal for Specialists in Group Work, 27,* 205–232.

Erikson, E. (1968). *Identity: Youth and crisis.* New York: W. W. Norton.

Evans, D. L. (2000). Bipolar disorder: Diagnostic challenges and treatment considerations. *Journal of Clinical Psychiatry, 61*(Suppl. 13), 26–31.

Even, C., Richard, H., & Thuille, J. (2007). Characteristics of voluntary participants versus non-participants in a psychoeducation program for euthymic patients with bipolar disorder. *Journal of Nervous and Mental Disease, 195*(3), 262–265.

Falloon, I. R. H., Boyd, J. L., & McGill, C. W. (1984). *Family care of schizophrenia.* New York: Guilford.

Fals-Stewart, W., Birchler, G. R., & Kelley, M. I. (2006). Learning sobriety together: A randomized clinical trial examining behavioral couples therapy with alcoholic female patients. *Journal of Counseling and Clinical Psychology, 74*(3), 579–591.

Famous quotes by author. (n.d.). Retrieved July 24, 2009, from www.yuni.com/quotes/emerson.html

Farmer, R. L. (2009). *Neuroscience and social work practice: The missing link.* Thousand Oaks, CA: Sage.

Feindler, E. L., & Starr, K. E. (2003). From steaming mad to staying cool: A constructive approach to anger control. *Reclaiming Children and Youth, 12*(3), 158–160.

Feld, R., Woodside, D. B., Kaplan, A. S., Olmsted, M. P., & Carter, J. C. (2001). Pretreatment motivational enhancement therapy for eating disorders: A pilot study. *International Journal of Eating Disorders, 11,* 97–110.

Feldstein, S. W., & Miller, W. R. (2007). Does subtle screening for substance abuse work? A review of the Substance Abuse Subtle Screening Inventory (SASSI). *Addiction, 102*(1), 41–50.

Fergusson, D., & Woodward, L. (2002). Mental health, educational, and social role outcomes of adolescents with depression. *Archives of General Psychiatry, 59,* 225–231.

Fingeret, M. C., Warren, C. S., Cepeda-Benito, A., & Gleaves, D. (2006). Eating disorder prevention research: A meta-analysis. *Eating Disorders, 14,* 191–206.

Finkel, S. I. (2001). Behavioral and psychological symptoms of dementia: A current focus for clinicians, researchers, and caregivers. *Journal of Clinical Psychiatry, 62*(Suppl. 21), 3–6.

Flannery, D. J., Vazsonyi, A. T., Liau, A. K., Guo, S., Powell, K. E., Atha, H., et al. (2003). Initial behavior outcomes for the PeaceBuilders universal school-based violence program. *Developmental Psychology, 39*(2), 292–308.

Floersch, J. (2003). The subjective experience of youth psychotropic treatment. *Social Work in Mental Health, 1*(4), 51–69.

Flory, V. (2004). A novel clinical intervention for severe childhood depression and anxiety. *Clinical Child Psychology and Psychiatry, 9*(1), 9–23.

Fonagy, P., Target, M., Cottrell, D., Phillips, J., & Kurtz, Z. (2002). *What works for whom? A critical review of treatments for children and adolescents.* New York: Guilford.

Franchini, L., Bongiorno, F., Spagnolo, C., Florita, M., Santoro, A., Dotoli, D., et al. (2006). Psychoeducational group intervention in addition to antidepressant therapy as relapse prevention strategy in unipolar patients. *Clinical Neurolopsychiatry: Journal of Treatment Evaluation, 3*(4), 282–285.

Frank, E. (2007). Interpersonal and social rhythm therapy: A means of improving depression and preventing relapse in bipolar disorder. *Journal of Clinical Psychology: In Session, 63*(5), 463–473.

Frank, J. D., & Frank, J. B. (1993). *Persuasion and healing: A comparative study of psychotherapy* (3rd ed.). Baltimore: Johns Hopkins University Press.

Fraser, M. W., Day, S. H., Galinsky, M. J., Hodges, V. G., & Smokowski, P. R. (2004). Conduct problems and peer rejection in childhood: A randomized trial of the making choices and strong families programs. *Research on Social Work Practice, 14*(5), 313–324.

Fristad, M. A., Goldberg-Arnold, J. S., & Gavazzi, S. M. (2002). Family psychoeducation: An adjunctive intervention for children with bipolar disorder. *Biological Psychiatry, 53*(11), 1000–1008.

Gallagher-Thompson, D., Coon, D. W., Solano, N., Ambler, B. A., Rabinowitz, Y., & Thompson, L. W. (2003). Change in indices of distress among Latino and Anglo female caregivers of elderly relatives with dementia: Site-specific results from the REACH National Collaborative Study. *The Gerontologist, 43*(4), 580–591.

Gallagher-Thompson, D., & DeVries, H. M. (1994). Coping with frustration classes: Development and preliminary outcomes with women who care for relatives with dementia. *The Gerontologist, 34*(4), 548–552.

Gallagher-Thompson, D., Lovett, S., Rose, J., McKibbin, C., Coon, D., Futterman, A., et al. (2000). Impact of psychoeducational interventions on distressed family caregivers. *Journal of Clinical Geropsychology, 6*, 91–110.

Gardner, H. (1999). *Intelligence reframed: Multiple intelligences for the 21st century.* New York: Basic Books.

Garfinkel, P. (1995). Classification and diagnosis of eating disorders. In K. D. Brownell & C. G. Fairburn (Eds.), *Eating disorders and obesity: A comprehensive handbook* (pp. 125–134). New York: Guilford.

Garner, D. M. (1997). Psychoeducational principles in treatment. In D. Garner & P. E. Garfinkel (Eds.), *Handbook of treatment for eating disorders* (2nd ed., pp. 145–177). New York: Guilford.

Gatz, J. L., Tyas, S. L., St. John, P., & Montgomery, P. (2005). Do depressive symptoms predict Alzheimer's disease and dementia? *Journal of Gerontology: Medical Sciences, 60A*(6), 744–747.

Gatz, M., Reynolds, C. A., Fratiglioni, L., Johansson, B., Mortimer, J. A., Berg, S., et al. (2006). Role of genetics and environments for explaining Alzheimer's disease. *Archives of General Psychiatry, 63*, 168–174.

Geller, R. E., & Goldberg, J. F. (2007). A review of evidence-based psychotherapies for bipolar disorder. *Primary Psychiatry, 14*(3), 59–69.

Gilbert, K. (1996). "We've had the same loss, why don't we have the same grief?" Loss and differential grief in families. *Death Studies, 20*, 269–283.

Gingerich, K., Turnock, P., Litfin, J., & Rosen, L. (1998). Diversity and attention-deficit hyperactivity disorder. *Journal of Clinical Psychology, 54*, 415–426.

Glick, B., & Goldstein, A. P. (1987). Aggression replacement training. *Journal of Counseling and Development, 65*(7), 356–362.

Glueckauf, R. L., Stine, C., Bourgeois, M., Pomidor, A., Rom, P., Young, M. E., et al. (2005). Alzheimer's rural care healthline: Linking rural caregivers to cognitive-behavioral intervention for depression. *Rehabilitation Psychology, 50*(4), 346–354.

Goldstein, E. (1995). *Ego psychology and social work practice* (2nd ed.). New York: Free Press.

Goldstein, M. J., & Doane, J. A. (1984). Interventions with families and the course of schizophrenia. In M. Alpert (Ed.), *Controversies in schizophrenia: Changes and constancies: Proceedings of the 74th annual meeting of the American Psychopathological Association, New York City, March 1–3, 1984* (pp. 381–397). New York: Guilford.

Goleman, D. (1998). *Working with emotional intelligence.* New York: Bantam Books.

Gonyea, J. G., O'Connor, M. K., & Boyle, P. A. (2006). Project CARE: A randomized controlled trial of a behavioral intervention group for Alzheimer's disease caregivers. *The Gerontologist, 46*(6), 827–832.

Good, T. L., & Brophy, J. E. (1997). *Looking in classrooms* (7th ed.). New York: Longman.

Goodman, S. H., & Gotlib, I. H. (1999). Risk for psychopathology in the children of depressed mothers: A developmental model for understanding mechanisms of transmission. *Psychological Review, 106*, 458–461.

Goodnick, P. J. (Ed.). (1998). *Mania: Clinical and research perspectives.* Washington, DC: American Psychiatric Press.

Greenberg, L., Fine, S. B., Cohen, C., & Larson, K. (1988). An interdisciplinary psychoeducation program for schizophrenic patients and their families in an acute care setting. *Hospital and Community Psychiatry, 39*(3), 277–282.

Greenfield, B. J., & Senecal, J. (1995). Recreational multifamily therapy for troubled children. *American Journal of Orthopsychiatry, 65*(3), 434–439.

Griffiths, C. A. (2006). The theories, mechanisms, benefits, and practical delivery of psychosocial educational interventions for people with mental health disorders. *International Journal of Psychosocial Rehabilitation, 11*(1), 21–28.

Hall, H. I., Song, R., Rhodes, P., An, Q., Karon, J., Kaplan, E. H., et al. (2008). Estimation of HIV incidence in the United States. *JAMA: Journal of the American Medical Association, 300*(5), 520–529.

Hansson, R. O., & Stroebe, M. S. (2007). The nature of grief. In R. O. Hansson & M. S. Stroebe (Eds.), *Bereavement in late life: Coping, adaptation, and developmental influences* (pp. 9–24). Washington, DC: American Psychological Association.

Hargie, O. D. W. (Ed.). (1997). *The handbook of communication skills.* New York: Routledge.

Hatfield, A. (1979). Help-seeking behaviors in families of schizophrenics. *American Journal of Psychiatry, 7*, 563–569.

Hayes, R., & Gantt, A. (1992). Patient psychoeducation: The therapeutic use of knowledge for the mentally ill. *Social Work in Health Care, 17*(1), 53–67.

Helgeson, V. S., Lepore, S. L., & Eton, D. T. (2006). Moderators of the benefits of psychoeducational interventions for men with prostate cancer. *Health Psychology, 25*(3), 348–354.

Hepburn, K. W., Tornatore, J., Center, B., & Ostwald, S. W. (2001). Dementia family caregiver training: Affecting beliefs about caregiving and caregiver outcomes. *Journal of the American Geriatrics Society, 49*(4), 450–457.

Hepworth, D., Rooney, R., Rooney, G. D., Strom-Gottfried, K., & Larsen, J. (in press). *Direct social work practice: Theory and skills* (8th ed.). Belmont, CA: Brooks/Cole.

Hester, R. K., Squires, D. D., & Delaney, H. D. (2005). The Drinker's Check-up: 12-month outcomes of a controlled clinical trial of a stand-alone software program for problem drinkers. *Journal of Substance Abuse Treatment, 28*(2), 159–169.

Hill, J. (2002). Biological, psychological and social processes in conduct disorders. *Journal of Child Psychology and Psychiatry, 43*(1), 133–164.

Hingson, R. W., Heeren, T., & Winter, M. R. (2006). Age at drinking onset and alcohol dependence. *Archives of Pediatrics and Adolescent Medicine, 160*, 739–746.

Hirschfeld, R. M. A., Lewis, L., & Vornik, L. A. (2003). Perceptions and impact of bipolar disorder: How far have we come? Results of the National Depressive and Manic Depressive Association's 2000 survey of individuals with bipolar disorder. *Journal of Clinical Psychiatry, 64*(2), 161–174.

Hobfoll, S., Freedy, R., Lane, C., & Geller, P. (1990). Conservation of social resources: Social support resource theory. *Journal of Social and Personal Relationships, 7,* 465–478.

Hoe, J., Hancock, G., & Livingston, G. (2006). Quality of life of people with dementia in residential care homes. *British Journal of Psychiatry, 188*(5), 460–464.

Hogarty, G. E., Flesher, S., Ulrich, R., Carter, M., Greenwald, D., Pogue-Geile, M., et al. (2004). Cognitive enhancement therapy for schizophrenia: Effects of a two-year randomized trial on cognition and behavior. *Archives of General Psychiatry, 61,* 866–876.

Holtkamp, K., Herpertz-Dahlmann, B., Vloet, T., & Hagenah, U. (2005). Group psychoeducation for parents of adolescents with eating disorders: The Aachen program. *Eating Disorders, 13,* 381–390.

Horne, A. M., Stoddard, J. L., & Bell, C. D. (2007). Group approaches to reducing aggression and bullying in school. *Group Dynamics: Theory, Research, and Practice, 11*(4), 262–271.

Horsley, H., & Patterson, T. (2006). The effects of a parent guidance intervention on communication among adolescents who have experienced the sudden death of a sibling. *American Journal of Family Therapy, 34*(2), 119–137.

Hughes, R. B., Nosek, M. A., Howland, C. A., Groff, J. Y., & Mullen, P. D. (2003). Health promotion for women with physical disabilities: A pilot study. *Rehabilitation Psychology, 48*(3), 182–188.

Hutchison, E. D. (2008). *Dimensions of human behavior: Person and environment* (3rd ed.). Los Angeles: Sage.

Ingersoll, K. S., Warner, C. C., & Gharib, S. (2002). *Motivational groups for community substance abuse programs.* Richmond, VA: Mid-Atlantic Addiction Technology Transfer Center.

Ingram, R., & Smith, L. T. (2008). Mood disorders. In J. E. Maddux & B. A. Winstead (Eds.), *Psychopathology: Foundations for a contemporary understanding* (2nd ed., pp. 171–197). New York: Routledge/Taylor and Francis Group.

James, R. K., & Gilliland, B. E. (2001). *Crisis intervention strategies* (4th ed.). Pacific Grove, CA: Brooks/Cole.

Jamison, C., & Scogin, F. (1995). The outcome of cognitive bibliotherapy with depressed adults. *Journal of Consulting and Clinical Psychology, 63*(4), 644–650.

Jedrziewskia, M. K., Lee, V. M., & Trojanowskia, J. Q. (2007). Lowering the risk of Alzheimer's disease: Evidence-based practices emerging from new research. *Alzheimer's and Dementia, 3*(2), 98–108.

Jewell, J. D., & Stark, K. D. (2003). Comparing the family environments of adolescents with conduct disorder or depression. *Journal of Child and Family Studies, 12,* 77–89.

Johnson, S. L., Winett, C. A., Meyer, B., Greenhouse, W. J., & Miller, I. (1999). Social support and the course of bipolar disorder. *Journal of Abnormal Psychology, 108,* 558–566.

Jones, L. V., & Hodges, V. G. (2001). Enhancing psychosocial competence among black women: A psychoeducational group model approach. *Social Work with Groups, 24*(3–4), 33–52.

Jones, R. S., Chow, T. W., & Getz, M. (2005). Asian Americans and Alzheimer's disease: Assimilation, culture, and beliefs. *Journal of Aging Studies, 20*(1), 11–25.

Jordan, C., Lewellen, A., & Vandiver, V. (1995). Psychoeducation for minority families: A social work perspective. *International Journal of Mental Health, 23*(4), 27–43.

Kallestad, J. H., & Olweus, D. (2003). Predicting teachers' and schools' implementation of the Olweus Bullying Prevention Program: A multilevel study. *Prevention and Treatment, 6*(1), 21–31.

Kalodner, C. R., & Coughlin, J. W. (2002). Psychoeducational and counseling groups to prevent and treat eating disorders and disturbances. In J. L. Delucia-Waack (Ed.), *Handbook of group counseling and psychotherapy* (pp. 481–496). Thousand Oaks, CA: Sage.

Kanter, J. (1980). *Coping strategies for families of the mentally ill.* Washington, DC: National Alliance for the Mentally Ill.

Karasu, T. B., Gelenberg, A., Merriam, A., & Wang, P. (2002). Practice guidelines for the treatment of patients with major depressive disorder. In *American Psychiatric Association practice guidelines for the treatment of psychiatric disorder: Compendium 2002* (2nd ed., pp. 463–545). Washington, DC: American Psychiatric Association.

Karp, D. A. (1995). *Speaking of sadness*. New York: Oxford University Press.

Kaslow, N. J., Collins, M. H., Rashid, F. L., Baskin, M. L., Griffith, J. R., Hollins, L., et al. (2000). The efficacy of a pilot family psychoeducational intervention for pediatric sickle cell disease (SCD). *Family Systems and Health, 18*(4), 381–404.

Kazdin, A. (2001). Treatment of conduct disorders. In J. Hill & B. Maughan (Eds.), *Conduct disorders in childhood and adolescence* (pp. 408–448). New York: Cambridge University Press.

Kellner, H., & Bry, B. H. (1999). The effects of anger management groups in a day school for emotionally disturbed adolescents. *Adolescence, 34*(136), 645–652.

Kelly, J., Myers, M., & Brown, S. (2002). Do adolescents affiliate with 12-step groups? A multivariate process model of effects. *Journal of Studies on Alcohol, 63*, 293–305.

Kerr, M. E., & Bowen, M. (1988). *Family evaluation: An approach based on Bowen theory*. New York: W. W. Norton.

Kessler, R. C., Chiu, W. T., Demler, O., & Walters, E. E. (2005). Prevalence, severity, and comorbidity of 12-month DSM-IV disorders in the National Comorbidity Survey Replication. *Archives of General Psychiatry, 62*, 617–627.

Kim, E. Y., Miklowitz, D. J., & Biuckians, A. (2007). Life stress and the course of early-onset bipolar disorder. *Journal of Affective Disorders, 99*(1–3), 37–44.

King, C. A., Kramer, A., Preuss, L., Kerr, D. C. R., Weisse, L., & Venkataraman, S. (2002). Youth-nominated support team for suicidal adolescents (version 1): A randomized controlled trial. *Journal of Consulting and Clinical Psychology, 74*(1), 199–206.

Klausner, E. J., Clarkin, J. F., Spielman, L., Pupo, C., Abrams, R., & Alexopoulos, G. S. (1998). Late-life depression and functional disability: The role of goal-focused group psychotherapy. *International Journal of Geriatric Psychiatry, 13*(6), 707–716.

Kolb, D. A. (1984). *Experiential learning: Experience as the source of learning and development*. Upper Saddle River, NJ: Prentice Hall.

Kopelowicz, A., Liberman, R. P., & Zarate, R. (2002). Psychosocial treatments for schizophrenia. In P. E. Nathan & J. M. Gorman (Eds.), *A guide to treatments that work* (pp. 201–226). New York: Oxford University Press.

Kotler, L. A., Cohen, P., Davies, M., Pine, D. S., & Walsh, B. D. (2001). Longitudinal relationships between childhood, adolescent, and adult eating disorders. *Journal of the American Academy of Child and Adolescent Psychiatry, 40*, 1434–1441.

Kovacs, M., Obrosky, S., Gatsonis, C., & Richards, C. (1997). First-episode major depressive and dysthymic disorder in childhood: Clinical and sociodemographic factors in recovery. *Journal of the American Academy of Child and Adolescent Psychiatry, 36*(6), 777–784.

Kownacki, R., & Shadish, W. (1999). Does Alcoholics Anonymous work? The results from a meta-analysis of controlled experiments. *Substance Use and Misuse, 34*, 1897–1916.

Kraaij, V., Arensman, E., & Spinhoven, P. (2002). Negative life events and depression in elderly persons: A meta-analysis. *Journals of Gerontology, Series B: Psychological Sciences and Social Sciences, 57B*(1), 87–94.

Kraft, M. K., Schubert, K., Pond, A., & Aguirre-Molina, M. (2006). Adolescent treatment services: The context of care. In H. Liddle & C. Rowe (Eds.), *Adolescent substance abuse: Research and clinical advances* (pp. 174–188). New York: Cambridge University Press.

Kreppner, J., O'Connor, T., & Rutter, M. (2001). Can inattention/overactivity be an institutional deprivation syndrome? *Journal of Abnormal Child Psychology, 29*(6), 513–529.

Kubler-Ross, E. (1997). *On death and dying: What the dying have to teach doctors, nurses, clergy, and their own families*. New York: Touchstone.

Kuhn, D., & Fulton, B. R. (2004). Efficacy of an educational program for relatives of persons in the early stages of Alzheimer's disease. *Journal of Gerontological Social Work, 42*(3–4), 109–130.

Kumpfer, K. L., Alvarado, R., Tait, C., & Whiteside, H. O. (2007). The Strengthening Families Program: An evidence-based, multicultural family skills training program. In P. Tolan, J. Szapocznik, & S. Sambrano (Eds.), *Preventing youth substance abuse: Science-based programs for children and adolescents* (pp. 159–181). Washington, DC: American Psychological Association.

Kymalainen, J. A., & Weisman de Mamani, A. G. (2008). Expressed emotion, communication deviance, and culture in families of patients with schizophrenia: A review of the literature. *Cultural Diversity and Ethnic Minority Psychology, 14*(2), 85–91.

Lahey, B., & Waldman, I. (2003). A developmental propensity model of the origins of conduct problems during childhood and adolescence. In B. Lahey, T. E. Moffitt, & A. Caspi (Eds.), *Causes of conduct disorder and juvenile delinquency* (pp. 76–117). New York: Guilford.

Lam, D., Donaldson, C., Brown, Y., & Malliaris, Y. (2005). Burden and marital and sexual satisfaction in the partners of bipolar patients. *Bipolar Disorders, 7*(5), 431–440.

Landsverk, S. S., & Kane, C. F. (1998). Antonovsky's sense of coherence: Theoretical basis of psychoeducation in schizophrenia. *Issues in Mental Health Nursing, 19,* 419–431.

Lang, F. R., & Fingerman, K. L. (Eds.). (2004). *Growing together: Personal relationships across the lifespan.* New York: Cambridge University Press.

Langstroem, N. (2002). Child neuropsychiatric disorders: A review of associations with delinquency and substance use. In R. R. Corrado (Ed.), *Multi-problem violent youth: A foundation for comparative research on needs, interventions, and outcomes: Series I. Life and behavioral sciences, Vol. 324* (pp. 91–104). Amsterdam: IOS Press.

Lara, M. A., Navarro, C., Acevedo, M., Berenzon, S., Mondragon, L., & Rubi, N. A. (2003). A psycho-educational intervention for depressed women: A qualitative analysis of the process. *Psychology and Psychotherapy: Theory, Research, and Practice, 77*(4), 429–447.

Lazarus, R. S. (2007). Stress and emotion: The new synthesis. In A. Monat, R. S. Lazarus, & G. Reevy (Eds.), *The Praeger handbook on stress and coping* (Vol.1, pp. 33–51). Westport, CT: Praeger/Greenwood Group.

Lazarus, R. S., & Lazarus, B. N. (1994). *Passion and reason: Making sense of our emotions.* New York: Oxford University Press.

LeDoux, J. (1996). *The emotional brain: The mysterious underpinnings of emotional life.* New York: Simon and Schuster.

Lee, J. A. B. (2001). *The empowerment approach to social work practice: Building the beloved community* (2nd ed.). New York: Columbia University Press.

Leff, J. P., Kuipers, L., & Berkowitz, R. (1983). Interventions in families of schizophrenics. In W. McFarlane (Ed.), *Family therapy in schizophrenia* (pp. 173–187). New York: Guilford.

Lenoir, M. E., Dingemans, P., Schene, A. H., Hart, A. A., & Linszen, D. H. (2002). The course of parental expressed emotion and psychotic episodes after family intervention in recent-onset schizophrenia: A longitudinal study. *Social Psychiatry and Psychiatric Epidemiology, 39*(2), 69–75.

Lensing, V. (2001). Grief support: The role of funeral service. *Journal of Loss and Trauma, 6*(1), 45–63.

Levinson, D. J. (1978). *The seasons of a man's life.* New York: Knopf.

Lewinsohn, P., & Essau, C. (2002). Depression in adolescents. In I. H. Gotlib & C. Hammen (Eds.), *Handbook of depression* (pp. 541–559). New York: Guilford.

Lewinsohn, P. M., Clarke, G. N., & Hoberman, H. M. (1989). The coping with depression course: Review and future directions. *Canadian Journal of Behavioral Sciences, 21*(14), 470–493.

Lewinsohn, P. M., Clarke, G. N., Rohde, P., Hops, H., & Seeley, J. R. (1996). A course in coping: A cognitive-behavioral approach to the treatment of adolescent depression. In E. D. Hibbs & P. S. Jensen (Eds.), *Psychosocial treatments for child and adolescent disorders: Empirically based strategies for clinical practice* (pp. 109–135). Washington, DC: American Psychological Association.

Lewinsohn, P. M., Forster, R., & Youngsen, M. A. (1992). *Control your depression.* New York: Simon and Schuster.

Lidz, T. (1975). *The origin and treatment of schizophrenic disorders.* London: Hogarth Press.

Lish, J. D., Dime-Meenan, S., Whybrow, P. C., Price, R. A., & Hirschfeld, R. (1994). The National Depressive and Manic-depressive Association (DMDA) survey of bipolar members. *Journal of Affective Disorders, 31*(4), 281–294.

Low, K. G., Charanasomboon, S., Lesser, J., Reinhalter, K., Martin, R., Jones, H., et al. (2006). Effectiveness of a computer-based interactive eating disorders prevention program at long-term follow-up. *Eating Disorders, 14,* 17–30.

Lukens, E. P., & McFarlane, W. R. (2006). Psychoeducation as evidence-based practice: Considerations for practice, research, and policy. In A. R. Roberts & K. R. Yeager (Eds.), *Foundations of evidence-based social work practice* (pp. 291–313). New York: Oxford University Press.

Lukens, E. P., & Prchal, K. (2002). Social workers as educators. In K. J. Bentley (Ed.), *Social work practice in mental health: Contemporary roles, tasks, and techniques* (pp. 122–142). Pacific Grove, CA: Brooks/Cole.

Lukens, E. P., Thorning, H., & Lohrer, S. (2004). Sibling perspectives on severe mental illness: Reflections on self and family. *American Journal of Orthopsychiatry, 74*(4), 489–501.

Lyketsos, C. G., Steinberg, M., Tschanz, J. T., Norton, M. C., Steffens, D. C., & Breitner, J. C. S. (2000). Mental and behavioral disturbances in dementia: Findings from the Cache County study on memory in aging. *American Journal of Psychiatry, 157,* 708–714.

Lynch, W. J., Roth, M. E., & Carrol, M. E. (2002). Biological basis of sex differences in drug abuse: Preclinical and clinical studies. *Psychopharmacology, 164,* 121–137.

Lynne, L. C., Cromwell, R. L., & Matthysse, S. (1978). *The nature of schizophrenia: New approaches to research and treatment.* New York: Wiley.

Mannion, E., Mueser, K., & Solomon, P. (1994). Designing psychoeducational services for spouses of persons with serious mental illness. *Community Mental Health Journal, 30*(2), 177–190.

Mannuzza, S., & Klein, R. (1999). Adolescent and adult outcomes in attention-deficit/hyperactivity disorder. In H. Quay & A. Hogan (Eds.), *Handbook of disruptive behavior disorders* (pp. 279–294). New York: Plenum.

Martin-Cook, K., Davis, B. A., Hynan, L. S., & Weiner, M. F. (2005). A randomized, controlled study of an Alzheimer's caregiver skills training program. *American Journal of Alzheimer's Disease and Other Dementias, 20*(4), 204–210.

Martin-Cook, K., Remakel-Davis, B., Svetlick, D., Hynan, L. S., & Weiner, M. F. (2003). Caregiver attribution and resentment in dementia care. *American Journal of Alzheimer's Disease and Other Dementias, 18*(6), 366–374.

Mason, S., & Vazquez, D. (2007). Making positive changes: A psychoeducation group for parents with HIV/AIDS. *Social Work with Groups, 30*(2), 27–40.

Masterman, S., & Reams, R. (1988). Support groups for bereaved preschool and school-age children. *American Journal of Orthopsychiatry, 58*(4), 562–570.

Maughan, B., & Rutter, M. (2001). Antisocial children grown up. In J. Hill & B. Maughan (Eds.), *Conduct disorders in childhood and adolescence* (pp. 507–552). New York: Cambridge University Press.

McClean, C., Greer, C., Scott, J., & Beck, J. (1982). Group treatment for parents of the adult mentally ill. *Hospital and Community Psychiatry, 33,* 564–569.

McClellan, J., McCurry, C., Snell, J., & DuBose, A. (1999). Early-onset psychotic disorders: Course and outcome over a two-year period. *Journal of the American Academy of Child and Adolescent Psychiatry, 38*(11), 1380.

McClendon, M. J., Smyth, K. A., & Neundorfer, M. M. (2004). Survival of persons with Alzheimer's disease: Caregiver coping matters. *The Gerontologist, 44*(4), 508–519.

McCrady, B. (2000). Alcohol use disorders and the Division 12 task force of the American Psychological Association. *Psychology of Addictive Behaviors, 14*(3), 267–276.

McDaniel, S. H., & Speice, J. (2001). What family counseling has to offer women's health: The examples of conversion, somatization, infertility treatment, and genetic testing. *Professional Psychology: Research and Practice, 32*(1), 44–51.

McFarlane, W. R. (2002). *Multifamily groups in the treatment of severe psychiatric disorders.* New York: Guilford.

McGuffin, P., Rijsdijk, F., Andrew, M., Sham, P., Katz, R., & Cardino, A. (2003). The heritability of bipolar affective disorder and the genetic relationship to unipolar depression. *Archives of General Psychiatry, 60,* 497–502.

McMahon, R. J. (1994). Diagnosis, assessment, and treatment of externalizing problems in children: The role of longitudinal data. *Journal of Consulting and Clinical Psychology, 62,* 901–917.

McMurtray, A. M., Ringman, J., & Chao, S. Z. (2006). Family history of dementia in early-onset versus very late-onset Alzheimer's disease. *International Journal of Geriatric Psychiatry, 21*(6), 597–598.

McPherson, M., Smith-Lovin, L., & Brashears, M. (2006). Social isolation in America: Changes in core discussion networks over two decades. *American Sociological Review, 71*(3), 353–375.

Meeks, T. W., Ropacki, S. A., & Jeste, D. V. (2006). The neurobiology of neuropsychiatric syndromes in dementia. *Current Opinion in Psychiatry, 19*(6), 581–586.

Mengelers, R., van Os, J., & Myin-Germeys, I. (2007). Childhood negative experiences and subclinical psychosis in adolescence: A longitudinal general population study. *Early Intervention in Psychiatry, 1,* 201–207.

Michalak, E. E., Yatham, L. N., Wan, D. D. C., & Lam, R. W. (2005). Perceived quality of life in patients with bipolar disorder. Does group psychoeducation have an impact? *Canadian Journal of Psychiatry, 50*(2), 95–100.

Miklowitz, D. J. (2006). Family-focused treatment of the suicidal bipolar patient. *Bipolar Disorders, 8*(5), 640–651.

Miklowitz, D. J. (2007). The role of the family in the course and treatment of bipolar disorder. *Current Directions in Psychological Science, 16*(4), 192–196.

Miklowitz, D. J., George, E. L., Axelson, D. A., Kim, E. Y., Birmhauer, B., Schenk, C., et al. (2004). Family focused treatment for adolescents with bipolar disorder. *Journal of Affective Disorders, 82*(Suppl. 1), s113–s128.

Miklowitz, D. J., & Goldstein, M. J. (1997). *Bipolar disorder: A family-focused treatment approach.* New York: Guilford.

Miklowitz, D. J., Simoneau, T. L., George, E. A., Richards, J., Kalbag, A., Sachs-Ericsson, N., et al. (2000). Family-focused treatment of bipolar disorder: One-year effects of a psychoeducational program in conjunction with pharmacotherapy. *Biological Psychiatry, 48,* 582–592.

Miklowitz, D. J., Wisniewski, S. R., Miyahara, M. W., Sachs, G. S., & Otto, M. W. (2005). Perceived criticism from family members as a predictor of the one-year course of bipolar disorder. *Psychiatry Research, 136*(2–3), 101–111.

Miller, A. L., & Glinski, J. (2000). Youth suicidal behavior: Assessment and intervention. *Journal of Clinical Psychology, 56*(9), 1132–1152.

Miller, G. E., & Prinz, R. J. (1990). Enhancement of social learning family interventions for childhood conduct disorder. *Psychological Bulletin, 108*(2), 291–307.

Miller, W., & Rollnick, S. (2002). *Motivational interviewing: Preparing people to change addictive behavior* (2nd ed.). New York: Guilford.

Minuchin, S. (1974). *Families and family therapy.* Cambridge, MA: Harvard University Press.

Minuchin, S., Lee, W., & Simon, G. M. (1996). *Mastering family therapy: Journeys of growth and transformation.* New York: Wiley.

Mirin, S., Batki, S., Bukstein, O., Isbell, P., Kleber, H., Schottenfeld, R., et al. (2002). Practice guideline for the treatment of patients with substance use disorders: Alcohol, cocaine, opioids. In *American Psychiatric Association practice guidelines for the treatment of psychiatric disorders: Compendium 2002* (pp. 249–348). Washington, DC: American Psychiatric Association.

Mitrani, V. B., & Czaja, S. J. (2000). Family-based therapy for dementia caregivers: Clinical observations. *Aging and Mental Health, 4*(3), 200–209.

Mittleman, M. S., Ferris, S. H., Shulman, E., Steinberg, G., & Levin, B. (1996). A family intervention to delay nursing home placement of patients with Alzheimer's disease: A randomized controlled trial. *Journal of the American Medical Association, 276,* 1725–1731.

Mittleman, M. S., Roth, D. L., Haley, W. E., & Zarit, S. H. (2004). Effects of a caregiver intervention on negative caregiver appraisals of behavioral problems in patients with Alzheimer's disease: Results of a randomized trial. *Journals of Gerontology, Series B: Psychological Sciences and Social Sciences, 59B*(1), 27–34.

Mizes, J. S., & Palermo, T. M. (1997). Eating disorders. In R. T. Ammerman & M. Hersen (Eds.), *Handbook of prevention and treatment with children and adolescents: Intervention in the real world context* (pp. 238–258). New York: John Wiley and Sons.

Moffit, T., Caspi, A., Rutter, M., & Silva, P. (2001). *Sex differences in antisocial behavior: Conduct disorder, delinquency, and violence in the Dunedin longitudinal study.* New York: Cambridge University Press.

Moffitt, T. (2003). Life-course persistent and adolescence-limited antisocial behavior: A 10-year research review and research agenda. In B. Lahey, T. Moffitt, & A. Caspi (Eds.), *Causes of conduct disorder and juvenile delinquency* (pp. 49–75). New York: Guilford.

Mohr, W. K., Lafuze, J. E., & Mohr, B. D. (2000). Opening caregiver minds: National Alliance for the Mentally Ill's (NAMI) provider education program. Archives of Psychiatric Nursing, 14(5), 235–243.

Monk, T. K., Flaherty, J., Frank, E., & Hoskinson, K. (1990). The Social Rhythm Metric: An instrument to quantify the daily rhythms of life. *Journal of Nervous and Mental Disease, 178*(2), 120–126.

Morano, C. L. (2003). Appraisal and coping: Moderators or mediators of stress in Alzheimer's disease caregivers. Social Work *Research, 27*(2), 116–128.

Morano, C. L., & Sanders, S. (2006). Exploring differences in depression, role captivity, and self-acceptance in Hispanic and non-Hispanic adult children caregivers. *Journal of Ethnic and Cultural Diversity in Social Work, 14*(1–2), 27–46.

Moren-Cross, J. L., & Lin, N. (2006). Social networks and health. In R. H. Binstock & L. K. George (Eds.), *Handbook of aging and the social sciences* (6th ed., pp. 111–126). Amsterdam: Elsevier.

Mueser, K. T., Corrigan, P. W., Hilton, D. W., Tanzman, B., Schaub, A., Gingerich, S., et al. (2002). Illness management and recovery: A review of the research. *Psychiatric Services, 53*(10), 1272–1284.

Muise, A., Stein, D., & Arbess, G. (2003). Eating disorders in adolescent boys: A review of the adolescent and young adult literature. *Journal of Adolescent Health, 33,* 427–435.

Murray, R. M., & Jones, P. B. (Eds.). (2003). *The epidemiology of schizophrenia.* New York: Cambridge University Press.

Mykelbust, H. R. (1973). Identification and diagnosis of children with learning disabilities: An interdisciplinary study of criteria. *Seminars in Psychiatry, 5*(1), 55–77.

National Alliance for the Mentally Ill. (1989). *Siblings and adult children's network: Background information and article booklet.* Arlington, VA: Author.

National Alliance for the Mentally Ill. (2009). *Education, training, and peer support programs.* Retrieved July 24, 2009, from www.nami.org/template.cfm?section=Education_Training_ and_Peer_Support_Center

Novaco, R. W. (2007). Anger dysregulation. In T. A. Cavell & K. T. Malcolm (Eds.), *Anger, aggression, and interventions for interpersonal violence* (pp. 3–54). Mahwah, NJ: Lawrence Erlbaum Associates.

Nowotny, P., Smemo, S., & Goate, A. M. (2005). Genetic risk factors for late-onset Alzheimer's disease. In C. F. Zorumski & E. H. Rubin (Eds.), *Psychopathology in the genome and neuroscience era.* (pp. 51–62). Washington, DC: American Psychiatric Publishing.

O'Connor, M. K. (2002). Using qualitative research in practice evaluation. In A. R. Roberts & G. J. Greene (Eds.), *Social workers' desk reference* (pp. 777–781). New York: Oxford University Press.

Orwin, R., Maranda, M., & Brady, T. (2001). *Impact of prior physical and sexual victimization on substance abuse treatment outcomes.* Report prepared under Contract No. 270-97-7016 for the Center for Substance Abuse Treatment. Fairfax, VA: Caliber Associates.

Ownby, R. L., Crocco, E., Acevedo, A., John, V., & Loewenstein, D. (2006). Depression and risk for Alzheimer's disease. *Archives of General Psychiatry, 63,* 530–538.

Panksepp, J. (2005). Affective consciousness: Core emotional feelings in animals and humans. *Consciousness and Cognition: An International Journal, 14*(1), 30–80.

Papassotriopoulos, A., Fountoulakis, M., Dunckley, T., Stephan, D. A., & Reiman, E. M. (2006). Genetics, transcriptomics, and proteomics of Alzheimer's disease. *Journal of Clinical Psychiatry, 67*(4), 652–670.

Parkinson, B., Fischer, A. H., & Manstead, A. S. R. (2005). *Emotion in social relations: Cultural, group, and interpersonal processes.* New York: Psychology Press.

Paulson, B. L., & Worth, M. (2002). Counseling for suicide: Client perspective. *Journal of Counseling and Development, 80*(1), 86–94.

Pegg, P. O., Auerbach, S. M., Seel, R. T., Buenaver, L. F., Kiesler, D. J., & Plybon, L. E. (2005). The impact of patient-centered information on patients' treatment satisfaction and outcomes in traumatic brain injury rehabilitation. *Rehabilitation Psychology, 50*(4), 366–374.

Peisah, C., Brodaty, H., & Quadrio, C. (2006). Family conflict in dementia: Prodigal sons and black sheep. *International Journal of Geriatric Psychiatry, 21*(5), 485–492.

Pekkala, E., & Merinder, L. (2002). Psychoeducation for schizophrenia. *Cochrane Database of Systematic Reviews, 2,* Art. No. CD002831. DOI: 10.1002/14651858.CD002831.

Peterson, C. B., Mitchell, J. E., Engbloom, S., Nugeent, S., Mussell, M. P., Crow, S. J., et al. (2001). Self-help versus therapist-led group cognitive-behavioral treatment of binge eating disorder at follow-up. *International Journal of Eating Disorders, 30*(4), 363–374.

Pharoah, F., Mari, J., Rathbone, J., & Wong, W. (2006). Family intervention for schizophrenia. *Cochrane Database of Systematic Reviews, 4,* Art. No.: CD000088. DOI: 10.1002/14651858.CD000088.

Phillipe, T., Lalloue, F., & Preux, P. (2006). Dementia patients' caregivers' quality of life: The PIXEL study. *International Journal of Geriatric Psychiatry, 21*(1), 50–56.

Phillips, R. E., Lakin, R., & Pargament, K. I. (2002). Development and implementation of a spiritual issues psychoeducational group for those with serious mental illness. *Community Mental Health Journal, 38*(6), 487–495.

Piaget, J. (1977). *The development of thought: Equilibration of cognitive structures.* New York: Viking Press.

Pilling, S., Bebbington, P., Kuipers, E., Garety, P., Geddes, J., Orbach, G., et al. (2002). Psychological treatments in schizophrenia: I. Meta-analysis of family intervention and cognitive behavior therapy. *Psychological Medicine, 32*(5), 763–782.

Pinquant, M., & Sorensen, S. (2006). Ethnic differences in stressors, resources, and psychological outcomes of family caregiving: A meta-analysis. *The Gerontologist, 45*(1), 90–106.

Plutchik, R. (2005). The nature of emotions. In P. W. Sherman & J. Alcock (Eds.), *Exploring animal behavior: Readings from American Scientist* (4th ed., pp. 85–91). Sunderland, MA: Sinauer Associates.

Pollio, D. E., North, C. S., & Foster, D. A. (1998). Content and curriculum in psychoeducation groups for families of persons with severe mental illness. *Psychiatric Services, 49*(6), 816–822.

Pollio, D. E., North, C. S., & Reid, D. L. (2006). Living with severe mental illness—what families and friends must know: Evaluation of a one-day psychoeducational workshop. *Social Work, 51*(1), 31–38.

Pollio, D. E., North, C. S., Reid, D. L., Eyrich, K. M., & McClendon, J. R. (2006). Differences in problems faced by families with a child coping with a serious emotional disorder or an adult member coping with mental illness. *Journal of Social Service Research, 32*(4), 83–98.

Pomeroy, E., Kiam, R., & Green, D. (2000). Reducing depression, anxiety, and trauma of male inmates: An HIV/AIDS psychoeducational group intervention. *Social Work Research, 24*(3), 156–167.

Pomeroy, E. C., Rubin, A., & Walker, R. J. (1995). Effectiveness of a psychoeducational and task-centered group intervention for family members of people with AIDS. *Social Work Research, 19*(3), 142–152.

Post, R. M., Leverich, G. B., King, Q., & Weiss, S. R. (2001). Developmental vulnerabilities to the onset and course of bipolar disorder. *Development and Psychopathology, 13*(1), 581–598.

Potvin, S., Sepehry, A. A., & Stip, E. (2006). A meta-analysis of negative symptoms in dual diagnosis schizophrenia. *Psychological Medicine, 36*(4), 431–440.

Rao, U., Ryan, N. D., Birmaher, B., Dahl, R., Williamson, D., Kaufman, J., et al. (1995). Unipolar depression in adolescents: Clinical outcome in adulthood. *Journal of the American Academy of Child and Adolescent Psychiatry, 34,* 566–578.

Rawson, R. A., Obert, J. L., McCann, M. J., & Marinelli-Casey, P. (1993a). Relapse prevention models for substance abuse treatment. *Psychotherapy: Theory, Research, Practice, Training, 30*(2), 284–298.

Rawson, R. A., Obert, J. L., McCann, M. J., & Marinelli-Casey, P. (1993b). Relapse prevention strategies in outpatient substance abuse treatment. *Psychology of Addictive Behaviors, 7*(2), 85–95.

Rea, M. M., Thompson, M. C., Miklowitz, D. J., Goldstein, M. J., Hwang, S., & Mintz, J. (2003). *Journal of Consulting and Clinical Psychology, 71*(3), 482–492.

Reinares, M., Vieta, E., Colom, F., Martinez-Aran, A., Torrent, C., Comes, M., et al. (2004). Impact of a psychoeducational family intervention on caregivers of stabilized bipolar patients. *Psychotherapy and Psychosomatics, 73*(5), 312–319.

Robin, A. L., Seigel, P. T., Moye, A. W., Gilroy, M., Dennis, A. B., & Sikand, A. (1999). A controlled comparison of family versus individual therapy for adolescents with anorexia nervosa. *Journal of the American Academy of Child and Adolescent Psychiatry, 38,* 1482–1489.

Robinson, W. D., Carroll, J. S., & Watson, W. L. (2005). Shared experience building around the family crucible of cancer. *Family Systems and Health, 23*(2), 131–147.

Rocco, P. L., Ciano, R. P., & Balestrieri, M. (2001). Psychoeducation in the prevention of eating disorders: An experimental approach in adolescent schoolgirls. *British Journal of Medical Psychology, 74,* 351–358.

Roehrig, M., Thompson, J. K., Brannick, M., & van den Berg, P. (2006). Dissonance-based eating disorder prevention program: A preliminary dismantling investigation. *International Journal of Eating Disorders, 39*(1), 1–10.

Roffman, R. (2004). Psychoeducational groups. In C. D. Garvin, L. M. Gutierrez, & M. J. Galinsky (Eds.), *Handbook of social work with groups* (pp. 160–175). New York: Guilford.

Rome, E., & Ammerman, S. (2003). Medical complications of eating disorders: An update. *Journal of Adolescent Health, 33,* 418–426.

Root, R. W., & Resnick, R. J. (2003). An update on the diagnosis and treatment of attention-deficit/hyperactivity disorder in children. *Professional Psychology: Research and Practice, 34*(1), 34–41.

Rose, S. M. (1990). Advocacy/empowerment: An approach to clinical practice for social work. *Journal of Sociology and Social Welfare, 17*(2), 41–51.

Rosen, A., & Proctor, E. K. (2002). Standards for evidence-based social work practice: The role of replicable and appropriate interventions, outcomes, and practice guidelines. In A. R. Roberts & G. J. Greene (Eds.), *Social workers' desk reference* (pp. 743–747). New York: Oxford University Press.

Rosenthal, R. N. (2004). Overview of evidence-based practice. In A. R. Roberts & K. R. Yeager (Eds.), *Evidence based practice manual: Research and outcome measures in health and human services* (pp. 20–28). New York: Oxford University Press.

Rothbaum, B. O., & Austin, M. C. (2000). Integration of pharmacotherapy and psychotherapy for bipolar disorder. *Journal of Clinical Psychiatry, 61*(Suppl. 9), 68–75.

Rouget, B. W., & Aubrey, J. (2007). Efficacy of psychoeducational approaches on bipolar disorders: A review of the literature. *Journal of Affective Disorders, 98*(1–2), 11–27.

Rudolph, K. D. (2008). Developmental influences on interpersonal stress generation in depressed youth. *Journal of Abnormal Psychology, 117*(3), 673–679.

Ruffolo, M. C., Kuhn, M. T., & Evans, M. E. (2005). Support, empowerment, and education: A study of multiple family group psychoeducation. *Journal of Emotional and Behavioral Disorders, 13*(4), 200–212.

Ruffolo, M. C., Kuhn, M. T., & Evans, M. E. (2006). Developing a parent-professional team leadership model in group work: Work with families with children experiencing behavioral and emotional problems. *Social Work, 51*(1), 39–47.

Ruitenberg, A., Ott, A., van Swieten, J. C., Hofman, A., & Breteler, M. M. B. (2001). Incidence of dementia: Does gender make a difference? *Neurobiology of Aging, 22,* 575–580.

Rummel, C. B., Hansen, W. P., Helbig, A., Pitschel-Walz, G., & Kissling, W. (2005). Peer-to-peer psychoeducation in schizophrenia: A new approach. *Journal of Clinical Psychiatry, 66,* 1580–1585.

Rushton, J., Forcier, M., & Schectman, R. (2002). Epidemiology of depressive symptoms in the national longitudinal study of adolescent health. *Journal of the American Academy of Child and Adolescent Psychiatry, 41*(2), 199–205.

Ryan, M. M., Lockstone, H. E., & Huffaker, S. J. (2006). Gene expression analysis of bipolar disorder reveals downregulation of the ubiquitin cycle and alterations in synaptic genes. *Molecular Psychiatry, 11*(10), 965–978.

Sachs, G. S., Printz, D. J., Kahn, D. A., Carpenter, D., & Docherty, J. P. (2000). *Medication treatment of bipolar disorder.* New York: McGraw-Hill.

Saldinger, A., Cain, A., Kalter, N., & Lohnes, K. (1999). Anticipating parental death in families with young children. *American Journal of Orthopsychiatry, 89*(1), 39–46.

Saldinger, A., Cain, A., Porterfield, K., & Lohnes, K. (2004). Facilitating attachment between school-aged children and a dying parent. *Death Studies, 28,* 915–940.

Saleeby, D. (1996). The strengths perspective in social work practice: Extensions and cautions. *Social Work, 41*(3), 296–305.

Saleeby, D. (Ed.). (1997). *The strengths perspective in social work practice.* White Plains, NY: Longman.

Samudra, K., & Cantwell, D. (1999). Risk factors for attention-deficit/hyperactivity disorder. In H. Quay & A. Hogan (Eds.), *Handbook of disruptive behavior disorders* (pp. 199–230). New York: Plenum.

Sands, J. R., & Harrow, M. (2000). Bipolar disorder: Psychopathology, biology, and diagnosis. In M. Hersen & A. S. Bellack (Eds.), *Psychopathology in adulthood* (2nd ed., pp. 326–347). Needham Heights, MA: Allyn and Bacon.

Sanson, A., & Prior, M. (1999). Temperament and behavioral precursors to oppositional defiant disorder and conduct disorder. In H. C. Quay & A. E. Hogan (Eds.), *Handbook of disruptive behavior disorders* (pp. 397–417). New York: Kluwer Academic.

Santora, P. B., & Hutton, H. E. (2008). Longitudinal trends in hospital admissions with co-occurring alcohol/drug diagnoses, 1994–2002. *Journal of Substance Abuse Treatment, 35*(1), 1–12.

Schoeman, L., & Kreitzman, R. (1997). Death of a parent: Group intervention with bereaved children and their caregivers. *Psychoanalysis and Psychotherapy: The Journal of the Postgraduate Center for Mental Health, 14*(2), 221–225.

Schotte, C. K., Van den Bossche, B., De Doncker, D., Claes, S., & Cosyns, P. (2006). A biopsychosocial model as a guide for psychoeducation and treatment of depression. *Depression and Anxiety, 23*(5), 312–324.

Scott, J., McNeill, Y., & Cavanaugh, J. (2006). Exposure to obstetric complications and subsequent development of bipolar disorder: Systematic review. *British Journal of Psychiatry, 189*(1), 3–11.

Seeman, M. V. (2003). Gender differences in schizophrenia across the life span. In C. I. Cohen (Ed.), *Schizophrenia into later life: Treatment, research, and policy* (pp. 141–154). Washington, DC: American Psychiatric Publishing.

Shechtman, A. (2000). An innovative intervention for treatment of child and adolescent aggression: An outcome study. *Psychology in the Schools, 37*(2), 157–167.

Shin, S. (2004). Effects of culturally relevant psychoeducation for Korean American families of persons with chronic mental illness. *Research on Social Work Practice, 14*(4), 231–239.

Siebenbruner, J., Englund, M. M., Egeland, B., & Hudson, K. (2006). Developmental antecedents of late adolescence substances use patterns. *Development and Psychopathology, 18,* 551–571.

Sierra, P., Livianos, L., Arques, S., Rojo, L., & Castelló, J. (2007). Prodromal symptoms to relapse in bipolar disorder. *Australian and New Zealand Journal of Psychiatry, 41*(5), 385–391.

Smith, D. H. (2007). Controversies in childhood bipolar disorders. *Canadian Journal of Psychiatry, 52*(7), 407–408.

Smith, T. E., Sells, S. P., Rodman, J., Coalitions, W., & Reynolds, L. R. (2003). *Reducing adolescent substance abuse and delinquency: Pilot research of a family-oriented psychoeducation curriculum.* Retrieved July 12, 2009, from http://www.difficult.net/research3.asp

Sobell, M. B., & Sobell, L. C. (2000). Stepped care as a heuristic approach to the treatment of alcohol problems. *Journal of Consulting and Clinical Psychology, 68*(4), 573–579.

Sparks, J. A., Duncan, B. L., & Miller, S. D. (2008). Common factors in psychotherapy. In J. L. Lebow (Ed.), *Twenty-first century psychotherapies: Contemporary approaches to theory and practice* (pp. 453–497). Hoboken, NJ: John Wiley and Sons.

Spence, S., Sheffield, J., & Donovan, C. (2003). Preventing adolescent depression: An evaluation of the problem solving for life program. *Journal of Consulting and Clinical Psychology, 71*(1), 3–13.

Stanton, M., & Shadish, W. R. (1997). Outcome, attrition, and family-couples treatment for drug abuse: A meta-analysis and review of the controlled, comparative models. *Psychological Bulletin, 122*(2), 170–191.

Stark, K. D., Reynolds, W. M., & Kaslow, N. J. (1987). A comparison of the relative efficacy of self-control therapy and a behavioral problem-solving therapy for depression in children. *Journal of Abnormal Child Psychology, 15*(1), 91–113.

Stark, K. D., Rouse, L. W., & Livingston, R. (1991). Treatment of depression during childhood and adolescence: Cognitive-behavioral procedures for the individual and family. In P. C. Kendall (Ed.), *Child and adolescent therapy: Cognitive-behavioral procedures* (pp. 165–206). New York: Guilford.

Steinberg, K. L., Roffman, R. A., Carroll, K. M., Kabela, E., Kadden, R., Miller, M., et al. (2002). Tailoring cannabis dependence treatment for a diverse population. *Addiction, 97*(Suppl. 1), 135–142.

Stice, E., Orjada, K., & Tristan, J. (2006). Trial of a psychoeducational eating disturbance intervention for college woman: A replication and extension. *International Journal of Eating Disorders, 39*(3), 233–239.

Strasser, F., & Strasser, A. (1997). *Existential time-limited therapy: The wheel of experience.* New York: Wiley.

Striegel-Moore, R. H., & Cachelin, F. M. (1999). Body image concerns and disordered eating in adolescent girls: Risk and protective factors. In N. G. Johnson, M. C. Roberts, & J. Worell (Eds.), *Beyond appearance: A new look at adolescent girls* (pp. 85–108). Washington, DC: American Psychological Association.

Stuart, C., Waalen, J. K., & Haelstromm, E. (2003). Many helping hearts: An evaluation of peer gatekeeper training in suicide risk assessment. *Death Studies, 27,* 321–333.

Subramanian, K., Hernandez, S., & Martinez, A. (1995). Psychoeducational group work for low-income Latina mothers with HIV infection. *Social Work with Groups, 18*(2–3), 65–78.

Substance Abuse and Mental Health Services Administration. (2009). *Evidence-based practices: Shaping mental health services toward recovery.* Retrieved April 1, 2009, from http://www.innovations.ahrq.gov/content.aspx?id=313

Sullivan, P. F., Neale, M. C., & Kendler, K. S. (2000). Genetic epidemiology of major depression: Review and meta-analysis. *American Journal of Psychiatry, 157*(10), 1552–1562.

Swan, J., Sorrell, E., MacVicar, B., Durham, R., & Matthews, K. (2004). "Coping with depression": An open study of the efficacy of a group psychoeducational intervention in chronic, treatment-refractory depression. *Journal of Affective Disorders, 82*(1), 125–129.

Swann, A. C. (2006). Neurobiology of bipolar depression. In R. S. El Mallakh & N. S. Ghaemi (Eds.), *Bipolar depression: A comprehensive guide* (pp. 37–68). Washington, DC: American Psychiatric Publishing.

Swartz, H. A., & Frank, E. (2001). Psychotherapy for bipolar depression: A phase specific treatment strategy. *Bipolar Disorders, 3*(1), 11–22.

Tantillo, M. (2006). A relational approach to eating disorders multifamily therapy group: Moving from difference and disconnection to mutual connection. *Families, Systems, and Health, 24*(1), 82–102.

Taylor, D. L., Siegel, J. E., Moran-Klimi, K., Lamdan, R. M., Shelby, R., & Hrywna, M. (2003). Psychological adjustment among African-American breast cancer patients: One year follow-up results of a randomized psychoeducational group intervention. *Health Psychology, 22*(3), 316–323.

Teri, L., McCurry, S. M., Logsdon, R., & Gibbons, L. E. (2005). Training community consultants to help family members improve dementia care: A randomized controlled trial. *The Gerontologist, 45*(6), 802–811.

Thomas, C., & Corcoran, J. (2001). Empirically-based marital and family interventions for alcohol abuse: A review. *Research on Social Work Practice, 11*(5), 549–575.

Titelman, P. (Ed.). (1998). *Clinical applications of Bowen family systems theory.* New York: Haworth.

Toseland, R. W., & Rivas, R. F. (2006). *An introduction to group work practice* (6th ed.). Needham Heights, MA: Allyn and Bacon.

Underwood, M. (2004). *Group interventions for treatment of psychological trauma: Module 10: Group interventions for bereavement following traumatic events.* New York: American Group Psychotherapy Association.

Vandiver, V. L. (2002). Step-by-step practice guidelines for using evidence-based practice and expert consensus in mental health settings. In A. R. Roberts & G. J. Greene (Eds.), *Social workers' desk reference* (pp. 731–738). New York: Oxford University Press.

Vaux, A. (1988). *Social support: Theory, research, and intervention.* New York: Praeger.

Vieta, E. (2005a). Improving treatment adherence in bipolar disorder through psychoeducation. *Journal of Clinical Psychiatry, 66*(Suppl. 1), 24–29.

Vieta, E. (2005b). The package of care for patients with bipolar depression. *Journal of Clinical Psychiatry, 66*(Suppl. 5), 34–39.

Vine, P. (1982). *Families in pain: Children, siblings, spouses, and parents of the mentally ill speak out.* New York: Pantheon.

Volpe, R. U. (1984). A psychoeducational program dealing with child abuse for elementary school children. *Child Abuse and Neglect, 8*(4), 511–517.

Vostanis, P., Feehan, C., Grattan, E., & Bickerton, W. (1996). Treatment for children and adolescents with depression: Lessons from a controlled trial. *Clinical Child Psychology and Psychiatry, 1*(2), 199–212.

Wachs, T. (2000). *Necessary but not sufficient.* Washington, DC: American Psychological Association.

Walker, D. D., Roffman, R. A., Stephens, R. S., Berghuis, J., & Kim, W. (2006). Motivational enhancement therapy for adolescent marijuana users: A preliminary randomized controlled trial. *Journal of Consulting and Clinical Psychology, 74*(5), 628–632.

Walker, R. J., Pomeroy, E. C., McNeil, J. S., & Franklin, C. (1994). Anticipatory grief and AIDS: Strategies for intervening with caregivers. *Health and Social Work, 21*(1), 49–57.

Walsh, J., & Connelly, P. R. (1996). Supportive behaviors in natural support networks of people with serious mental illness. *Health and Social Work, 21*(4), 296–303.

Walters, G. (2002). The heritability of alcohol abuse and dependence: A meta-analysis of behavior genetic research. *American Journal of Drug and Alcohol Abuse, 28,* 557–584.

Wardle, J., Williamson, S., McCaffrey, K., Sutton, S., Taylor, T., Edwards, R., et al. (2003). Increasing attendance at a colorectal cancer screening: Testing the efficacy of a mailed, psychoeducational intervention in a community sample of older adults. *Health Psychology, 22*(1), 99–105.

Warmbrod, M. (1986). Counseling bereaved children: Stages in the process. *Social Casework: Journal of Contemporary Social Work. 67*(6), 351–358.

Waslick, B. D., Kandel, B. A., & Kakouros, B. S. (2002). Depression in children and adolescents: An overview. In D. Shaffer & B. D. Waslick (Eds.), *The many faces of depression in children and adolescents* (pp. 1–36). Washington, DC: American Psychiatric Publishing.

Weaver, H. N., & Brave Heart, M. Y. (1999). Examining two facets of American Indian identity: Exposure to other cultures and the influence of historical trauma. *Journal of Human Behavior in the Social Environment, 2*(1–2), 19–33.

Weiss, G., & Trokenberg-Hechtman, L. (1993). *Hyperactive children grown up: ADHD in children, adolescents, and adults.* New York: Guilford.

Weiss, L., Katzman, M., & Wolchik, S. (1985). *Treating bulimia: A psychoeducational approach.* New York: Pergamon Press.

Weisz, J. R., Southam-Gerow, M. A., Gordis, E. B., & Connor-Smith, J. (2003). Primary and secondary control enhancement training for youth depression: Applying the deployment-focused model of treatment development and testing. In A. E. Kazdin & J. R. Weisz (Eds.), *Evidence-based treatments for children and adolescents* (pp. 165–183). New York: Guilford.

Woodward, L. J., Fergusson, D. M., & Horwood, L. J. (2000). Driving outcomes of young people with attentional difficulties in adolescence. *Journal of the American Academy of Child and Adolescent Psychiatry, 39,* 627–634.

Yager, J., Anderson, A., Devlin, M., Egger, H., Herzog, D., Mitchell, J., et al. (2002). Practice guideline for the treatment of patients with eating disorders. In *American Psychiatric Association practice guidelines for the treatment of psychiatric disorders: Compendium 2002* (pp. 697–766). Washington, DC: American Psychiatric Association.

Young, S. E., Rhee, S. H., Stallings, M. C., Corley, R. P., & Hewitt, J. K. (2006). Genetic and environmental vulnerabilities underlying adolescent substance use and problem use: general or specific? *Behavior Genetics, 36*(4), 603–615.

Youngstrom, E. A., Findling, R. L., Youngstrom, J. K., & Calabrese, J. R. (2005). Toward an evidence-based assessment of pediatric bipolar disorder. *Journal of Child and Adolescent Psychiatry, 34*(3), 433–448.

Zabinski, M. F., Wilfley, D. E., Calfas, K. J., Winzelberg, A. J., & Taylor, C. B. (2004). An interactive psychoeducational intervention for women at risk of developing an eating disorder. *Journal of Consulting and Clinical Psychology, 72*(5), 914–919.

Zambelli, G., & DeRosa, A. (1992). Bereavement support groups for school-age children: Theory, intervention, and case example. *American Journal of Orthopsychiatry, 62*(4), 484–492.

Zaretsky, A., Rizvi, S., & Parikh, S. V. (2007). How well do psychosocial interventions work in bipolar disorder? *Canadian Journal of Psychiatry, 52*(1), 14–20.

Zastrow, C. H. (2006). *Social work with groups: A comprehensive workbook* (6th ed.). Belmont, CA: Thomson Brooks/Cole.

Ziabreva, I., Perry, E., & Perry, R. (2006). Altered neurogenesis in Alzheimer's disease. *Journal of Psychosomatic Research, 61*(3), 311–316.

Zimmerman, M. A. (2000). Empowerment theory: Psychological, organizational, and community levels of analysis. In J. Rappaport & E. Seidman (Eds.), *Handbook of community psychology* (pp. 43–65). New York: Kluwer Academic/Plenum.

Zimmerman, M. A., Israel, B. A., Schulz, A., & Checkoway, B. (1992). Further explorations in empowerment theory: An empirical analysis of psychological empowerment. *American Journal of Community Psychology, 20*(6), 707–727.

Zisook, S., & Shuchter, S. R. (2001). Treatment of the depressions of bereavement. *American Behavioral Scientist, 44*(5), 782–792.

Zvolensky, M. J., Lejuez, C. W., & Eifert, G. H. (2000). Prediction and control: Operational definitions for the experimental analysis of anxiety. *Behaviour Research and Therapy, 38*(7), 653–663.

Index

About the Author

Joseph Walsh is professor of social work and affiliate professor of psychology at Virginia Commonwealth University. He has been a direct service practitioner in the field of mental health for many years, first in a psychiatric hospital and later in community mental health center settings. He has provided services to general outpatient populations, but has mostly specialized in services to persons with serious mental illness and their families. Since 1993, Joe has been teaching courses in generalist practice, clinical practice, human behavior, research, and social theory. He continues to provide direct services to clients at the university's Center for Psychological Services. He has published widely in social work and related journals on topics related to clinical practice and is the author of several other books, two published by Lyceum, including *Short-term Existential Intervention in Clinical Practice* (2007), with Jim Lantz, and *Endings in Clinical Practice: Ensuring Closure Across Service Settings* (2nd edition, 2007).

16398490R00138

Printed in Great Britain
by Amazon